Crystal Reports For Dummies

W9-CZI-663

Cheat Sheet

The Crystal Reports toolbar

Button	Function
	Create a new report.
	Open an existing report.
	Save the report.
	Preview the report in the Preview Tab.
	Print the report to a printer.
	Export the report to a file or e-mail.
	Refresh the report data.
	Activate the Report Expert.
	Search for a record on the current report.
	Undo an action.
	Zoom in and out of your report.
	Insert database, formula, parameter, and group name fields.
	Insert a text object.
	Insert a summary.
	Insert a line.
	Insert a box.
	Insert a picture.
	Insert a graph/chart.
	Insert a subreport.
	Insert a Cross-Tab.
	Set selection criteria.
	Set record sort order.
	Format any section of the report.
	Define links between tables.
	Get context-sensitive help.

The Crystal Reports format bar

Button	Function
B	Change the selected data to boldface.
I	Italicize the selected data.
U	Underline the selected data.
A	Increase the font size of the selected data one point each time you click the button.
A	Decrease the font size of the selected data one point each time you click the button.
	Align the selected data flush left.
	Center the selected data.
	Align the selected data flush right.
$	When a number field is selected, it places a currency symbol with the number.*
,	When a number field is selected, it places a thousands separator in the number.*
%	When a number field is selected, it places a percentage sign with the number.*
	When a number field is selected, adds one decimal place to the number.
	When a number field is selected, subtracts one decimal place from the number.
	Arranges field objects automatically.
	Applies a professionally designed style to the entire report.

Note: The program refers to your setting in the International section of the Control Panel (Windows 3.*x*, Windows NT) or the Regional section of the Control Panel (Windows 95).

...For Dummies®: Bestselling Book Series for Beginners

Crystal Reports 6 For Dummies®

Cheat Sheet

Seeing the data in the Preview Tab

Crystal Reports has two ways to view a report. One is the Design Tab, in which you see the placeholders for the fields, and the other is the Preview Tab, in which real data is inserted into the report from the source database. When you begin creating a new report, only the Design Tab is visible. To see the Preview Tab:

1. **Click the Preview button (or choose File➪Print Preview).**

   Crystal Reports adds the Preview Tab and shows you a WYSIWIG view of the report: What You See Is What You Get. When you print the report to paper, it should match very closely the Preview Tab layout.

Getting zoomed!

Zooming in allows you to take a closer look at the formatting of your reports — and to make those teeny-tiny adjustments that make a good report a great one. You can do this in either Design or Preview, but Preview is much more interesting. To take a closer look at your report:

1. **Open the View menu and choose Zoom to get the Magnification Factor dialog.**

2. **To see more detail, type a number greater than 100 in the Magnification Factor box (you can enter up to 400 as the zoom factor).**

   You have two other choices:

   - Fit Whole Page, which zooms out the view so that you see the entire page at once.
   - Fit One Dimension, which reformats the view so that the entire width of the report is in view.

   To return the view to normal, click the Reset button in this same dialog box.

Inserting a field in a new report

Most of the time, you will insert fields into the Details section.

1. **Choose File➪New to get the Report Gallery dialog box.**

2. **Click the Custom button and then the Data File button.**

3. **In the Choose Database File dialog box, locate the database that you want to use as the source for your report, click the database file name, and click OK.**

   A new report form appears and the Insert Fields dialog box appears.

4. **In the Insert Fields dialog box, locate the field you want to insert into the report and click the field name.**

5. **Click the Insert button, at the bottom of the Insert Fields dialog box.**

6. **Move the mouse pointer to the section of the report in which you want the field data to appear.**

   Note: If you are really good with the mouse, just drag and drop!

Creating a group

Groups are a powerful way to arrange records in your report. For example, grouping records by salesperson would make a sales report easy to create.

1. **With the report open, choose Insert➪Group.**

   The Insert Group dialog box opens.

2. **Select the field upon which you wish to group the records.**

   The field *does not* have to be part of the report.

3. **Choose the Sort Order for the groups and click OK.**

...For Dummies®: Bestselling Book Series for Beginners

™

BESTSELLING BOOK SERIES

References for the Rest of Us!®

Are you intimidated and confused by computers? Do you find that traditional manuals are overloaded with technical details you'll never use? Do your friends and family always call you to fix simple problems on their PCs? Then the *...For Dummies*® computer book series from IDG Books Worldwide is for you.

...For Dummies books are written for those frustrated computer users who know they aren't really dumb but find that PC hardware, software, and indeed the unique vocabulary of computing make them feel helpless. *...For Dummies* books use a lighthearted approach, a down-to-earth style, and even cartoons and humorous icons to dispel computer novices' fears and build their confidence. Lighthearted but not lightweight, these books are a perfect survival guide for anyone forced to use a computer.

Already, millions of satisfied readers agree. They have made *...For Dummies* books the #1 introductory level computer book series and have written asking for more. So, if you're looking for the most fun and easy way to learn about computers, look to *...For Dummies* books to give you a helping hand.

IDG BOOKS WORLDWIDE

CRYSTAL REPORTS 6

FOR

DUMMIES®

CRYSTAL REPORTS 6 FOR DUMMIES®

by Douglas J. Wolf

IDG BOOKS WORLDWIDE

IDG Books Worldwide, Inc.
An International Data Group Company

Foster City, CA ◆ Chicago, IL ◆ Indianapolis, IN ◆ New York, NY

Crystal Reports 6 For Dummies®

Published by
IDG Books Worldwide, Inc.
An International Data Group Company
919 E. Hillsdale Blvd.
Suite 400
Foster City, CA 94404
www.idgbooks.com (IDG Books Worldwide Web site)
www.dummies.com (Dummies Press Web site)

Library of Congress Catalog Card No.: 97-71809

ISBN: 0-7645-0178-X

Printed in the United States of America

10 9 8 7 6

1O/QZ/QS/ZZ/IN

Distributed in the United States by IDG Books Worldwide, Inc.

Distributed by Macmillan Canada for Canada; by Transworld Publishers Limited in the United Kingdom; by IDG Norge Books for Norway; by IDG Sweden Books for Sweden; by Woodslane Pty. Ltd. for Australia; by Woodslane (NZ) Ltd. for New Zealand; by Addison Wesley Longman Singapore Pte Ltd. for Singapore, Malaysia, Thailand, and Indonesia; by Norma Comunicaciones S.A. for Colombia; by Intersoft for South Africa; by International Thomson Publishing for Germany, Austria and Switzerland; by Distribuidora Cuspide for Argentina; by Livraria Cultura for Brazil; by Ediciencia S.A. for Ecuador; by Ediciones ZETA S.C.R. Ltda. for Peru; by WS Computer Publishing Corporation, Inc., for the Philippines; by Contemporanea de Ediciones for Venezuela; by Express Computer Distributors for the Caribbean and West Indies; by Micronesia Media Distributor, Inc. for Micronesia; by Grupo Editorial Norma S.A. for Guatemala; by Chips Computadoras S.A. de C.V. for Mexico; by Editorial Norma de Panama S.A. for Panama; by Wouters Import for Belgium; by American Bookshops for Finland. Authorized Sales Agent: Anthony Rudkin Associates for the Middle East and North Africa.

For general information on IDG Books Worldwide's books in the U.S., please call our Consumer Customer Service department at 800-762-2974. For reseller information, including discounts and premium sales, please call our Reseller Customer Service department at 800-434-3422.

For information on where to purchase IDG Books Worldwide's books outside the U.S., please contact our International Sales department at 317-596-5530 or fax 317-596-5692.

For information on foreign language translations, please contact our Foreign & Subsidiary Rights department at 650-655-3021 or fax 650-655-3281.

For sales inquiries and special prices for bulk quantities, please contact our Sales department at 650-655-3200 or write to the address above.

For information on using IDG Books Worldwide's books in the classroom or for ordering examination copies, please contact our Educational Sales department at 800-434-2086 or fax 317-596-5499.

For press review copies, author interviews, or other publicity information, please contact our Public Relations department at 650-655-3000 or fax 650-655-3299.

For authorization to photocopy items for corporate, personal, or educational use, please contact Copyright Clearance Center, 222 Rosewood Drive, Danvers, MA 01923, or fax 978-750-4470.

About the Author

Douglas J. Wolf is the author of over 25 other computer software books, ranging from *Quick and Easy Guide to 123* to *ACT! for Windows*. He is the President of Wolf's Byte Productions, which produces video and CD-ROM training on various software products. He is an ACT! Certified Consultant. For more information, or to contact him, browse his Web site at www.howtosoftware.com.

He has also been a political consultant, a radio talk show host, and a Pop Warner football coach, and he plays a mean game of tennis. He collects words in his spare time.

ABOUT IDG BOOKS WORLDWIDE

Welcome to the world of IDG Books Worldwide.

IDG Books Worldwide, Inc., is a subsidiary of International Data Group, the world's largest publisher of computer-related information and the leading global provider of information services on information technology. IDG was founded more than 30 years ago by Patrick J. McGovern and now employs more than 9,000 people worldwide. IDG publishes more than 290 computer publications in over 75 countries. More than 90 million people read one or more IDG publications each month.

Launched in 1990, IDG Books Worldwide is today the #1 publisher of best-selling computer books in the United States. We are proud to have received eight awards from the Computer Press Association in recognition of editorial excellence and three from Computer Currents' First Annual Readers' Choice Awards. Our best-selling ...For Dummies® series has more than 50 million copies in print with translations in 31 languages. IDG Books Worldwide, through a joint venture with IDG's Hi-Tech Beijing, became the first U.S. publisher to publish a computer book in the People's Republic of China. In record time, IDG Books Worldwide has become the first choice for millions of readers around the world who want to learn how to better manage their businesses.

Our mission is simple: Every one of our books is designed to bring extra value and skill-building instructions to the reader. Our books are written by experts who understand and care about our readers. The knowledge base of our editorial staff comes from years of experience in publishing, education, and journalism — experience we use to produce books to carry us into the new millennium. In short, we care about books, so we attract the best people. We devote special attention to details such as audience, interior design, use of icons, and illustrations. And because we use an efficient process of authoring, editing, and desktop publishing our books electronically, we can spend more time ensuring superior content and less time on the technicalities of making books.

You can count on our commitment to deliver high-quality books at competitive prices on topics you want to read about. At IDG Books Worldwide, we continue in the IDG tradition of delivering quality for more than 30 years. You'll find no better book on a subject than one from IDG Books Worldwide.

John Kilcullen
Chairman and CEO
IDG Books Worldwide, Inc.

Steven Berkowitz
President and Publisher
IDG Books Worldwide, Inc.

VIII WINNER
Eighth Annual
Computer Press
Awards ≥1992

IX WINNER
Ninth Annual
Computer Press
Awards ≥1993

X WINNER
Tenth Annual
Computer Press
Awards ≥1994

XI WINNER
Eleventh Annual
Computer Press
Awards ≥1995

Dedication

I want to dedicate the hard work of creating this book to my lovely and talented and oh so sensuous wife, Gloria. She made this book possible by writing some and editing most.

Author's Acknowledgments

Let me begin by acknowledging the folks at Seagate Software who got this book off the ground, Julia Elkins and Ian Galbraith. Next the technical people who patiently read this tome for errors, Kathryn "purple" Hunt and Kathy Thomson. Finally, thanks to Keith Thomson for his brilliant insights when I called for help.

To the IDG Books team, starting with Jill Pisoni who had the foresight to approve this project, Darlene Wong (she sends the checks), Bill Helling, the patient master of the edits, and Tammy Castleman and Christa Carroll who make random prose coherent. They wore out at least two leather whips on me.

All of the people involved were indispensable members of the project and I am sincerely grateful for their involvement.

Publisher's Acknowledgments

We're proud of this book; please register your comments through our IDG Books Worldwide Online Registration Form located at `http://my2cents.dummies.com`.

Some of the people who helped bring this book to market include the following:

Acquisitions, Development, and Editorial

Project Editor: Bill Helling

Senior Acquisitions Editor: Jill Pisoni

Associate Permissions Editor:
Heather Heath Dismore

Copy Editors: Tamara S. Castleman,
Christa Carroll

Technical Editors: Kathryn Hunt,
Kathy Thomson

Editorial Manager: Mary Corder

Editorial Assistant: Chris H. Collins

Production

Project Coordinator: Sherry Gomoll

Layout and Graphics: Angela F. Hunckler,
Todd Klemme, Jane E. Martin,
Anna Rohrer, Brent Savage, Deirdre Smith

Proofreaders: Sandra Profant, Kelli Botta,
Michelle Croninger, Joel K. Draper,
Karen York

Indexer: Richard S. Shrout

General and Administrative

IDG Books Worldwide, Inc.: John Kilcullen, CEO; Steven Berkowitz, President and Publisher

IDG Books Technology Publishing: Brenda McLaughlin, Senior Vice President and
Group Publisher

Dummies Technology Press and Dummies Editorial: Diane Graves Steele, Vice President and
Associate Publisher; Mary Bednarek, Director of Acquisitions and Product Development;
Kristin A. Cocks, Editorial Director

Dummies Trade Press: Kathleen A. Welton, Vice President and Publisher; Kevin Thornton,
Acquisitions Manager

IDG Books Production for Dummies Press: Michael R. Britton, Vice President of Production
and Creative Services; Cindy L. Phipps, Manager of Project Coordination, Production Proofreading, and Indexing; Kathie S. Schutte, Supervisor of Page Layout; Shelley Lea, Supervisor
of Graphics and Design; Debbie J. Gates, Production Systems Specialist; Robert Springer,
Supervisor of Proofreading; Debbie Stailey, Special Projects Coordinator; Tony Augsburger,
Supervisor of Reprints and Bluelines

Dummies Packaging and Book Design: Patty Page, Manager, Promotions Marketing

♦

The publisher would like to give special thanks to Patrick J. McGovern,
without whom this book would not have been possible.

♦

Contents at a Glance

Cartoons at a Glance

By Rich Tennant

"THAT'S RIGHT, DADDY WILL DOUBLE YOUR SALARY IF YOU MAKE HIM MORE DATABASES."

page 67

page 229

page 171

page 7

page 101

page 319

page 277

Fax: 978-546-7747 • E-mail: the5wave@tiac.net

Table of Contents

Introduction

*W*elcome to *Crystal Reports 6 For Dummies*. This book is about one of the best-kept software secrets. Seagate Crystal Reports has been bundled with a wide variety of other software products for several years, and therefore you have not seen it on the software best-seller list. Yet it is a best-seller. If you have used Visual Basic or an accounting package, you have probably seen the product and wondered how to get it to work.

This book covers what you need to know to begin creating reports that not only look good but actually have data that make sense to the person reading them. The good news is that it is not difficult. In fact, creating reports is quite easy after you understand a few basic concepts such as how a report is laid out and where you insert the records, summaries, totals, and headings.

About This Book

I have written more than 25 books on computer software and have been an ACT! consultant for many years. One constant in my experience is the lack of an easy way to generate reports from the data in databases. Crystal Reports solves that problem.

But most folks do not use a report writer every day. At the end of the month or quarter, all of a sudden you or the boss needs a report on sales activity of a product or sales force, and you are in crunch time trying to figure out how to get the report you want without that creeping feeling of desperation. So I have designed the book to allow you to easily turn to the page you need to find the necessary steps for success. Therefore, the book is targeted to beginners and intermediate users. You do not have to read this book cover to cover; just grab the chapter or subject you require, and read that. The structure is such that if you are a true beginner, you can start with the first few chapters and get a report out the door. If you have written your own database application, you can go to Chapter 7 on formulas and discover the elements necessary to convert your data to a format Crystal can use.

You need not be a database expert to use Crystal Reports. If you understand how to start programs in Windows 95 and know what data you want to use in reports, you should be in great shape!

Foolish Assumptions

I have made a few. First, that you are familiar with the rudiments of using a computer and Windows 95 — like a mouse is not an animal and Windows has nothing to do with panes (although *pains* may be accurate). Second, that you have, or someone has, installed Crystal Reports and that you have worked with some sort of database program from which you want to garner reports. I do not assume that you understand how databases are con-structed — I cover that in Chapter 1. Last, I trust that you have discovered that a computer is stupid — that is, it only does what you ask it to do, and on top of that, it requires that you learn a special language to communicate with it. That is why the phrase "user-friendly" ranks up there with "the check is in the mail" on the list of oft-quoted fibs.

How This Book Is Organized

In this book, I try to present the steps to creating reports and then adding enhancements in the sequence most new users would. You may find other ideas as to the topics you want to approach and in what order, so glance through the following chapter descriptions, and empower yourself.

Note: The screenshots in this manual will show the Crystal Reports screen as you would see if you are using Windows 95 or Windows NT 4. If you are using a different version of Windows, your screen may look slightly different (for example, Windows 95 and Windows NT will show a check mark when a check box is turned on whereas other versions of Windows will show an x). Don't worry about this; you follow the same steps throughout this manual in any and all versions of Windows unless otherwise noted.

Part I: What You Need to Know to Survive

Chapter 1: Setting the Table

Not everyone comes to the report-creation process skilled at using and understanding databases. So read this chapter if you have never had to create a database but have only entered data into one. This chapter gives you an idea of how the information is stored and why it is done that way.

Chapter 2: Creating a Simple Report

This chapter takes you through the beginning stages of creating a report, including how to determine the type of report you want and how to start inserting database information into a report. I also give you an introduction to an easy way to generate reports with the Crystal Reports Experts.

Chapter 3: Crystal Reports: Basic Skills

The text in a report refers to the stuff you may add that is separate from the database information, such as headings, titles, and footers A report is only as good as the information it conveys, and the text objects make the report more easily understood.

Part II: Manipulating Records

Chapter 4: Selecting Records

When you access a database, you may want all of the records that are in the database or just a certain type of record. This chapter shows you how to pick the ones you want.

Chapter 5: Sorting and Grouping Records

You can manipulate database records in a number of ways. This chapter covers changing the sort order and creating groups.

Part III: Formatting and Formulas for Success

Chapter 6: Graphing Data

This chapter shows you more on how to add pizzazz to your reports to make them more readable — and the information more accessible.

Chapter 7: Using the Crystal Formula Language

A powerful tool, formulas are the way to convert data, combine data from different tables, and perform calculations on data in tables. After you have learned the concept of how to construct and insert formulas into a report, you reach a higher plane of reporting.

Chapter 8: Using Conditional Formatting

Want a record (such as those that are negative numbers or group) formatted depending on the information contained? This chapter is where you find the steps to do so.

Part IV: Putting On Some Finishing Touches

Chapter 9: Formatting Sections of a Report

This chapter offers a further look at applying formatting based on the information in a report section, making it easy to highlight good news — or downplay bad news.

Chapter 10: Creating Presentation-Quality Reports

How about adding pictures, logos, and OLE objects to the report? Find out how in this chapter.

Part V: Creating Specific Types of Reports

Chapter 11: Creating a Cross-Tab Report

A cross-tabulation report allows you an entirely different look at your database information. It's used frequently in market research as adjunct to survey data. A cross tabulation can deliver new insights into your customers and prospects. Crystal Reports makes the process of creating a cross tabulation easy.

Chapter 12: Creating a Summary Report

A summary report is one that prints or displays only the summary information developed by the report process. In other words, when the boss wants only the bottom line, Crystal Reports can deliver. This chapter shows you how to create such a report.

Chapter 13: Linking to Other Databases

Links are a way of combining information from a variety of tables, in a variety of ways. In this chapter, I explain the best ways to join data from different tables.

Part VI: Disseminating Reports without a Hitch

Chapter 14: Distributing Reports

This chapter covers compiling, mailing, and exporting your reports, including posting a report to a Web site.

Chapter 15: Setting Your File Options

Each time you create a report, there are some automatic settings that determine the size of text, where files are saved and so on. Each of the settings can be customized to give you complete control of the look of your reports.

Part VII: The Part of Tens

Chapter 16: Ten Questions to Ask before You Create a Report

Revel in ten questions that — if asked — make creating any report easier.

Chapter 17: Ten Tricks to Enhance Reports

Shine with ten proven means of adding appeal to a report.

Conventions Used in This Book

Taking a leap, I have ignored the Geneva Convention, so often invoked on *Hogan's Heroes,* and have employed the following:

When the instructions say choose File menu and Save, it means that you are to use your mouse to click (using the left mouse button) on the File menu name and then, from the menu that appears, select the Save option. The underlined letter is another means of making the choice. For example, pressing the Alt key and holding it down while pressing the F key also opens the menu.

Occasionally, you will be asked to type text or a number to make an example work. Whenever that's the case, the text you are to enter appears in **bold type**.

When you read "select the text," that means you are to click and hold the left mouse button and drag it over the text until it is highlighted, and then release the mouse button.

There are also times when you are asked to select an option that is not a menu item but is a choice that must be clicked with the left mouse button. The selection is displayed in the following typestyle: equal to, sum

At no point do I ask you to refer to the Crystal Reports manual. The manual is very comprehensive, if a bit dry. When you get the reporting basics down, you can peruse it for the advanced topics that I don't cover.

Icons Used in This Book

To help you find quickly the information you want to read, or at least to make that information a little more memorable, I've strategically strewn icons throughout this book. Here is the lowdown on the little pictures:

The information beside this icon is a good piece of information to know: Save time, avoid delays, get ahead, and prosper with these tidbits.

Not that Crystal Reports is dangerous or anything (unless you drop the official User's Guide on your foot), but this icon can warn you about things that keep you out of trouble.

If you are interested in the technical and advanced stuff, this icon is the place to go for such information. But you shouldn't need a Ph.D. from MIT to follow along.

This icon reminds you to remember information that it signals. Keep this stuff somewhere in memory or at least written down on the back of envelopes in the top-right drawer of your desk.

If you want to appreciate what Crystal Reports can do, this icon will point them out for you. Some things may seem like magic.

The information beside this icon is considered basic, common knowledge to have in order to function within Crystal Reports. Sort of like the time you were forced in fifth grade to memorize all the provinces of Canada or the 50 U.S. state capitals so that you could function in life. Basic, common knowledge.

Where to Go from Here

With a cloud of dust and a hearty "Hi-ho Silver away!" you are on your journey to go where no report writer has gone before. I promise to make it an easy journey, with few delays and much productivity.

Part I
What You Need to Know to Survive

In this part . . .

You know that sooner or later you're going to have to finish that report that your boss asked for. This part shows you how to get something in the boss's hands pretty quick. Really. It's pretty easy to use Seagate Crystal Reports even though the MIS department bought the program and dropped it in your lap with a slight sneer. Open a report and pop in a few fields and you're in business. Add a couple of titles, and people will think you are an undiscovered genius. I'm not kidding. It happened to a friend of a relative of a guy that my brother knows. He started creating reports with Crystal Reports and, before you know it, he got a good-paying-annual-raise-three-weeks-off-dental-care-plan-never-get-fired government job. You could be next!

Chapter 1

Setting the Table

*W*hat is life without reports? Every business has a database of some sort, and from those databases, people expect reports. The problem is, most of the products, such as Paradox, Access, ACT!, dBASE, and Peachtree, to name a few, have report-creating capabilities that are limited and clumsy. In addition, corporate users want to create reports on databases that may be in SQL (Structured Query Language), Oracle, or another mainframe database.

Seagate Crystal Reports will create terrific-looking reports from the data you have from almost any format. Before starting the program, I want to show you how data is stored in products such as Access, Paradox, or FoxPro so that you have an understanding of how Crystal Reports works with your data.

In the Beginning, a Table

When you create a database in virtually any program, a *table* is created into which the data is entered. This is true whether you enter data into a *form screen* (a screen resembling an invoice or other paper type form) or into tabular fields, which is like a spreadsheet with rows and columns.

What do you see when you look at a real world table? Food! Me too. But in a computer, a table is a structure for storing information. You view the table you sit down to at Thanksgiving from above. You see the turkey, mashed potatoes, gravy, and so on as individual items *on* the table.

Not so with a database table. You look at computer tables from the *side*. So, across the top of the table is a list of fields, and underneath the table top are legs (usually more than the four that a dinner table has). Figure 1-1 shows a computer table.

Figure 1-1:
A computer
table.

Record	Turkey	Mashed Potatoes	Pie
Alex	6	10	6
Ilsa	2	2	1
Gloria	1	3	3

Because the view is from the side, the top of the table has the column headings, which in this example are Record, Turkey, Mashed Potatoes, and Pie. In a computer database, these would be the *field names* that are in the database.

The names on the left are the individual names (or *records,* in database terms): Alex, Ilsa, and Gloria. In some databases, this column would hold a unique identifier number such as the record number or a person's Social Security number.

A Thanksgiving table is held up by legs of some sort. In a computer database, the table legs separate the individual pieces of data. In Figure 1-1, the number of servings of turkey eaten by Alex (6) is separated by the table leg from the number of servings of mashed potatoes (10) and the number of pieces of pie (6).

A database record consists of the individual pieces of data that run from left to right across and underneath the table top. So, Alex, Ilsa, and Gloria are individual records.

The field names in your database are more likely to be First Name, (Fname), Last Name, (Lname), Address 1, (Add1), Address 2, (Add2), City, State, and Zip as shown in Figure 1-2. The names are shortened for simplicity, although if you do not know what the abbreviations stand for, things are actually more confusing.

Figure 1-2:
A sample
database
table.

Record#	Fname	Lname	Add1	Add2	City	State	Zip
1	Doug	Wolf	1st	Street	NY	NY	10025
2	Gloria	Lenares	2nd	Place	SF	CA	90024

Form Follows Function

As I mentioned earlier, the database you work with may resemble a form. Figure 1-3 shows a database program into which records are entered into the table via a form. Each of the fields in this form are the same as the table headings.

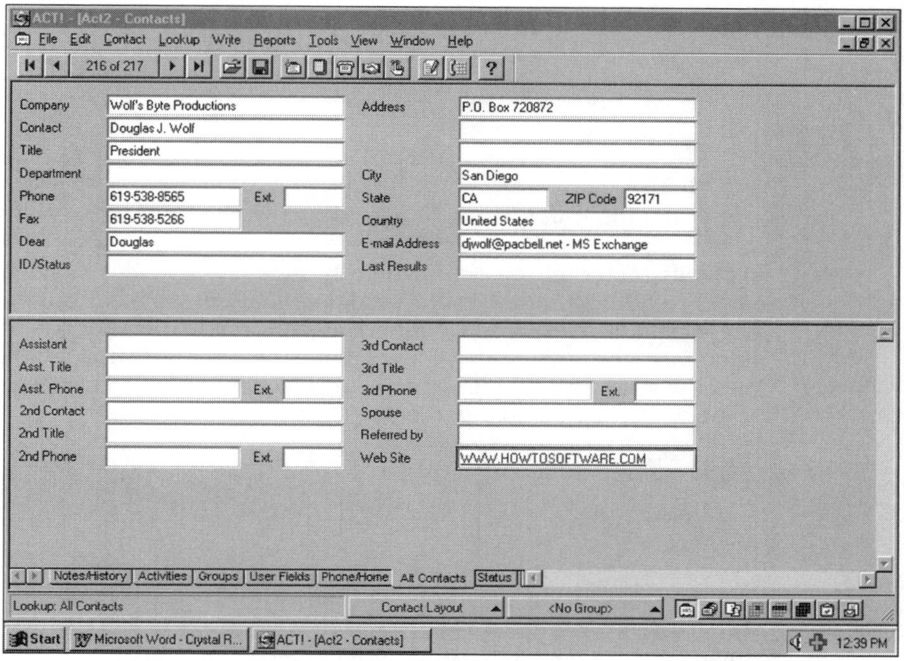

Figure 1-3:
Form view
of a
database.

So, as you can see, no matter how you enter data into a database, all the information ends up in a table. That is where Crystal Reports comes in.

After you enter thousand of records, any database makes finding and editing one or several an easy task. You can even sort the records by zip code. But, suppose that you want to send a direct mail piece to each of the customers, using bulk mail. The Post Office has strict rules about how the mail is sorted and grouped. Crystal Reports can easily sort and compile a report that shows you how many customers you have in each zip code and sort them in the proper order. In other words, Crystal Reports starts where the reports built in to whatever program you are using as a database leave off.

Table for . . . One or More?

Now consider how a real database is constituted. Suppose that your company has products with repeat sales. That is, you sell the same things over and over to the same customer base. If you were the architect of the company's electronic database (in computer lingo, a *systems design engineer,* harumph), sooner or later you would notice that every time the customer ordered, essentially the same data is needed to fill the order.

Retyping the customer name, address, and so on with every order would be a great waste of time, not to mention re-entering the product information such as price. The solution: Use several tables to hold the data.

1. Customer information
2. Product Information
3. Order information

In the customer information table, you have the specifics of where to ship, where to bill, and so on. Each customer would be assigned a unique customer number. Next, you would create a product table that has each product listed by name and number including the price so that the database calculates the cost. Last, you create the order when the customer places an order. In the order, you are going to enter:

1. Customer number
2. Product number and quantity

If you have constructed your database properly, the correct customer and product information is entered for you and the order is complete. This scenario is very typical. Your report may need to involve several tables or a single table from a database. So remember this:

A database can consist of a single table but most likely consists of several interconnected tables.

Keep this fact in mind while working through the examples in the text. I begin with a single table, show off the Crystal Reports attributes as best I can, and then move onto using multiple tables to make a report in Chapter 13.

If you are working on standard PC-type databases (such as dBASE, FoxPro, and Paradox), each table is a separate file stored on a local or network drive. Therefore, each time you need a table for you report, you add another physical file — a .dbf file for a dBASE database, for example. But think again about that pesky SQL and a related term — relational databases. A *relational database* is a database designed on the relational model and contains many tables within one database. To obtain information from these tables, an application uses or "talks" SQL. Examples of common relational databases are Oracle, Sybase, and DB2. The interface to SQL or relational databases from Crystal Reports is ODBC.

Plan the Report

The first thing you need to do before starting Crystal Reports is sit down with a piece of paper and decide what you want in the report. Admittedly, at this point visualizing the exact layout of the report may be difficult, but you or the Dilbert-like person demanding the report be on his desk by Friday should have a clear idea of what you want to appear in the report. Keep in mind that Crystal Reports allows for the creation of myriad mathematical formulas — from simple totals, averages, and maximum and minimums to expressions that Einstein would have admired. You can include graphs, footers, headers, and so on. So, if you anticipate computational needs instead of adding them after the report is constructed, you will save time — and that is the stuff life is made of.

If you are creating a complex report — one that will involve several tables, determine which fields from each table you will be using and how they will be linked. In Chapter 13, I show you a terrific Crystal Reports tool for linking disparate tables.

The other benefits of Crystal Reports, such as the nifty formatting of numbers or text or adding your company logo, can be added at any time — so no need to worry about planning those enhancements right now.

What makes a report?

When you look at a professionally prepared paper report, it usually has a report header, page headings, the details of the individual page, and a report footer.

So does Crystal Reports. Every report that you create will have standard layout sections. The trick to understanding how Crystal Reports transfers the paper world to your computer desktop is to think this way: *All of the parts of a paper report are represented in the Crystal Reports report window.* In other words, Crystal Reports layers the parts of a paper report onto the computer window so that you can see all the parts at the same time — from title section to summary section.

Crystal Reports uses the information in existing databases. It does not create new databases, nor does it affect the data in the source database itself. If you are working on a large database such as a mainframe Oracle database with 200,000 records, Crystal Reports is designed to let you access the records you need to create the report outline, and then when the design is finished, you can broaden the selection of records to include more records and more data.

Report distribution

The point of creating reports is distribution of the information. Not only can you print, fax, or e-mail a report, but Crystal Reports also provides a way for you to create a report file that anyone can run on her computer, enabling her to examine the report in detail.

The origin of Crystal Reports (from the book of Relation, Chapter 1, Verse 1)

Now in that time, a mighty tribe of Programmers existed known as dBASE nerds. They dwelt in the land of Southern California, known for its fine beaches and beautiful weather. But the dBASE nerds did not surf, nor did they spend much time in the Eden-like climate. Verily, the dBASE nerds were mighty storers of information, creating databases that only the high priests of the tribe could understand. And the people cried out, "You dBASE nerds have created these mighty storehouses of data, but we cry for reports! Reports with cross tabs and graphs and lots of fancy fonts." The Programmer High Priests were sore afraid, and asked themselves, "What can we do? We have the knowledge of getting data in, but we cannot get it out! We shall be broken into 16 and even 32 bits! Is no one among us able to satisfy the thirst for reports?"

And much lamenting and wailing occurred about their lack of reports. But they knew not what to do. So in this time a small tribe in the northern lands known as Canada had a tribe of Programmers, too. They were known as the Crystals. These Crystals were skilled in the ways of the database and had the secret knowledge of reports. And lo and behold, from them sprang forth code that took data to a place it had never been. The code created reports so easily that the people were amazed, and their e-mail and faxes chattered with the news. Verily they asked the Crystals for a name for this stupendous code. The wise men of Crystal gathered in council and thought long and hard; much pasta and hops were consumed. Then, after their deliberation, they drew their tribe unto them and declared: "We hereby exclaim the name of our code to be CRYSTAL REPORTS! Go forth from this place and spread the word that a new way of creating reports now exists among us. Truly we have been blessed! And a book shall be struck, so that all of the unwashed, known as *Dummies*, shall come to have knowledge of Crystal Reports and the world shall be made good. We have said it; so it shall be. "

Chapter 2

Creating a Simple Report

- -

In This Chapter
▶ Starting Crystal Reports
▶ Accessing a database
▶ Inserting fields
▶ Previewing a report
▶ Moving objects
▶ Using guidelines
▶ Using Crystal Reports Experts

- -

*I*n this chapter, you plumb the depths of opening a database and inserting its fields into a report. You also look at the way Seagate Crystal Reports allows you to easily see what your report looks like by using the Preview.

Starting Crystal Reports

When you install Crystal Reports on your computer, it adds the Crystal Reports program to a Crystal Reports program group. Now, how you start Crystal Reports depends on what "flavor" of Microsoft Windows you are using. Are you using Windows 95, Windows NT 3.51 or 4.0, Windows for Workgroups, or just plain old Windows?

If your computer is running Windows 95 or Windows NT 4.0, to start Crystal Reports just do the following:

Note: Don't forget that the screenshots in this book show Crystal Reports in Windows 95.

1. Click the Start menu.

2. Select Programs.

Windows 95 displays a list of programs installed on your computer.

3. Click Seagate Crystal Reports 6.0.

A sub-menu appears. If you have the Professional version of 6.0, you see a series of programs you can run.

4. Click 16- or 32-bit Crystal Report Designer.

If you are using any other version of Windows (Windows for Workgroups, Windows NT 3.51, or Windows 3.1), your original computer screen will have the Crystal Reports program group visible in the Program Manager. Just do the following:

1. If the Crystal Reports program group is not already maximized (if you can see a bunch of icons/pictures within the program group, it is maximized), double-click it to make it maximized.

2. Double-click the 16- or 32-bit Crystal Reports icon.

When you start Crystal Reports, a dialog box opens that gives you several choices. You can start creating a New Report, Open an existing Report, or Cancel. You can turn off the Welcome dialog box if you would rather not see it. To do so, click in the box next to Show welcome dialog at startup, so that no check mark appears. Just because you turn it off doesn't mean you've worn out your welcome; you simply have to use the File menu to get going. The Welcome dialog box appears in Figure 2-1.

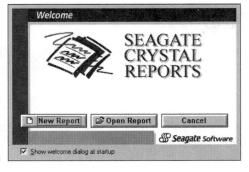

Figure 2-1:
The Crystal Reports startup dialog box greets you.

For the example that I want to use, the choice is New Report.

1. Click the New Report button.

The next dialog box is the Report Gallery, as shown in Figure 2-2. The Report Gallery is a collection of report formats from which you can choose to begin creating a report.

Report creating options

In Crystal Reports, you have three options when creating reports: Experts, Another Report, or Custom.

Experts: Ah, it's an oxymoron; you don't have to be an expert to use an Expert. Experts are similar to Microsoft's Wizards. You are walked through each step in the report creation process. It's quick, it's easy, and it's foolproof — you won't forget any major steps. Business users love experts and usually use experts to quickly start a report that they can then fine-tune. Power users still use Experts because they're quick, and then the power users just go from there. See "Using the Gallery Report Experts" at the end of this chapter for more information on working with Experts.

Another Report: Ever opened up a word-processing document, started to modify it with the intention of saving it under a different name, and then forgot? Oops. The Another Report option makes sure this never happens. You get a "new, clean" version of the original report and never have to worry about overwriting or ruining the original.

Custom: With this option you can build the report from the ground up. It gives you a ton of control — you do what you want, when you want. It's normally used by people who like to build the report from the ground up. And working with the custom option is a great way to learn about Crystal Reports. See where I'm going with this? I use the Custom option through the majority of this book to teach you all the fun, juicy stuff.

Figure 2-2:
The Report
Gallery
dialog box.

The Report Gallery offers you the opportunity to begin creating a specific type of report right away. To learn more about the various types and how to use the Report Gallery, see "Using the Report Gallery Experts," later in this chapter.

2. Go ahead and click the Custom button.

This button reveals a further set of reports from which to choose, as you see in Figure 2-3.

Ah, what button, what button?

Data File: Use this option when you want to use a standard PC type database in your report (for example, MS Access, FoxPro, or dBASE).

SQL/ODBC: Use this option when you want to use a Structured Query Language database in your report (MS SQL Server, Oracle, Sybase). And you also click this button if you are using any data that is accessed via Microsoft's Open Database Connectivity (ODBC) Some examples are Informix, DB2/2, Lotus Notes, and Excel.

Dictionary: When you think of Dictionary, you probably think of the Webster's version that translates unknown words. A Crystal Dictionary translates what can be very complicated data in a way the average Joe can understand. If a dictionary exists for you to use (and

someone has to have created it for you), you use this option.

Okay, but what if you've read all this and still don't know what button to hit on your computer? There are two ways you can solve this mystery:

✔ If there is a technical person in your organization or another Crystal Reports user, they may be able to help you — if you ask them nicely. It may even be worth a café latté.

✔ If you need to solve this problem on your own, refer to the Data Source chapter of the Crystal Reports User Guide or search on "Data Sources and Databases Index" in the Crystal Reports online help. Look up the database you're working with and voilà — problem solved.

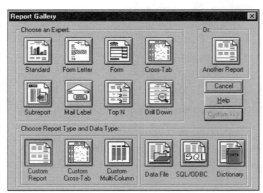

Figure 2-3:
The Report Gallery dialog box with the Custom Report types button exposed.

At this point, you have a choice. The example report in this chapter uses a database that was created for general use. If you have a specific database from which you want to create a report, you can open it instead. The Data File button allows you to open the database you want — and the one I want, so that is your next step.

3. Click the Data File button.

Crystal Reports opens the Choose Database File dialog box you see in Figure 2-4.

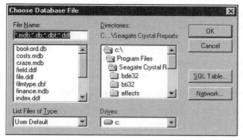

Figure 2-4:
The Choose Database File dialog box.

Crystal Reports can open virtually any type of data file. Remember that a database can consist of one or many tables. The example database I am using has several tables, but mine has only one to start with, an Access database named CRAZE. Figure 2-5 shows the CRAZE database as it looks in Access.

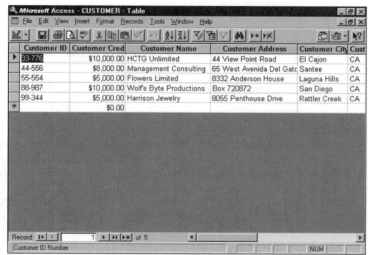

Figure 2-5:
The CRAZE database in Access.

Note: In this book, most of the time, I am going to use the sample data that comes with Crystal Reports. It is a Microsoft Access database called CRAZE.MDB. It contains all the information that the Craze

Mountain Bike Company wants to track for its customers, orders, suppliers, and so on. Even if you have not ridden a bicycle since Grade two, this data should be easy enough to relate to. Many customers need to track and report on data of this type.

Within the table are the field names — Customer ID, Customer Credit ID, Customer Name, and so on (the field names go further across to the right than the screen can show). These are the field names that Crystal Reports finds when you open this database table.

4. **To open the database you want, click the drop-down arrow in the List Files of Type box. Select the kind of database you want to open (you have to know the name and extension of the database).**

   You may have to switch to a different file folder and/or drive to locate your database. Or you may have to click the Network button to locate the database on a network drive.

   You are probably thinking: "I thought Windows 95 did away with those short, cryptic file names." Gotcha! When you name a file, the name can be in recognizable English, but Windows 95 waves a magic wand and creates an underlying filename in the old DOS 8.3 (eight characters, a period, and three more characters) format, such as BILGATES.MDB or KINGBILL.HRM.

5. **Double-click the file named CRAZE.MDB.**

   The Select Tables dialog box appears. This is an advanced feature of Crystal Reports that I cover in Chapter 13.

6. **For the moment, skip this advanced stuff by clicking Customer, then OK.**

   Crystal Reports opens the report window and the Insert Fields dialog box, as shown in Figure 2-6, and displays the individual field names from the CUSTOMER table.

Before going further, think about what you've done and what you are going to do. You have opened an Access database that consists of several tables. Crystal Reports uses the Insert Fields dialog box to list the field names of the CUSTOMER table in the Report window. At this point, you can select the field names and place them in your report. When you do so, Crystal Reports knows that you want to use the data from the records in the CUSTOMER table to create your report.

The Report Design Tab

You are on the brink of creating your first report. Before inserting field names, a trip around the Report Design Tab is in order. Remember, Crystal Reports is an electronic version of a paper report and therefore has the same basic components. So look at the report sections in Figure 2-7.

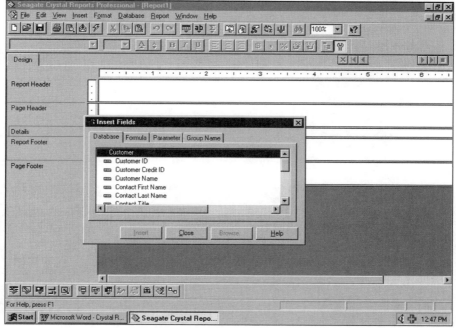

Figure 2-6:
The Report
window
with the
Insert Fields
dialog box.

✔ **Report Header:** This section represents the title or front page of the report. In this section, you insert a title, perhaps a graph, and maybe even a company logo. This section prints once at the beginning of the report.

✔ **Page Header:** This section represents the header that appears at the top of every page of the report. It also contains the field names for the columns of data in the body of the report.

✔ **Details:** This section represents the portion of the report that has the individual records from the database. It appears small in the Design Tab, but it is the section that holds the most data. This section prints one time for every record in the database.

✔ **Report Footer:** This section represents the portion of the report in which you can print grand totals and cross-tabulations. It appears once, at the end of the report.

✔ **Page Footer:** This section represents the portion of the report that prints at the bottom of every page. It can contain page numbers, the report name, and so on.

Although you cannot see initially the following sections in the Design Tab, Crystal Reports adds two more sections if you create groups of data. After you get comfortable with simple reports, you may want to add grouping (see Chapter 5) to your arsenal. A *group* is a subset of the records in the report.

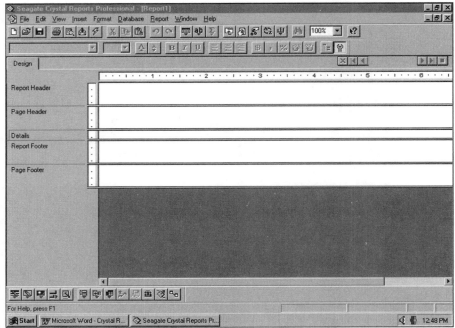

Figure 2-7:
The various
sections in
the Report
Design Tab.

 ✔ **Group Header:** This section contains the group name field, and you can insert a graph, cross-tabulations, and summaries. It prints once at the beginning of each group.

 ✔ **Group Footer:** This section is a special footer that contains a summary value for the group and prints at the end of each group (and can contain other information).

Note: I've tried to give you some examples of what you can place in various sections, but you can be quite creative. For example, Crystal Reports puts the Group Name in the Group Header and the group totals in the Group Footer, but you can do just the opposite.

Inserting Data Fields

Every table consists of fields. In those fields is the information about which you want to report. Crystal Reports needs to have you pick the fields that you want in your report and then place them on the Report Design Tab. In this example report, you may want to include the business name of the customer, the city in which the customer is located, the state, and the total of last year's sales — in all, a total of four fields. The steps to insert fields are the same with every report:

1. **After you start Crystal Reports, select the database that you want to use for the report.**

2. **From the Insert Fields dialog box, select the table you want to use.**

   The Insert Field dialog box opens.

3. **Click the field name you want to include.**

4. **Click the Insert button.**

5. **Move the pointer to the section of the report where you want the field to appear.**

6. **Click the mouse button.**

   The field is inserted at that point.

When you last left the Craze Mountain Bikes database, you had opened CRAZE.MDB, which is the database, and double-clicked the CUSTOMER table, which revealed the list of field names in CUSTOMER, as shown in Figure 2-8.

Figure 2-8:
The Insert
Fields
dialog box
and
Customer
database
fields.

To insert the Customer Name field into the Report Design Tab:

1. **Click the field name Customer Name.**

   At the bottom of the dialog box, the Insert and Browse buttons become active. More on the Browse button in the section "Browsing Data" later in this chapter.

2. **Click the Insert button.**

   A funny thing happens! The mouse pointer becomes the international sign for stop — a circle with a line drawn through it. You have not violated any international treaty! Crystal Reports is simply telling you that you have a field attached to the pointer and it is ready for insertion but not in the section where the mouse is currently positioned (your next step).

3. **Drag the pointer toward the top of the screen.**

When the pointer is positioned over the Design layout, the pointer once again transforms. This time, it is a long rectangle, meaning that the field can be properly inserted, as shown in Figure 2-9.

4. **Position the rectangle in the Details section of the Design Tab as it is in Figure 2-9.**

5. **Click the mouse button to finish the insertion.**

The result appears in Figure 2-10.

After you insert a field, the name of the field is represented by a series of Xs. The number of Xs alerts you to the length of the field you have inserted and that the field is a text field. The length of the field comes from the database field, not from Crystal. So a single field can go all the way across from left to right. (I show you how to shorten a long field in a moment.)

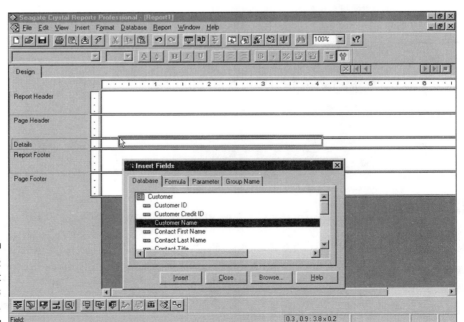

Figure 2-9:
The Insert
Fields
rectangle.

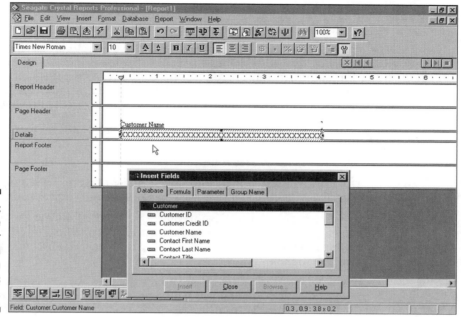

Figure 2-10:
The
Customer
field
inserted in
the Details
section.

Control and shift to select multiple fields at once

If you want to quickly place a couple of fields on the report in one step:

1. **Click the first field in the Insert Fields dialog box to select it.**

2. **Ctrl+Click on second and subsequent fields to select them as well.**

   Now when you insert, you will be inserting multiple fields.

If you want to quickly insert a number of adjacent fields:

1. **Click the first field in the Insert Fields dialog box to select it.**

2. **Shift+Click the last field you want to insert.**

   Notice how all fields between the two selected are now highlighted. Now when you insert, you will be inserting all highlighted fields.

Taking a Preview

The next step is to see the result of placing the field into the design. Crystal Reports has a very powerful feature called Preview, which works in conjunction with the Design Tab. As you make changes in the report of virtually any kind, including inserting fields, adding formatting or formulas, and so on, you can see the effect of the change immediately by going to the Preview Tab.

To Preview a change in a report, do the following:

1. Click the Print Preview button.

The Print Preview button looks like a sheet of paper with a magnifying glass over the top. Figure 2-11 shows the Preview that results.

As you can see, Crystal Reports has opened the Preview Tab and inserted the actual data from the Customer Name field into the report, adding the name of the field to the top of the list of customer names as a column heading.

When you start creating a new report, the Preview Tab is not displayed. Only the Design Tab appears. You must first generate a report by using the Print Preview button.

Figure 2-11:
A Preview
of the first
field you
inserted.

2. **Now that you have seen the Preview of the report, switch back to the Design Tab. Click the Design Tab at the top of the window.**

Voilà, back in the Design Tab.

You need to understand this concept: In the Design Tab, you are working with placeholders for the data; in the Preview Tab, you are working with actual data itself.

This two-window view of a report, the Design Tab and the Preview Tab, is what sets Crystal Reports apart from many other report writers. By switching back and forth between the two, you can build a report exactly as you want it because you can see the changes as quickly as you make them!

One other point to make is that when you are working in Preview, the response time of your computer may slow because you are using real data. As you make changes, the page has to be modified.

Inserting a Second Field

Adding a second field follows the same procedure as inserting the initial field, except that you have to position the field in the Details section in a different location. Crystal Reports assumes that you are going to continue to add fields to the report, so the Insert Fields dialog box is still open.

 If you closed the dialog box accidentally, click the Insert Fields button.

In this report, the plan is to include the customer name, the city in which the customer is located, the state, and the total of last year's sales. To this point, you have inserted the customer name. The next field to insert is the city field:

1. **Click and hold the mouse button on the City field name in the Insert Fields dialog box.**

2. **Drag the mouse pointer into the Detail section of the report, and position the rectangle to the right of the placeholder for the Customer Name.**

3. **Release the mouse button.**

The second field is inserted into the report as shown in Figure 2-12.

4. **Preview the new object by clicking the Preview Tab.**

The report preview appears in Figure 2-13.

Everything you place on a report, from fields to text to graphics, is referred to as *objects* in Crystal Reports lexicon. So you have inserted two objects: the Customer Name field and the City field.

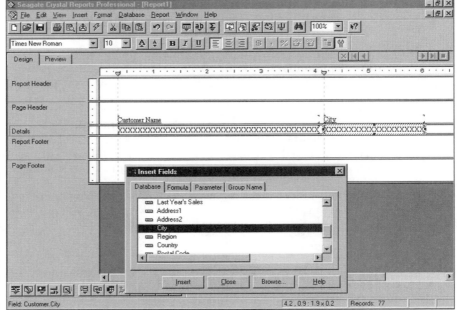

Figure 2-12:
The second field, City, is inserted into the Report Design window.

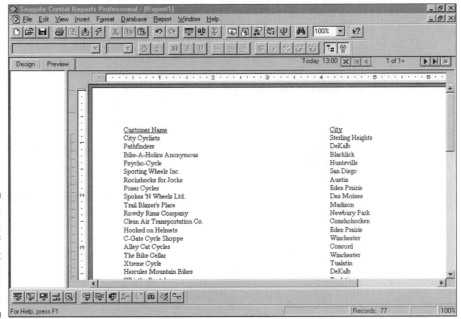

Figure 2-13:
The Preview of a report with a second field inserted.

Browsing Data

Many databases have multiple tables and multiple fields. In that situation, you can't be expected to remember exactly which table has the field you need to complete a report.

Before inserting a field into a report, you can look at a sampling of the data in the field and see whether it is the correct data and whether or not it is of a format that will work properly.

When you use Browse Field Data, you get a sampling of data. You will see the first 500 unique values for the field you are browsing. "Unique" meaning that if you are browsing on a City field, you would only see Vancouver once, even if there were 100 records from Vancouver. It is considered a sampling because Crystal is not showing you all the data, just a sampling. Would you really want to see the Order Number for a million records?

To Browse field data, do the following:

1. **In the Insert Fields dialog box, click the field name that you want to view.**

2. **Click the Browse button.**

   Crystal Reports opens a dialog box showing you the actual data from the field and listing the type of data it is. An example appears in Figure 2-14.

At the top of the dialog box it says that the Type is String and that the field length is 15. Of course, this information means nothing to you if you have not worked with data types. The "Type" and "Length" sections that follow may be helpful to you if this is the case.

Why use an X at all?

Crystal Reports tries to leave enough room for the worst case scenario. So, it needs to leave enough room to print the largest characters in width, which is the capital letter X. That's why the field is often so large.

The fact that Xs appear indicate that the field is a string. 5s will appear if the field is a number or currency field. Mar 3, 1996 represents a date field, and true represents a Boolean field. The size is an approximation of the worst case scenario (just in case all the characters were the largest proportional character "X"). That way, no characters are cut off. Crystal Reports is trying to make sure no information is not shown — it's trying to be smart.

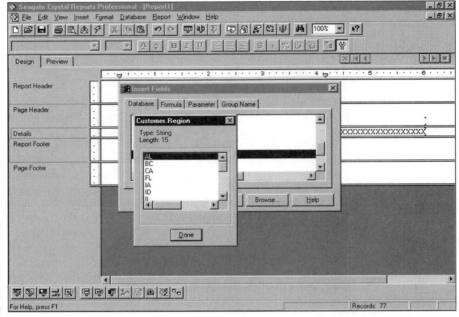

Type

A data type that is *string* means that it is a character field. A character field has nothing to do with personal values. Rather, it is a field where you can enter *letters* or *numbers*. So a character field may have 12345 or ABCDE and be a valid entry. This property is important because you cannot calculate a total for a character field (you can summarize a string but you can't sum). Now, you may be thinking: "If the field can have numbers, why can't I get a total?" The answer goes back to the type, which allows you to *mix* numbers and letters. The database designer decided that this field would be allowed to have either numbers or letters in the field. If the designer had designated the field as being Number, instead of String, you could perform calculations because no letters would have been allowed into the field.

Length

The second piece of information that the Browse process yields is the *length* of the field. Again, this length has been determined by the designer of the database, not by Crystal Reports. In this example, the length is 15 characters, which means 15 letters or numbers or a mixture of the two can be entered into the field. So when you inserted the field name Customer Name into the Details section of the report, Crystal Reports inserted 15 Xs as a visual indicator of how much space it was allowing for the field information.

This allocation does not mean that the data in the field *is* that long — only that the designer of the database allowed that much space. So you may find as you construct reports that the length allowed for the field is too much for the report. You can shorten the space allowed.

Changing the field length in the Design Tab

Often the length of the field in the database is a waste of space. That is, the data is never long enough to warrant the space allowed. A good example is the Region field shown in Figure 2-14. Scrolling through the data, you can see that all the record entries were two characters. In this case, the designer was using Region as the name for a field that most Americans would name State. However, some countries may have a longer name to indicate region — therefore the extra 13 characters. Because you can see that none of the records in this database have an entry longer than two characters, you can safely shorten the field.

Here's how to change the length of a field after it is selected:

1. **In the Design window, position the mouse pointer on the far right side of the placeholder that you want to change.**

   The mouse pointer changes to a small (tiny, even) two-headed arrow, pointing left and right. This transformed pointer indicates that you can change the size of the rectangle along the horizontal.

2. **Hold down the mouse button, and drag the mouse to the left.**

   The rectangle shrinks in size as you do. (If the whole rectangle moves, the pointer switched to a four-headed arrow, and you have moved the entire field. Drag the mouse back to where it was, and try again.)

3. **Release the mouse button after you have resized the field to your liking.**

   In Figure 2-15, the City field has been resized to a much shorter length.

4. **Click the Print Preview button, or the Preview Tab, to see the result of resizing.**

When you're resizing a field, click the field and then hold down the Ctrl key as you click the heading. By doing so, you resize both the field and the heading in one step.

In the example report, the City field, although shortened, is still a long way to the right of the Customer Name field. To add more fields to the report, having the two fields closer together would be better (take another look at Figure 2-13).

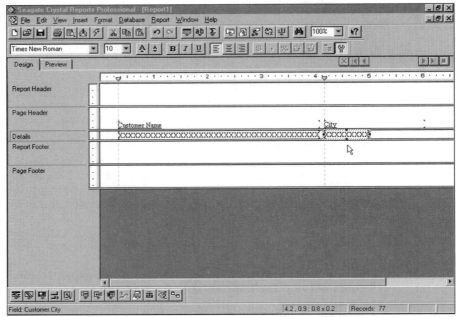

Figure 2-15:
The City
field
resized.

Changing field length in the Preview Tab

As you look at the report in the Preview Tab, how to change the length of a field is not as readily apparent as in the Design window. You can do it — you only have to click in the field.

To change a field length from the Preview Tab, do the following:

1. **Click the field.**

   Crystal Reports displays the report outline, as shown in Figure 2-16. The outline of the field length appears.

2. **Move the mouse pointer to the right side of the rectangle so that the pointer becomes an arrow pointing left and right.**

3. **Drag the pointer to the left, until the field is reduced to the desired length.**

4. **Release the mouse button.**

   If the whole rectangle moves, the pointer switched to a four-headed arrow, and you have moved the entire field. Drag the rectangle back to where it was, and try again.

In Figure 2-17, see the Customer Name field at a reduced size, from the Preview Tab.

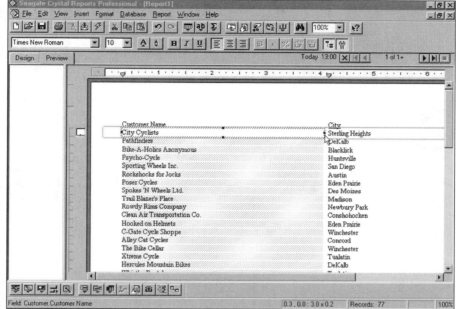

Figure 2-16:
You can see
Design
parameters
in the
Preview
mode, too.

Figure 2-17:
The
Customer
Name field
reduced in
the Preview
Tab.

Moving a Field in the Preview Window

With the size of a field reduced, more distance exists between the two fields, which means that you can move the City field to the left, leaving more room for more fields that you may want to add.

The Preview Tab accurately reflects what you will see on paper when the report is printed. If you have many fields in the report, besides reducing the length of individual fields, you can also change the print orientation to *landscape,* which means the report prints along the 11-inch edge of a piece of paper as opposed to the standard 8¹/₂-inch edge. As you work with a report, you may want to change the page orientation or even the page size. You can do this at any point by selecting File⇨Printer Setup and changing the paper size, page orientation, or even the printer used.

To move a field in the Preview Tab, do the following:

1. **Click the field.**

   When you place the cursor over the field, Crystal Reports displays the formatting outline, as shown in Figure 2-18.

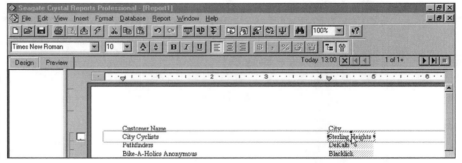

Figure 2-18:
The Field format outlined.

2. **Hold down the mouse button, and drag the field to the left.**

3. **Release the mouse pointer after the field is positioned correctly.**

   Figure 2-19 shows the City field moved to the left.

Well, the field has moved all right, but the column header, City, has not. The reason is that when you insert a field into a report, Crystal Reports assumes that you want to use the field name as the column header in the report. So it inserts the name, too. But you can move the header name, either in Design or Preview mode. Because you can change the name, it is not directly connected to the field itself. So it doesn't move with the field, either. To see the way this works, try the following:

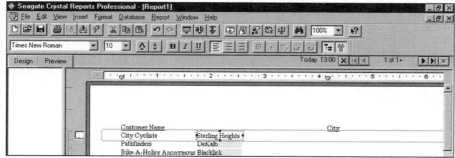

Figure 2-19:
The City
field, moved
to the left.

1. **Click the Design Tab.**

2. **Click on the City text object in the Page Header section.**

   In Figure 2-20, you can't tell that the name of the column is a separate
   object! Because it a separate object, you can edit and manipulate it
   separately from the field itself.

You can move a field and its heading separately. Seems like a lot of work,
doesn't it? You could save yourself a step by clicking the field, Ctrl+clicking
the column heading, and then moving them both at once.

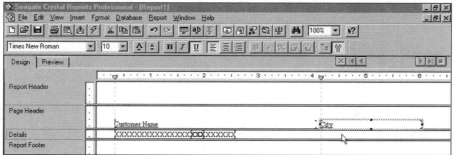

Figure 2-20:
The City
text
selected in
the Design
Tab.

Using a Guideline to Position Objects

Crystal Reports gives you a tool to line up the field header with the field.
Notice the vertical line that borders the left edge of the Customer Name text
field? Crystal Reports created this guideline when the field was inserted.

Here's how to move a vertical guideline:

1. **Click the guideline end in the ruler at the top of the window (it's the
   little upside-down triangle).**

2. **Hold the left mouse button down, and drag the guideline to the desired position on the ruler, in this example to the 2-inch mark.**

3. **Release the mouse button.**

A funny thing about a guideline is that objects that are *attached* to the guideline line themselves up to it. In other words, you can use the guideline to arrange and align a series of objects in a report.

To attach an object to a guideline, do the following:

1. **In the Design Tab, click the object you wish to align.**

2. **Hold the mouse button down, and drag the object so that its left edge is on the guideline.**

3. **Release the mouse button.**

You observe no changes in the object itself when it is attached to the line. To see whether an object is attached, click on the guideline end and drag it to the right or left. The object should move with the line.

Aligning a Field Name with a Field

In this example, I show you how to align the field header, City, with the field itself. Before doing that, however, I have a quick example on field sizes. Earlier in this chapter, in "Changing the field length in the Design Tab," I show you how to reduce the size of a field in the report. That section explains that the field header is automatically added to the report when you insert the field, but that the field header is a separate *object*. So Crystal Reports creates a text field for the header with the same number of spaces as the field itself. In the case of the City field name, it has 20 spaces allotted to it, even though the field name City is only 4 characters in length.

The logical thing to do before aligning the object is to reduce the number of spaces the field name uses to match its corrresponding object field.

1. **In the Design Tab, click the text object.**

2. **Position the mouse pointer at the right side of the rectangle until the two-headed arrow appears.**

3. **Click and drag the field outline until only the text is visible within the rectangle.**

4. **Release the mouse button.**

In the example report, I have reduced the size of both the Customer Name and City text boxes. This reduction makes them easier to work with, particularly the Customer Name, because it was a very large field. In Figure 2-21, both objects are selected, after being resized.

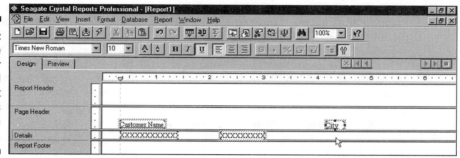

Figure 2-21:
The Customer Name and City text fields reduced in size.

Time to align the City text object and its concomitant field. (A great word! Throw this into the next conversation with the boss, and watch the eyebrows. It means things that are connected together, like the IRS and money, politicians and lying, computers and confusion. . . .)

I have already moved the vertical guideline to the 2-inch mark.

1. **Click and drag the City text box so that its left edge is aligned with the vertical guideline.**

2. **Click the City field, and drag it so that its left edge is aligned to the vertical guideline.**

   The results appear in Figure 2-22.

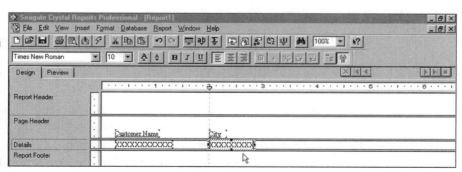

Figure 2-22:
The City text box and City field aligned to the vertical guideline.

Remember, to test the guideline, click and hold the mouse button on the guideline head in the ruler line, and drag the mouse right to left.

Using Guidelines in Preview

After aligning the objects, go back to Preview by clicking the Preview Tab. I want to show you how to use guidelines in this tab. The reason for using guidelines in this tab is the same as in the Design Tab — to line up objects. Remember, Crystal Reports allows you to arrange the report layout in either Design or Preview mode. The difference is that in Preview, you are working with real data and not placeholders. (So the performance of your computer may be diminished. In other words, stuff takes longer to happen in Preview than it does in Design, but in Preview you can see the actual report.)

To turn on guidelines in the Preview Tab, do the following:

1. **Choose File⇨Options.**

2. **In the dialog box that appears, click the Layout tab.**

   The dialog box opens, as in Figure 2-23.

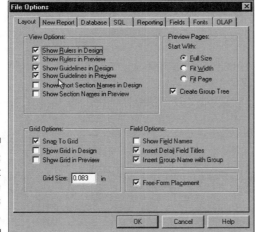

Figure 2-23:
The Layout
tab of the
File Options
dialog box.

A number of options are on this tab. Your concern is the single option, Show Guidelines in Preview. No check mark appears in front of that option, indicating that it is set to off.

3. **Click the box in front of the Show Guidelines in Preview option.**

4. **Click OK.**

   Not too hard, was it? Back in Preview, you can see whether the change has taken effect. Click the City text header object. The guidelines should appear, as in Figure 2-24.

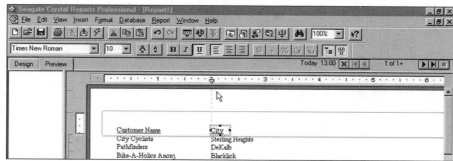

Figure 2-24:
The
guidelines
appear in
the Preview
Tab.

Other guidelines using grids

In addition to the vertical guidelines, you can create horizontal guidelines, too. You have no limit to the number of guidelines you can have in a report.

Grids

A *grid* is a cross section of horizontal and vertical lines. (In fact, the term *gridiron* as a synonym for a football field comes from the fact that at one time, the football field had vertical *and* horizontal lines.) Crystal Reports has a grid, too, which can aid in the placement of objects in the report. In fact, the gridlines have a property known as *Snap to Grid,* which means that when objects are placed they snap into alignment vertically and horizontally. This feature is terrific for those reports that require many objects beyond simple text headers and fields. The switch for turning this property off and on is in the same dialog as the guidelines (which I discuss in "Using Guidelines in Preview," earlier in this chapter).

Turning on the grid

Here's how to turn on the display of the grid:

1. **Choose File⇨Options.**

   The File Options dialog box opens.

2. **Click the Layout tab.**

3. **Click the Show Grid in Design and/or the Show Grid in Preview option.**

4. **Click OK.**

   The grid appears, as in Figure 2-25.

Using the Report Gallery Experts

As you start creating new reports, you have two broad options. After you select the File⇨New option, you can choose a Report Expert or the Custom option from the Report Gallery dialog box. The Custom option assumes that you know something about creating reports and do not need the guidance of the experts or that you prefer the control of creating your own reports from the ground up.

Looking at the Report Gallery

You must also have some knowledge of Crystal Reports if you choose the Custom Report, Custom Cross-tab, and the Custom Multi-Column reports. However, what if you know the type of report you want but need help? Crystal Reports provides an "expert" to guide you through the steps needed to create the report. Thus, the second path is to use the Crystal Reports built-in experts! Users new to Crystal Reports love the Report Creation Experts because, within a few minutes, they can create very powerful reports. Even techies sometimes start their reports using a Report Expert.

Take a look at the Report Gallery.

1. **Close any reports you have open (by selecting File⇨Close).**

2. **Choose File⇨New (or click the New Report button).**

   The Report Gallery dialog box appears as in Figure 2-26.

Figure 2-26:
The Report
Gallery
dialog box.

At the beginning of this chapter, you use the Custom option and then you choose Data File to create a report from scratch. Now take a different path. The Report Experts are available on the following report types, and here is a brief explanation of each type:

- **Standard:** This button takes you through the steps to create a standard report, which you will see the steps to in a moment.

- **Form Letter:** Form letters are a common task that people want to create using their database information. Crystal Reports helps you insert the fields you want in the form letter — for example, the address fields and perhaps a field that has an amount due for a bill, a start date for a project, or whatever is appropriate for your business. Then you can import a text file as the body of the letter.

- **Form:** Do you have a form that you use all the time and it would be much better if it were computerized? Use this expert to create a computer form of your paper form.

- **Cross-Tab:** A Cross-Tab is a report that reveals information in your database in a *by* manner. An example is tabulating sales for a product *by* store. These have a spreadsheet-like look. Chapter 11 covers Cross-Tabs in detail.

- **Subreport:** A subreport is a report that runs inside a master report. The concept of a subreport is that the subreport can be using entirely unrelated database information from the master report. So it could be a graph that shows the total sales for the company, while the master report shows the sales for a specific division.

- **Mail Label:** Generally, getting names to align properly on labels from a database is very tricky. Creating a mailing label from the names in your database is the task of this expert.

- **TopN:** A TopN report reveals the top salespeople in your company, the top performing states in terms of sales, or, conversely, the bottom performing products or states. Chapter 5 covers this type of report.

- **Drill Down:** A drill-down report is a technique for finding detailed information behind a number. For example, if you have a total in your report, the total can be drilled down to show the individual values that compose the total.

Stepping out with an Expert: A Standard Report

The advantage of using the Report Experts is that you cannot miss a step accidentally. That is, you are walked through the correct process necessary to creating the report. I expand upon these reports and their steps in subsequent chapters. Because each of these types of reports have some aspects in common and some specific to the type of report, I derive the following sequence from the Standard Report Expert.

From the Report Gallery dialog box, if you click the Standard button, the Create Report Expert dialog box appears, as in Figure 2-27.

Figure 2-27:
The Create Report Expert dialog box with the Data tab selected.

At the top of this dialog box are a series of tabs. You can select a tab at any time if you know you want to jump ahead to that tab. Otherwise, the Expert steps you through each tab in order.

Data

The initial tab in this dialog box is the Data tab. This tab is used to select the database from which you are going to create the report. The options for selecting a database source are listed in the dialog box. The steps to select a database table are covered earlier in this chapter.

After selecting a database file, Crystal Reports gives you the opportunity to add another database table to the report. This option is for those instances in which the report will include data from unique database files.

Links

The next tab is the Links tab. This tab only appears when you have selected several unique tables. The Visual Linking dialog box appears, allowing you to create the necessary links between and among the tables. Linking tables is covered in detail in Chapter 13.

Fields

At this point, you select the individual fields you want in the report. This subject is also covered earlier in this chapter (see "Inserting Data Fields").

Sort

After adding the fields to your report, the next tab is Sort. Crystal Reports is offering you the opportunity to sort the report records by the field of your choice. This tab allows you to also group the records, such as by state or by product. Sorting and grouping records are the subjects of Chapter 5.

Total

Next, Crystal Reports assumes that you want some subtotals, summaries, and grand totals included in the report. So if you have selected a field such as Sales, you can create a subtotal for that field, particularly if you have grouped the sales field by state or product. Adding subtotals is covered in this chapter and in Chapter 7.

TopN

The TopN tab provides a tool for determining which groups have the top five sales numbers, the top ten salespeople, or any other top number you need (you must have a group with a subtotal for this to work). If you were Casey Kasem, you would want the top ten hit songs for the past week listed. You can bypass this tab if your report does not use the TopN feature. Chapter 5 deals with TopN Sorts and other types of sorting and grouping.

Graph

Inserting a graph into your report is available via the Graph tab. Crystal Reports has its own graph editor; therefore you can create virtually any type of graph and annotate to fit your needs and then insert it directly into your report, as brilliantly described in Chapter 6. If you don't require a graph in the report, simply skip this tab.

Select

The Select tab is next, and this is an important aspect of Crystal Reports. As you design your report, you may not want all the records in the source database to be part of the report. You may want only records of last month's sales or only the records of sales of ski boots. The Select tab allows you to use only the records you want, as detailed in Chapter 4.

Style

The Standard Report expert concludes with a choice of report formats, selected from the Style tab. That is, taking all the choices you have made to this point, Crystal Reports includes several handy layouts for formatting the report data. You can take a look at each of the layouts in the dialog box. After choosing a Style, you can then proceed to Preview the report, which is a WYSIWYG (what you see is what you get) view of the report. I cover using a variety of formatting techniques in Chapters 8 and 10.

Why you should use an Expert

Not all the Experts arrive at the report in the same manner, but I would advise using them for the reason I stated earlier: They lead you step-by-step through the process, thereby eliminating any worry about forgetting a step. Not that you wouldn't get a report without using an Expert, but, on your own, you may not get the exact report you want.

In addition, now you can return to the Report Expert to modify reports. After you preview your report, how do you go about fine-tuning it? Once the Report Expert creates the report, you can manually modify it using what you read about in this book. For example, you could modify the record selection or insert another field onto the report.

 But you may find it quicker to return to the Report Expert and make your changes there. To do this, simply click the Report Expert button or select the Report Expert command from the Report menu.

Chapter 3
Crystal Reports: Basic Skills

- -

In This Chapter

▶ Opening a saved report

▶ Inserting text objects

▶ Formatting text objects

▶ Moving among pages in a report

▶ Magnifying the report window

- -

*A*fter inserting fields, the next natural step is to add text to define and enhance your report. Text objects, as they are called in Seagate Crystal Reports, can be formatted in a number of ways, so I take a look at that, too. Finally on my agenda is a quick tour of how to move from page to page in a report.

Opening a Saved Report

In Chapter 2, I create a report into which I insert two fields. I then save the report with the brilliant and unique name, ch2. Here's how to open a saved report, using my report as an example:

1. **Open Crystal Reports.**

   The Welcome dialog box appears, as in Figure 3-1. (If you have clicked off the <u>S</u>how welcome dialog at startup box, you do not see this — see separate steps that apply to you later in this section.)

2. Click the Open Report button.

Crystal Reports opens the aptly named Open dialog box, as in Figure 3-2. (You can see my saved report — ch2 — in the lower-left corner.)

Figure 3-2:
The Open
dialog box.

3. Select (by clicking) the report that you want.

I click ch2, of course.

4. Click Open.

The report appears on your desktop, as mine does in Figure 3-3.

If you have problems opening the file, make sure that the Files of type box in the Open dialog box lists Crystal Reports. Second, make sure that you clicked the report name so that the name appears in the File name field *before* you clicked the Open button. One other possibility is that you saved the report in a folder other than the CRW folder, and you have to locate the report by checking other folders.

Figure 3-3:
Doug's ch2
report
opened.

If you have shut off the Welcome dialog box, open a saved report this way:

1. **After starting Crystal Reports, click the File menu.**
2. **From the File menu, select Open.**

   The Open dialog box appears.
3. **Click the name of the report you want.**
4. **Click Open.**

Inserting Text Objects

A *text object* is a type of object that you can insert into a report to describe what is in the report, to highlight a particular record, or to add a description. The most common use of a text object is the title for the report. Text objects can be added in the Design or Preview Tab. My advice is to add text objects in the Design Tab for reasons that soon become obvious.

When you insert fields from a database table, Crystal automatically adds the field name as the header for the column. The header is a text object; therefore, you can modify it by clicking it and typing a new name or by changing its font style.

With Windows 95, you can add more text to the names of the reports you create, and Crystal Reports also provides a means to add descriptive text to a report, as described in Chapter 17.

Adding a text object

Adding a text object from the Design Tab is easier because of the layout guides available, including the ability to see exactly to which section of the report the text object is being added, and in Preview the program slows considerably because you are working with live data. So all you need to do is click the Design Tab (which appears as in Figure 3-4).

The title for a typical report normally appears on the first page of that report. The Report Header section is where you place objects that you want to appear on the title page of the report, because this section of the report is designed to print once. Remember that everything that is part of a report is considered an *object*.

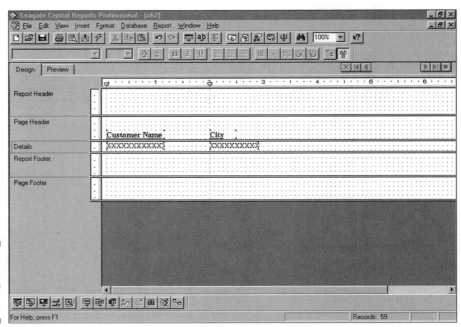

Figure 3-4:
The Design Tab view of the report.

To insert a text object in the Report Header section of a report:

1. **Click the Insert menu.**

2. **Click Text Object.**

   The mouse pointer has a rectangle outline attached, as shown in
   Figure 3-5.

Figure 3-5:
A rectangle
attached to
the pointer
— getting
ready to
insert a text
object.

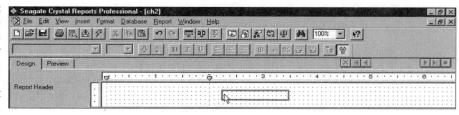

3. **Move the rectangle until it is positioned where you want the left edge
   of the title object to begin.**

   Simply click the left mouse button, causing Crystal Reports to open the
   text box and ruler guide.

   In Figure 3-6, I have clicked the mouse button. Crystal Reports opens
   the text ruler above the text box. But you do not have to worry about
   getting the size exactly correct, because Crystal Reports is intelligent
   and resizes the text box for you as you type!

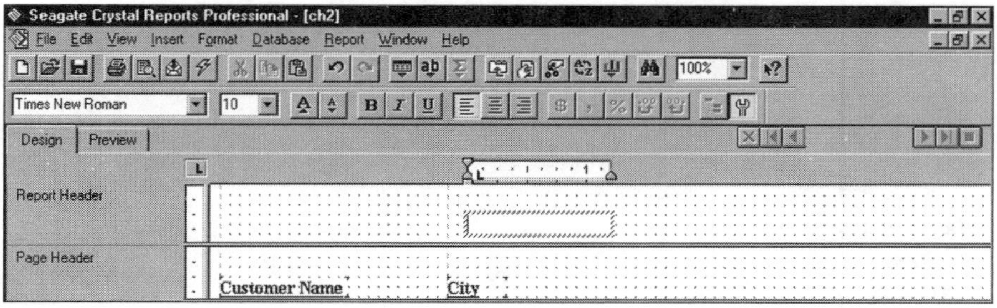

Figure 3-6:
A text box
ready for
text, with a
ruler line
above it.

4. **The insert text cursor is flashing in the text box. Type the text you want for your title.**

   For me the title is **Doug's Brilliant Report.**

   If you have been creating the text object along with me, notice that the text box expands automatically to accommodate the length of the text being entered.

5. **To finish a text object entry, simply click on another part of the report.**

Previewing the text object

After you insert a text object, click the Preview Tab to see how the text object looks in relation to your report (something like Figure 3-7). The Preview Tab gives you an accurate view of how any change to the report actually looks when printed. If you'd like to turn off the grid background, select File⇨Options Layout and use the Options Layout dialog box.

The title may be great, but it is too small for this or any report. Crystal uses a 10-point font by default, so the next logical step is to increase the size of the title. Check Chapter 15 (on file options), which shows you how to set the default sizes and styles of Crystal Report objects.

Figure 3-7:
The title text object in the Preview Tab.

Editing a text object

You can make changes to a text object in the Design Tab or Preview Tab. But the Design Tab offers more layout guides, and I recommend using it.

To modify a text object:

1. Click the Design Tab.

2. Click the text object that you want to modify.

3. Right-click that object.

The menu appears, as in Figure 3-8.

Figure 3-8:
The text
object
format
menu.

You can right-click to open a similar menu for other types of objects, too.

The top of the menu tells you which kind of object you have selected — in this case, text. Under that, is a list of options from which you can select. Edit Text Object puts the insertion point into the text field and re-opens the ruler, as Figure 3-6 shows.

4. Select the second choice (Format Text), which opens the dialog box in Figure 3-9.

This dialog has a myriad of options, which I touch upon as needed. At the top of the dialog are the tabs for different format options. In this example, I want to change the font of the title.

5. Click the Font tab.

The dialog box changes to reflect your selection, as in Figure 3-10. Table 3-1 outlines the various elements of the dialog box.

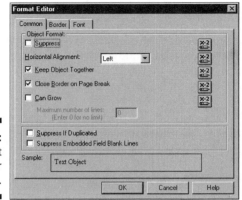

Figure 3-9:
The Format
Editor
dialog box.

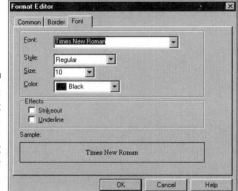

Figure 3-10:
The Font
tab
selected in
the Format
Editor
dialog box.

Table 3-1   Fields That Can Change the Appearance of Your Text

Feature Name	What It Does
Font	To select a font, click the down arrow and click the font style you want. Crystal Reports shows you the selection in the Sample field at the bottom of the dialog. The fonts from which you can choose are determined by the fonts installed on your system.
Style	Click the down arrow in the style menu to select Bold, Italic, Bold Italic, or Regular.
Size	This option interests me most at this point. I want the title to be bigger. You have two options: You can type in the point size you desire, or you can click the down arrow and select a value from the list. In this example, I enter 20 as the point size.

Feature Name	What It Does
Color	Click the down arrow to select a color for the text.
Strikeout	Check the box for strikeout.
Underline	Check the box for underline.

6. To modify the text, make the selection(s) you want.

7. Click OK.

In my example, I simply changed the point size to 20. You can see the change in the Design Tab, but click the Preview Tab for a better look, as in Figure 3-11. In order to see the text, I had to expand the text box.

Note that in Figure 3-11, several outlines appear, one around the title and another across the top of the page. The outline around the title defines the area of the text object, and the outline across the top of the page defines the Report Header section.

Adding a border and drop shadow to the title

In addition to simply changing the size of the text, you can modify the look of the text object. In this example, I show you how to add a border and then a drop shadow to the title, giving a 3D effect. I am working in the Preview Tab.

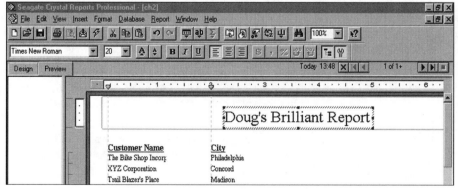

Figure 3-11:
The title size changed to 20 points.

To add a border to a text object:

1. **Right-click the text object.**

2. **From the menu, select the Change Border option.**

   The Border tab appears in the Format Editor dialog box in Figure 3-12.

Figure 3-12:
The Format
Editor
dialog box,
with the
Border tab
selected —
ready to
add a
border of
your
choosing.

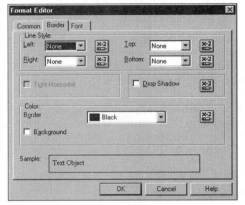

Most of the time, you want the border completely around the text object, but not always. So Crystal gives you the option of picking which of the sides of the rectangle to include in the border. If you really get fanciful, you can combine different fonts and type sizes with one or more borders for a variety of effects.

In Chapter 8, I show you how to use another option in this dialog box. The small icon that has an X+2 on it is a *conditional formatting tool,* meaning that you can have Crystal Reports execute a formula that determines whether or not the particular border is visible. The practical aspect of this tool is that a report's title can be easily identified by formatting that causes it to appear when printed. For example, if the report shows a net loss in the number of products sold, the border can be printed in a special color (red comes to mind) and with double-lined borders.

3. **Click the pull-down arrow next to the rectangle side that you want to be visible (Left, Right, Top, or Bottom), and select the type of border that you want to appear.**

   Crystal previews the border change at the bottom of the dialog box.

4. **If you want a drop shadow, with or without any border, click in the Drop Shadow check box.**

5. **Click OK.**

   The results appear in Figure 3-13.

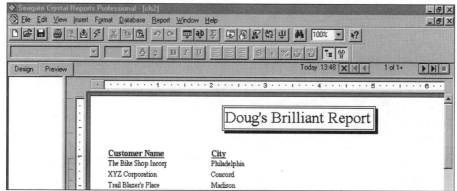

Figure 3-13:
A double-
lined border
with a drop
shadow
added to my
title object.

Adding other fields

To this point, the database fields that I have inserted into the report have been text objects. (Once inserted into the report, they become objects.) To add another layer to a report, add a field with numbers in "Adding a Number Field," later in this chapter. The process is identical in either case, but numeric fields can be formatted in a number of ways that text database fields cannot. In addition, the Customer table has a Region field that you can use to group the records, as described in Chapter 5, so I show you how to add that field, too.

Moving a field in a report

Consider the current layout of the report. At present, the Customer Name field precedes the City field. In the database, you also have a Region field, which is a larger area than the City. So putting the Region field the farthest to the left makes sense, followed by the City and then the Customer Name field.

To move a field in a report:

1. **Click the Design Tab.**
2. **Click the field name in the Page Header — in this case, Customer Name.**
3. **Press and hold the Ctrl key.**
4. **Click the database field in the Details section, directly underneath the column heading.**

   Because you press the Ctrl key after you select an object, Crystal assumes that you want to select several objects. So both the column header and column records are selected and can be moved at the same time. Figure 3-14 shows both objects selected.

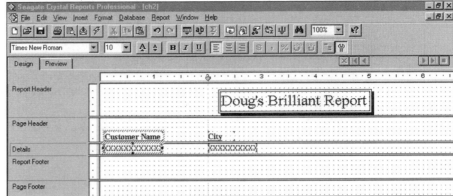

Figure 3-14:
The column
head and
column
details both
selected.

5. Click and hold either of the objects already selected.

6. Drag the mouse to the right.

As you do, you see an outline of the objects moving with the mouse pointer.

7. After they are moved to the position you want, release the mouse button.

In Figure 3-15, the two objects that represent the column head of Customer Name and the details have been moved to the right of the City field.

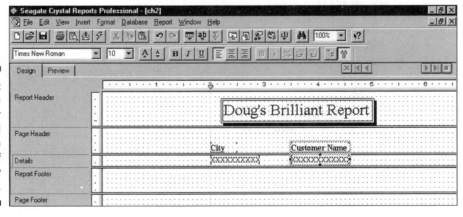

Figure 3-15:
The
Customer
Name field
moved to
the right of
the City
field.

Now I want to add the Region field and insert it where the Customer Name field was.

To add a field to a report:

1. If you are in the Preview Tab, click the Design Tab.

2. Click the Insert Fields button.

The Insert Fields dialog box appears.

3. Click the field name you want to insert.

In this case, it's the Region field.

4. Click Insert.

5. Position the mouse pointer so that the field outline is right next to the left margin of the report.

You know that you have reached the left margin when Crystal does not let you drag the object any farther.

6. Click the mouse button.

Figure 3-16 shows the results.

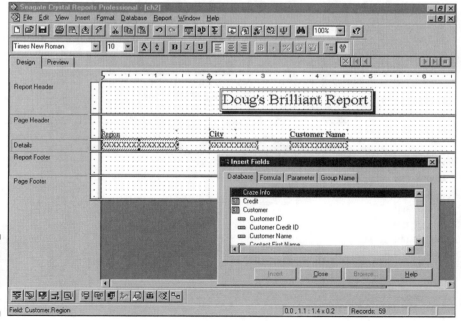

Figure 3-16:
The Region field added to report.

Adding a Number Field

No difference exists between adding a number field and adding a text field. I just thought that the topic of adding a number field deserves its own section in this book. In this example, I add the field named Last Year's Sales to the Design Tab. This particular field consists of numbers, formatted as currency.

1. **If the dialog box is not already open, click the Insert Fields button.**

2. **Scroll the list to locate the Last Year's Sales field name.**

   Note that the fields are not listed in alphabetical order; rather, they are listed in the order they occur in the database.

3. **Click the Last Year's Sales field name, and then click Insert.**

4. **Position the field outline so that the field is inserted at the far right of the report.**

   The newly added field does not have a series of XXXs to indicate the length and kind of field, as a text field does. Rather, the numbers $55,555.56 appear, as in Figure 3-17.

Figure 3-17:
You just added the Last Year's Sales field to the Design Tab.

To check the look of the report and see how the printed report will look, click the Preview Tab. The new report appears in Figure 3-18.

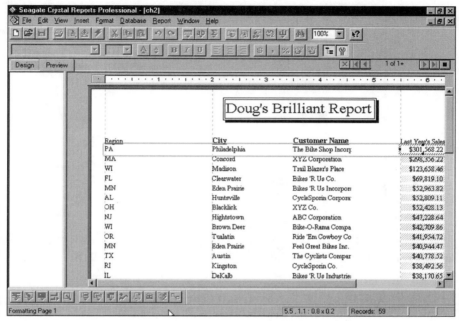

Figure 3-18:
A preview
of the
report with
new fields
added.

Aligning Columns and Headers

This formatting exercise is easier to execute in the Preview Tab than in Design. You can select the column head and the field containing the records, and thereby align the two objects so that the column head is *centered* over the records.

To align a column header with the records below it:

1. **Select the column header by clicking it.**

2. **Press and hold the Ctrl key, and then click the field.**

   Figure 3-19 shows the two selected together.

Figure 3-19:
Two objects
selected,
ready for
alignment.

3. **Open the Format menu (which you see in Figure 3-20) by right-clicking on the records.**

Note that the top of the menu indicates that this is a multiple object selection.

Figure 3-20:
The Format
menu.

4. **Click the Format Objects option.**

The Format Editor dialog box appears, as in Figure 3-21. (If the Common tab is not on top, click it.) The procedure you want — centering the column head — is considered a Horizontal alignment.

5. **Click the down arrow in the Horizontal Alignment box.**

6. **Select the Center option.**

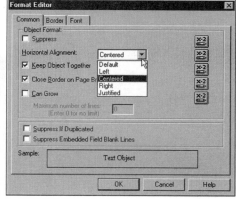

Figure 3-21:
The Format
Editor
dialog box
helps you
with
horizontal
alignment.

7. Click OK.

Figure 3-22 shows the results of the change.

You have to admit that it looks much better this way. When you become a little cocky, you can hold down the Ctrl key and select all the column headers and all the records and center them all at once! Crystal recognizes each of the individual headers and columns and aligns them properly.

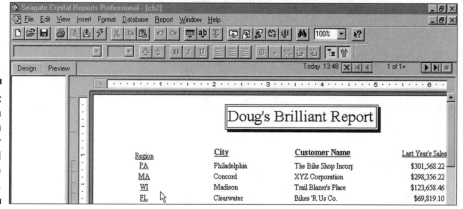

Figure 3-22:
The Region
column
header
centered
over the
records.

Getting the Numbers Formatted

With the text in good shape, time to move on to the newly inserted number field. Because the field is numeric, the formatting choices are broader than text, as you might expect. This procedure is easy to execute in the Preview Tab.

To format number fields, click the Preview Tab.

1. **Click the field in the number column you want to format.**

 In this example, that's Last Year's Sales.

2. **Right-click the mouse.**

 The menu in Figure 3-23 appears.

Figure 3-23:
With a
right-click,
you have
the Format
menu for
numbers.

3. **Select the Format Field option.**

 The Format Editor dialog box appears, as in Figure 3-24.

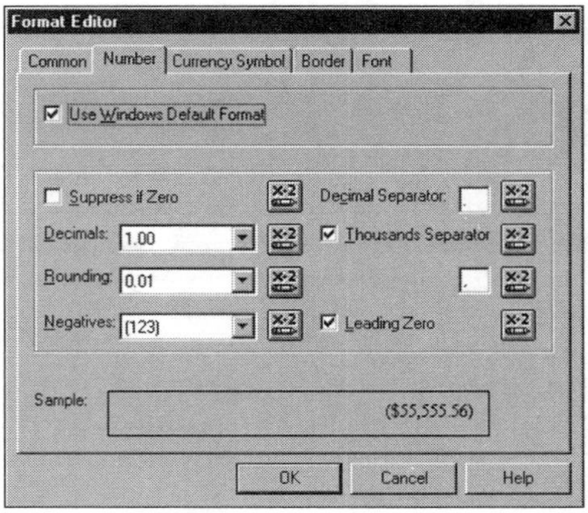

Figure 3-24:
The Format
Editor
dialog box
for number
fields.

For this example, I am only concerned with a single setting, which is the number of Decimals printed. Currently, the column of numbers includes two decimal places, which are unnecessary clutter. Also note that if the check box next to Use Windows Default Format is checked, those Windows defaults about printing numbers are at work in Crystal Reports. Making a change, though, is easy.

To change the number of decimal places displayed and printed:

1. **Click the down arrow in the Decimals field.**
2. **Click the 1 value, indicating that no decimals follow each numeral.**
3. **Click OK.**

Figure 3-25 shows the reformatted numbers.

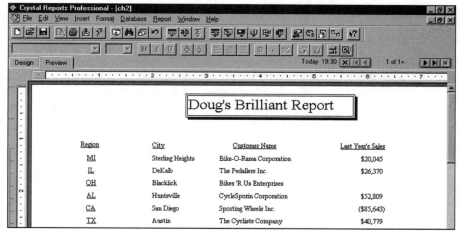

Figure 3-25:
The number column with zero decimals displayed.

Moving from Page to Page in a Report

Frequently, your reports run more than a single page when printed. When you create them in Crystal Reports, it allows you to view a single page at a time. So you need to know how to move from the current page to a previous or following page. The approach is quite easy. At the top-right corner of the Preview Tab is a series of three boxes, followed by numbers and then three more boxes. You can see them in Figure 3-26. The common term for these kinds of buttons is *VCR buttons,* because they imitate the buttons on your VCR to an extent. (By the way, my VCR clock shows the correct time. Look for my next book, *VCR Clocks For Dummies.*)

Look at Figure 3-26 and Table 3-2 to discover how these buttons work.

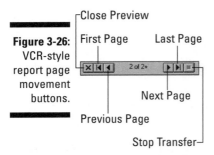

Figure 3-26:
VCR-style
report page
movement
buttons.

┌Close Preview

First Page   Last Page

Next Page

Previous Page

Stop Transfer┘

Table 3-2	VCR Buttons in the Preview Tab
Button	*Function*
Close Preview	The first button closes the Preview Tab. You may want to do so if your system resources (computer memory) are running low and Crystal Reports starts to slow down.
First Page	This button causes Crystal Reports to display the first page of the report.
Previous Page	This button causes Crystal Reports to display the page previous to the current page.
Next Page	This button causes Crystal Reports to display the page following the current page.
Last Page	This button causes Crystal Reports to display the final page in the report.
Stop Transfer	At the far right is a button that only operates when Crystal Reports is reading the database to get or refresh records. If you open the Preview Tab and find that it is taking a long time for the report to appear, click this button to stop records from being transferred to the report.

Magnifying the Page

As you add more and more objects to a page, the clutter may overwhelm even the sharpest eye. Or you may have added a combination of objects and need to see them close up before printing. For just these sorts of situations, Crystal Reports gives you a means to *zoom* in on an area of the report.

To zoom your report in or out:

   1. At the right end of the toolbar, click the downward-pointing arrow to view the Zoom Control drop-down list (see Figure 3-27).

Figure 3-27:
Using
the Zoom
Control
drop-down
list.

From this drop-down list, you can select a percentage that will either zoom in on the report (if you choose a percentage greater than 100%) or zoom out (if you choose a percentage less than 100%).

Or, choose View⇨Zoom.

The Magnification Factor dialog box appears (see Figure 3-28).

Figure 3-28:
The
Magnification
Factor
dialog box
for
zoooooming.

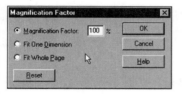

2. Set the Magnification Factor, either enlarging or shrinking:

- To enlarge, type a larger value in the field provided.

    The default value is 100 percent. So if you increase the value, you zoom in on the report. You can enter a number as large as 400. When you do, the report looks like the one in Figure 3-29. It gives you an idea of the ease with which you can see detail using this method.

- To shrink, decrease the number.

    You may do so in order to see the entire page at one time. Figure 3-30 is an example of a 40 percent magnification factor.

The reasons for viewing the entire page are more apparent after you have added headers and footers and summary data, discussed in Chapter 9. Looking at the entire page may save you the chore of printing the report to check the formatting.

Figure 3-29:
Report
zoomed 400
percent.

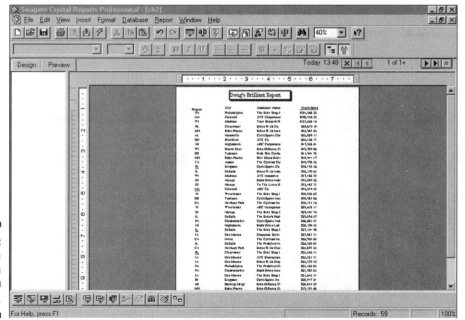

Figure 3-30:
Page
magnification
set at 40
percent.

Part II
Manipulating Records

The 5th Wave   By Rich Tennant

"THAT'S RIGHT, DADDY WILL DOUBLE YOUR SALARY IF
YOU MAKE HIM MORE DATABASES."

In this part . . .

Stage two, and the whole department is on pins and needles wondering whether your next report is going to discover that the entire west coast sales division is a bunch of slackers who talk a good game but do not sell anything. Of course, everyone knows that everything loose rolls west, but who would have thought all those salaries were going to pay for hot tubs and Moet and Chandon! Outrageous! Well, this part of the book gives you the power to ferret out the wheat from the chaff, the men from the boys, and the quick from the, er, not so quick.

Chapter 4
Selecting Records

· ·

· ·

*W*hen you create a report, you may or may not want every record in the database to be in the report. You can limit the number of records, and you can specify which records to include. This chapter gives you the lowdown on selecting records.

What Is Selecting Records?

When you are generating a report, you have to access an existing table in order to create the report. A problem arises when the table consists of thousands of records. You may want a report that consists of records from a specific geographic area, records from a certain sales division, or records only of the products in which you are interested. That is the primary reason to use record selection. This load is not so noticeable in the Design Tab, but a large number of records greatly affects performance in the Preview Tab. The folks at Seagate Software anticipated your needs and built in a way for you to select only a few records in order to design the report or to have only the records that fit the report criteria.

The Select Expert

The Select Expert is a tool that walks you through the process of selecting the records you want to include in the report. Think of the process as filtering the data in the field. If the data is of a certain size, it passes through the filter to be included in the report. If not, it is not included in the report.

Open the Select Expert by clicking the Select Expert button on the toolbar. You can also open the Select Expert by choosing Report⇨Select Expert. The Choose Field dialog box then appears, as in Figure 4-1.

If you have a database field selected prior to clicking the Select Expert, you bypass the Choose Field database and go directly to the Select Expert by using the field you highlighted.

Notice two things in this dialog box. First, because I have a report open on the screen, Crystal Reports lists the fields that are part of the report, as possible candidates for record selection. Second, Crystal Reports also displays field names from the source database table, with good reason. The record selection process is not restricted to the fields in the report. You can use *any* field from the table as the filter. So even though your report may include the fields you want, you can restrict the records included using an entirely different field. Most of the time, though, you use a field that is in the report as the record filter.

In the following example, I have opened a report that includes a field that has sales numbers. I am going to use that field to restrict which records are included in the report.

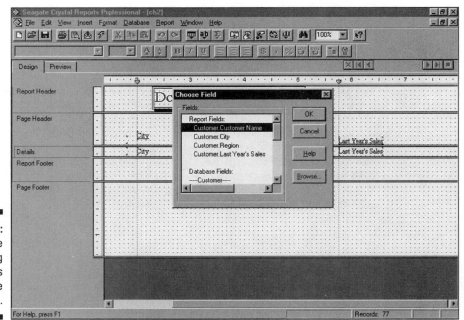

Figure 4-1:
The Choose Field dialog box awaits your wise choice.

To use the Select Expert:

1. **Open the report for which you want to select records.**

2. **Click the Select Expert button, or choose Report⇨Select Expert.**

   If you had a database field selected prior to clicking the Select Expert, you bypass the Choose Field database and go directly to the Select Expert by using the field that you highlighted.

3. **In the Choose Field dialog box, click the field you want to use as the record filter. (Click Browse to view the data in the field.)**

   The Select Expert dialog box appears.

4. **Enter the filters you want by using the drop-down boxes.**

5. **Click OK.**

6. **Click Refresh data.**

   Crystal Reports asks you whether you want to use saved data or refreshed data. In most cases, select refreshed — which means that Crystal Reports rereads the data in the table you are using for the report.

7. **Click OK.**

Those are the basic steps. Now see what happens to a report when you use the Select Expert. In my report, which includes four fields, one is named Last Year's Sales. Say that you want to restrict the records to those that have a number greater than $50,000 in Last Year's Sales. Here are the steps:

1. **Open the report.**

   In my case, I have opened the report named ch3.

2. **Click the Select Expert button.**

3. **In the Choose Field dialog box, click the Last Year's Sales field.**

4. **Click OK.**

   The Select Expert dialog box opens, as shown in Figure 4-2.

Figure 4-2:
The Select
Expert
dialog box.

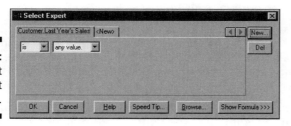

5. **To make sure that the field has the data upon which you want to filter, click Browse, as I have done in Figure 4-3.**

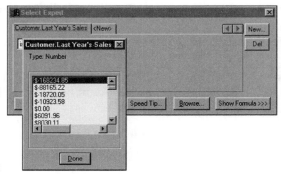

Figure 4-3:
Last Year's
Sales data
browsed.

Browsing data here lets you double-check that this is the field on which you'd like to base your record selection. Press Done when finished.

So looking at the next drop-down list, find the option to make the selection work. Figure 4-4 shows the drop-down list opened.

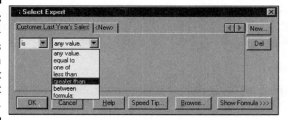

Figure 4-4:
The drop-
down list is
opened in
the Select
Expert
dialog box.

6. **Okay, remembering that you want the records that have sales greater than $50,000, click the greater than syntax, which is inserted into the field.**

At this point, the criteria reads LAST YEAR S SALES IS GREATER THAN.

Note: If you select the greater than or less than option, notice you get a check box or equal to. When this is selected, you will also include on your report all records that match the value. In this example, when you turn on the or equal to check box, you include on the report records that have Last Year's Sales amount of exactly $50,000 or higher.

So far so good. When you enter the greater than syntax, Crystal Reports opens an edit box to the right. This box is for entering a number, completing the criteria. Crystal Reports allows you to take a look at the data again: Click the down arrow at the far right of the edit box. (This method is the alternative way of getting browse data.) The data appears, as in Figure 4-5.

Figure 4-5:
The Field data is revealed — you can look at it to decide your criteria.

The final step is to enter the number. You have two ways to do so.

7. Simply type the number you want in the box, or reveal the field data and click a number there.

In this example, no number is exactly 50,000, so I type the value. In Figure 4-6, I have entered **50000** into the field. Note that you should *not* include a comma as a separator. Crystal Reports does not interpret the comma as part of a number.

Figure 4-6:
50000 entered into the previously blank field.

The criteria reads LAST YEAR S SALES IS GREATER THAN 50000. The subject-verb agreement may be suspect, but the criteria syntax is correct.

8. Click OK.

Crystal Reports pops up a dialog box that asks an important question. In a moment, I explain the reason for what I tell you to do here. The dialog box you see asks whether the report should use the current set of saved records, or refresh the data. Figure 4-7 shows this dialog box.

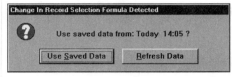

Figure 4-7:
The dialog box that lets you choose saved or refresh data.

9. **Click Refresh Data.**

If you are in the Preview Tab, pressing Refresh does just that and no further input is required from the user, but if you are in the Design Tab, Crystal Reports doesn't ask you if you want to save or refresh until you ask to go to the Preview Tab. Remember, you must be in Preview to see the change.

10. **Click the Preview button to see the results.**

Figure 4-8 shows the new, highly filtered report.

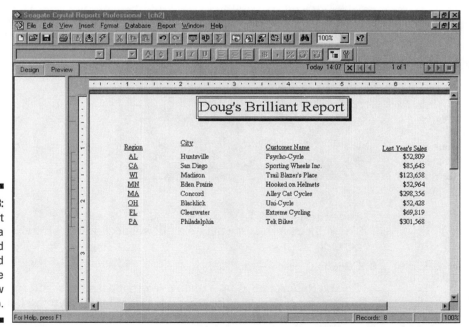

Figure 4-8:
A report with a filtered record in the Preview Tab.

Saved or refreshed data

In order not to burden the computer system where your data resides and to speed up report creation, Crystal Reports only reads the data from the tables you have included in a report when necessary. Now, on your home computer, you may not think that this feature would be a big deal. It probably is not. However, in a setting in which you are creating reports from a shared database, such as a network with SQL servers, having Crystal Reports reading the shared database at every turn would slow your report-building process.

So why does Crystal Reports sometimes ask the immortal question: Use saved data? Crystal Reports has some built-in smarts and won't bug you for an answer to this question when it knows it is necessary to get more data for the report by going back to the database. It is only when Crystal Reports is not sure if rereading the database is necessary that it asks you to decide. And how do you determine how to answer the question?

If you are narrowing your record selection, click Use Saved Data. For example, perhaps when you first built your record selection you included all records with sales greater than 0. If you change the record selection to sales greater than 50,000, you can select Use Saved Data because you are narrowing the record selection.

If you are not positive that you are narrowing the record selection, click Refresh Data just to be safe.

Select the Refresh data on every print option by choosing File⇨Options and then the Reporting tab (see Figure 4-9).

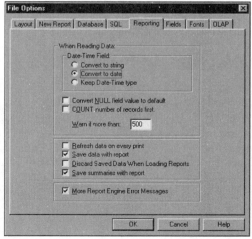

Figure 4-9:
Choosing
File⇨
Options
and the
Reporting
tab allows
you to
refresh data
every time
you print.

Crystal Reports considers printing to be of any kind: Print previewing, actual printing to hard copy, or saving the report to a file.

Refreshing the report on demand

Because Crystal Reports saves the records with the report, and time may pass between the time you create the report and the time you plan to use it again, Crystal Reports provides a button to cause it to re-read the records for the report. To refresh report data, do one of the following:

- ✔ Click the Refresh button on the toolbar.
- ✔ Choose <u>R</u>eport➪Refresh Report <u>D</u>ata.

Crystal Reports provides an indicator for you so that you know exactly when you last refreshed your report data. In Figure 4-10, you can see the numbers that indicate the most recent update.

Figure 4-10:
The pointer showing you the report date indicator.

Record selection and case sensitivity

Record selection is *case sensitive.* What does this mean for your reports? If the abbreviation for California is entered as CA, ca, or Ca in your database, what records would be included in your report if your record selection is Equal to "CA"? The report would only include those records where the Region is exactly "CA" and won't include any other version (ca, Ca, or cA). This is one reason you may want to use the Browse Field Data button in the Select Expert — to find out how the data is stored.

When working with SQL/ODBC data, you have the ability to select whether or not you want record selection to be case sensitive or insensitive. By default the option is not selected and your SQL/ODBC record selection will be case sensitive. The Case-Insensitive SQL Data option (available under File➪Options➪Database or from File➪Report Options) is where you set whether you want a case-sensitive or case-insensitive record selection. This option will only be available when your database server supports case insensitivity.

If the report was refreshed several *weeks* ago, Crystal Reports displays the date and time of the last refresh exactly.

Select Expert options

Now that you have an idea of how the filtering process works, Table 4-1 presents other ways in which you can filter records. Remember, you do not have to use a field that is in the current report; any field in the database table works.

Table 4-1	Filtering Parameters
Filter	*What It Does*
any value	When you see this option, you have no record selection for the field. It's the same as saying, "Give me all records on the report, I don't care about the sales amount."
equal to	Filters records so that only an exact match passes through. For example, if you want to see only records that are from California, the field data is equal to CA (assuming the name for California is entered as an abbreviation).
one of	Allows you to specify records that match values from a series. So you can enter one of CA, MN, or BC. This filter only allows records that are from CA, MN, or BC to pass through to the report.
greater than or less than	Allows you to filter records in which the field value is less than a value you choose, or greater than a value of your choice. So you can use this filter to cut off records that are at the extremes.
or equal to	With either the greater than or less than, you will get a check box where you can determine if you want to include the equal to value itself on the report.
between	Selects those records that fall into a range that you want. You can enter between 20,000 and 75,000 to get only those records.
starting with	Selects records using a text field. So if you want all records that have a field entry beginning with the letter S, this is the filter to use. Further, if you want to find records that begin with SON, you can do so by entering the three characters.

(continued)

Table 4-1 *(continued)*

Filter	What It Does
like	Although the world now sees computers through Windows 95, in the background are still ways to use tricks that are from the DOS era. For example, the entry D*G (an asterisk) filters records that have any entries in the field that begin with D and end with G. So the words DOG, DOUG, DARING, and DECIDING all pass through this filter. The asterisk is called a *wildcard* character because it matches any character and any number of characters. This works with text data only. Another type of wildcard is the "?" which is a question mark. It will match any character, but only one at a time. So, the D?G filter would retrieve records like DOG, DIG. The word DOING would not be retrieved because more than one letter appears between the D and G, not just one.
formula	Creates complex filters or filters that do not fit the format of the other filter tools. Chapter 7 is devoted to the Crystal Reports formula language, and the lessons there can be used here to select records. Figure 4-11 shows the formula for a filter. The Formula Editor portion of the dialog box is opened by clicking Show Formula (which then changes to Hide Formula). Even if you have not specified a formula overtly, Crystal Reports creates a formula for every type of record selection that you create. Note in Figure 4-11 that you have a button to access the Formula Editor. In Chapter 7, I explain the concepts of using formulas.

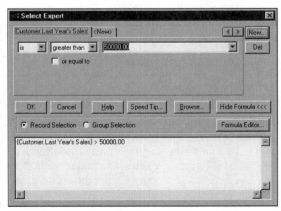

Figure 4-11: A view of the formula that Crystal Reports created automatically exposed in the Select Expert dialog box.

Filter	What It Does
`in the period`	Conducts date range searches. Suppose that you are trying to create a report for a recurring date range. This selects records for which the value in the date field falls within the date range specified. When you select this condition, the dialog box displays a scroll list of all Crystal Reports date ranges. Select the range you want from the list. Include all records in which the date falls within the calendar first quarter of the year. Dates from January 1 to April 30 (including January 1 and April 30) will be included; all other dates will be excluded. *Note:* The `in the period` option always evaluates the record selection relative to your computer's current date. For example, the LastFullMonth option will give you the preceding calendar month. If you preview your report on April 1st, 1997, you will see all data for March 1997.
`is not`	But what if you want to include all records except those where the region is CA? After you choose an option in the second box other than Any Value, you can go back to the first box and change *is* to *is not*. This option is available for any option other than `any value` and `formula`. Remember this; you'll use it at some point.

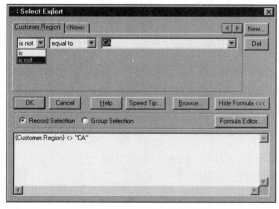

Figure 4-12: `is not` displayed in the Select Expert dialog box — it filters for data that is not CA.

Selecting records on more than one field

With a beginning grasp of the record selection process on a single field, the next question is how to use two or more fields to create a compound record selection. An example is a report that includes only records from a certain region and with sales over a certain amount. You have two ways to approach this type of selection. You can create the first filter and execute it, and then reopen the Select Record Expert and add the second filter. Or you can create both filters in one step. The advantage of the two-step process is that you can check your work step-by-step by previewing the records at each step to make certain that they are what you want.

To create both filters in one step:

1. **In an open report, click the first field you want to use for a filter.**

 2. **Click the Select Expert button.**

The field name already appears in the dialog box.

Note: You may have noticed that this is a different way of getting to the Select Expert with the field you want to work with. If you have a database field selected on your report when you go to the Select Expert, Crystal Reports assumes that is the field you want to work with. A great little shortcut.

3. **Enter the filter criteria.**

4. **Click New at the top of the Select dialog box.**

5. **Select the field you want to use for the second filter.**

6. **Enter the filtering criteria.**

7. **Click OK.**

In this example, filter the records so that the report includes only CA (California) with sales from last year greater than 10,000:

1. **In the Design Tab, click the Region field.**

2. **Click the Select Expert button.**

3. **In the dialog box, select** equal to **and** CA.

4. **Click New.**

Crystal Reports opens the Choose Field dialog box, from which you can select a field already in the report or any field from the table.

5. **Select Last Year's Sales, select the** greater than **filter, and enter a value of** 10000.

The completed two-field criteria appear in Figure 4-13.

In the Select Expert, click the Show Formula button to see the entire record selection. I've let Crystal Reports do most of the work. I just dropped down a few boxes, and Crystal Reports has translated this into a formula your database will understand. Sometimes you will want to view this formula to see the Big Picture — how the record selection looks as a whole.

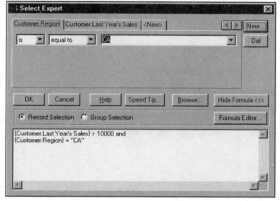

Figure 4-13:
Two filters
set and
ready to go.

6. **Click OK.**

Crystal Reports filters the records and displays those meeting the criteria in the Preview Tab as shown in Figure 4-14.

This tool is powerful and can be used in many ways to fine-tune the reports you create, so that only the records you want are included. Adding a third or fourth filter follows the same procedure as adding a second.

Figure 4-14:
Filtering
produces a
report with
California
records and
sales
greater
than 10,000.

Region	City	Customer Name	Last Year's Sales
CA	San Diego	Sporting Wheels Inc.	$85,643
CA	Newbury Park	Rowdy Rims Company	$30,131
CA	Irvine	Changing Gears	$26,706
CA	Irvine	Off the Mountaing Biking	$25,000
CA	Santa Ana	Tyred Out	$18,126
CA	Newbury Park	Bike Shop from Mars	$25,873

Removing Record Selection

After selecting records for a specific report you can save the report or print it. If you want to use the same table to create a different report, but need to have access to all the records, you can remove the filter. To remove a Select Expert filter:

1. **Click the Select Expert button.**

   The Select Expert dialog box appears.

2. **Click the filter tab that you wish to remove.**

3. **Click the Del button, which deletes that filter.**

4. **Continue deleting filters until the records you want can be part of the report.**

5. **Click OK.**

   Crystal Reports asks you if you want to use saved data or refresh the data.

6. **Click Refresh Data.**

   Crystal Reports re-runs the filter and adds back any records that were previously excluded.

The Select Expert is meant to make your life simple. Just point and click to create your record selection. This will probably be sufficient for most reports, but you can get more sophisticated if you need to. See Chapter 7 for more info.

Chapter 5

Sorting and Grouping Records

- -

In This Chapter

▶ Sorting records

▶ Inserting groups

▶ Inserting summaries or subtotals

▶ Inserting a Grand Total

▶ Modifying a group

▶ Doing a TopN Sort

- -

*W*ith an existing report, you may wish to sort the records by one or several fields, such as by state or by salesperson. Or you may want to group the records. Suppose that you are creating a sales report and want to group the records by sales region. Within that region, you also want to sort by the amount of sales, and calculate subtotals for each region. In this chapter, you discover the steps to sort and group.

 In Figure 5-1, you see a typical report that has a series of records, as yet without any grouping or any discernible sort order. The process of sorting and grouping is best accomplished in Preview mode. So, change to that mode by clicking the Preview Tab, or click the Preview button.

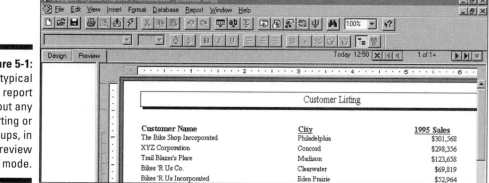

Figure 5-1:
A typical
report
without any
sorting or
groups, in
Preview
mode.

Sorting Records

The first thing you can do with any set of records is to add a sort order. In any report, the steps to change the sort order are as follows:

 1. **Choose Report⇨Sort Records (or click the Sort Order button on the toolbar).**

The Record Sort Order dialog box opens, as in Figure 5-2.

Figure 5-2:
The Record
Sort Order
dialog box.

On the left of the dialog box, Crystal Reports lists the fields in the report that can be used to perform a sort. In this example, four fields are available, three on the left and one on the right. Your report may have more or fewer fields available for sorting.

2. **Select a field to use for the sort, and click Add.**

3. **Select the sort order: Ascending or Descending.**

4. **Click OK.**

Breaking Ties

Taking the idea a bit further, if you have several records that have identical values in the field upon which you have sorted, you can add a second sort field to break the tie. As an example, if you have a set of records that are sorted primarily by the City field, the possibility exists that several records are from the same city. In the example report, several records have Conshocken as the city. So adding a second sort, Last Year's Sales in descending order, shows the records sorted first by the name of the city and then by the sales volume.

To add a second sort value:

1. **Open the Record Sort Order dialog box by choosing <u>R</u>eport⇨Sort <u>R</u>ecords (or by clicking the Sort button).**

2. **Click the field name you want as the second sort value, click <u>A</u>dd, and select D<u>e</u>scending as the sort order.**

   In this example, click the Last Year's Sales field.

3. **Click OK.**

   Now the records are sorted at two levels, as you can see in Figure 5-3. The Conshocken records are sorted from the largest sales amount to the least.

For a sort to work, the field *must* be included in the report.

The number of sorts you can perform is limited only by the number of fields and the sense it makes. If you do too much sorting, you become, well, out of sorts.

If you perform a sort but then want to return to the previous sort order, click the Undo button on the toolbar.

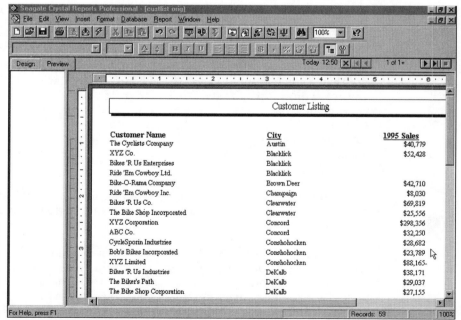

Figure 5-3:
Records
sorted
on two
levels —
city and
sales.

Inserting Groups

Groups provide a handy way to arrange records in a myriad of ways, in order to determine sales strategies, distribution points, under- or over-performing salespeople, and so on. You are probably way ahead of me in thinking of the ways you can create that one report that you used to have to do by hand or wanted to have but could never coax out of your database.

If you change your mind after creating (inserting) a group or decide to use another grouping method, you can easily remove the group and replace it with another. Deleting a group is covered later in this chapter.

In any report, the grouping process follows the same steps:

1. **Choose Insert⇨Group.**

2. **From the Insert Group dialog box, select the field upon which you want the records grouped.**

3. **Select the sort order that you want to occur after the grouping.**

You have two other options, and they have to do with how the groups print on paper. The first option, Keep Group Together, keeps grouped records contiguous on the same printed page. Crystal Reports calculates whether the next group can fit on what remains of the current page and, if not, begins printing the group on the page following. Clicking the option, which inserts an X in the box, turns this feature on.

Now you come to another option. Suppose that the group of records is longer than a single printed page? The second option, Repeat Group Header, when turned on, causes Crystal Reports to print the Group Header at the top of each new page.

The best way to use these options is to click OK and see the results of the grouping, and if the records do cover more than a page, decide how to best divide the groups.

If you are unhappy with the results of a grouping and decide for whatever reason to remove the group, Crystal Reports cannot undo such a move. You must recreate the group.

In this example, the CUSTLIST database has been opened. The records are grouped by the Customer Region field. In the cold, frozen north, in a country far away known as Canada, *region* is considered to be the same as *state*. So don't let this naming convention throw you. You can use this field to create the group despite the fact that the Customer Region is not part of the *printed* report. The Customer Region is part of the *table* that was accessed to create the report and so is accessible for grouping records in the report.

How to add a group using a field not in the report:

1. Click the down arrow and select the field listed as `Customer.Region.`

2. Click the down arrow and select the sort order, as in Figure 5-4.

You can choose a number of ways beyond the standard sorts to arrange the records within a group. In this case, choose `ascending`.

Figure 5-4:
Selecting
the sort
order in the
Insert
Group
dialog box.

3. Click OK.

Figure 5-5 shows the result.

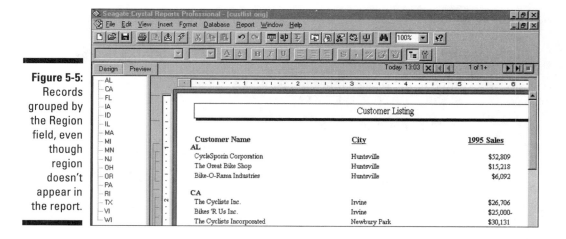

Figure 5-5:
Records
grouped by
the Region
field, even
though
region
doesn't
appear in
the report.

As you can see, the grouping effect is to arrange the records by region, which in this particular database is the same as state. Note, too, that the Group Header name is automatically placed at the upper left of the group. So the first group has AL as its header, which in this case stands for Alabama. The second grouping is headed by CA (for California). Within each individual group, the records are in data-entry order (the way that they were placed in the database).

Group Tree Options

On the far left side of the Preview window you see the list of groups that have been created. This list is called the Group Tree, and it makes it easy to move to the group associated with the records. For example, to see the detail records associated with a particular region, you simply click on the group name, and the Preview window shows the page that contains those records. In addition, the Group Tree can be used to create a Drill Down preview window. A Drill Down is a subset of detail records from the report and has its own tab at the top of the Preview window. Click on a group name, and then *right-click* to open the popup menu. Two choices appear, Hide and Drill Down. Click Drill Down and the report preview will include a tab with the group name; only the records associated with this group are displayed. You may drill down as many groups as you wish. When you print the report, only the main report in Preview prints. To print a Drill Down, you must click the Drill Down tab and then click the Printer icon. The other option available when you right-click the Group Tree is the Hide option, which closes the Group Tree. You may want to do this if you need more space in the Preview window to see your report columns. To restore a closed Group Tree, choose View⇨Group Tree.

Viewing Groups in the Design Window

Switch to the Design Tab, and take a look at the way adding a group changes the underlying report structure.

1. **Click the Design Tab.**

2. **On the left edge of the report is the name** Group Header #1**. Right-click that name.**

   The shortcut menu appears, as in Figure 5-6.

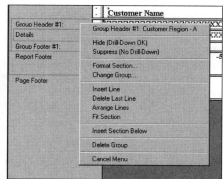

Figure 5-6:
The shortcut menu for the Group Header.

Note that in the Design Tab, the Group section surrounds the Details section of the report. This arrangement makes sense because the groups are created by arranging the individual records in the Details section of the report. Also, the menu tells you the name of the file used to make the group and the sort order, A for ascending.

Deleting or undoing a group

If the results of a grouping are not what you had expected, you can undo the group or delete the group. In the case of undoing, you create a *toggle,* that is, you can undo the group and then turn the group back on without having to go through the steps to create the group.

- ✔ To undo a group, choose Edit➪Undo.
- ✔ To Redo a Group, choose Edit➪Redo Group.

If you use any formatting or formula commands after using undo on a group, the toggle is no longer available, because Crystal Reports then assumes you want to undo only the most recent action.

Deleting a group

Deleting a group is a permanent way to remove a group, if the grouping is entirely unsatisfactory.

1. **Choose Edit➪Delete Group.**

   After you select this option, Crystal Reports pops open an alert box warning you that deleting a group cannot be undone.

2. **Click OK to proceed.**

Inserting a Total

With the records separated by region, or whatever grouping you have chosen, you can add calculations for each group in the form of a subtotal and a summary. The difference is the type of data you choose. Numbers can be calculated, whereas text such as names cannot be added together, but they can be counted. Crystal Reports distinguishes between a subtotal and a summary in this way: A subtotal works only on number or currency fields. A summary works on all data types.

A total can be inserted in the Design or Preview Tabs. In this example, I add a total to Last Year's Sales, in order to see the total amount of sales by region.

To add a total to a number field:

1. **Click the field in Details that has the numbers you want to calculate.**

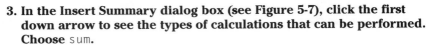

2. **Choose Insert⇨Summary (or click the Insert Summary button).**

3. **In the Insert Summary dialog box (see Figure 5-7), click the first down arrow to see the types of calculations that can be performed. Choose** sum.

   The list necessarily changes based on the type of field selected.

   In the second box, Crystal automatically inserts any grouping you have performed as the sorting and grouping to be used. You can make a change to this sort/group by clicking the down arrow and choosing a new field upon which to sort and/or group.

4. **Make sure that** Group #1: Customer.Region-A **appears.**

5. **Click OK.**

   Figure 5-8 shows the result of adding the summary to the CUSTLIST report.

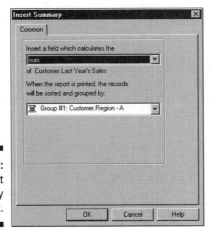

Figure 5-7:
The Insert Summary dialog box.

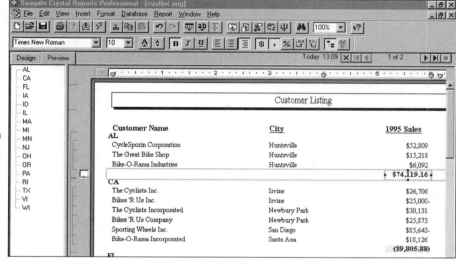

Figure 5-8:
The
CUSTLIST
report with
new
summary
totals.

In this example, the totaling is calculated on a *number* field. Another example of using summary totals is *counting* the number of records in a particular group. This requires that you use a different type of calculation, named *count*.

To count the number of records in a report or by group:

1. Click a field that you have not already used for a summary.

In this example, select the City field.

2. Choose Insert⇨Summary (or click the Insert Summary button).

And don't forget that you can also right-click to open the Insert Summary dialog box. If you right-click, select the Insert Summary option.

3. In the Insert Summary dialog box, select the calculation you want.

In this example, choose the count calculation.

4. You can modify the group setting.

If you have already created a group, it appears.

5. Click OK.

See the results in Figure 5-9.

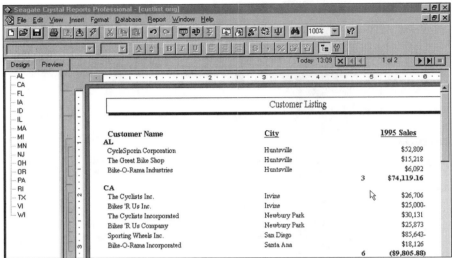

Figure 5-9:
Records
counted by
group.

In this example, the number of records per group is calculated and the result inserted between the groups. For the first group, AL, you see three records. With a small group such as this, you could have counted the records yourself. But as your report grows in length, the number of records can become overwhelming, and after all, this work is what *computers* are supposed to do, not people.

In the two previous examples, you have discovered how to total a series of numbers and to generate a count of records by group. I want to take the example a step further by showing you how to calculate the total of Last Year's Sales for the entire report and a total count of all records in the report.

Inserting a numeric grand total

Grand totals generally print at the end of the report, although you can insert them anywhere in the report.

You can insert the grand total from any page in a report, but you must move to the last page in order to see the total . You do not have to have any other totals, such as by groups, in order for this to process properly, but you must be in the Preview Tab to see the result.

To insert a grand total:

1. **Click on the field, in Details, for which you want to create a grand total.**

In this example, select the Last Year's Sales field. Do not select a field for which you have already created a grand total (although it is possible to insert the results of a grand total in more than one place in a report).

2. Right-click, and then from the shortcut menu, click Insert Grand Total. Or choose Insert➪Insert Grand Total.

After you select Insert Grand Total, the Insert Grand Total dialog box opens.

3. In the dialog box, select the type of calculation.

In this example, select sum, as in Figure 5-10.

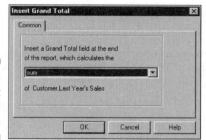

Figure 5-10:
The Insert
Grand Total
dialog box.

4. Click OK.

5. To see the result of the calculation, go to the last page of the report by clicking the far-right page control button (Last Page) in the upper-right part of the window.

You may have to scroll down the page, using the vertical scroll bar control on the right side of the window.

Figure 5-11 shows the results.

TX			
The Cyclists Company	Austin		$40,779
		1	
VI			
The Bike Shop Inc.	Winchester		$30,939
ABC Incorporated	Winchester		$29,618
Ride 'Em Cowboy Industries	Winchester		$12,014
		3	
WI			
Bike-O-Rama Company	Brown Deer		$42,710
Trail Blazer's Place	Madison		$123,658
XYZ Industries	Madison		$37,489
Ride 'Em Cowboy Co.	Madison		
		4	
			1,715,611.16

Figure 5-11:
A grand
total added
at the end
of the
report.

To check and see whether the number is correct, that is, whether it calculated the field you chose, right-click the number to see the definition, as in Figure 5-12.

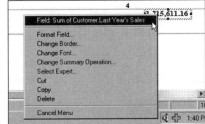

By right-clicking the value for any summing operation, you can verify that the calculation is what you desired. Also, this shortcut menu allows you to change the summary operation if desired.

Inserting a grand total for text

The next total that is useful for any report is a grand total of the number of records in the report. Crystal Reports indicates the number of records in a report, in the Preview Tab at the bottom right of the window. But it does not automatically *print* the number of records in a report. The grand total usually prints at the end of the report, but you can insert it into the Report Header. You must be in Preview to see the result.

To insert the grand total of the number of records in a report:

1. **Click a field in the report that you have not already used to tally a grand total. (Do not suppose that you cannot grand total a field twice, but for this example use a field without a grand total.)**

2. **Right-click, and from the menu that appears, select Insert Grand Total.**

   The Insert Grand Total dialog box appears.

3. **Select** count **as the type of calculation you want.**

4. **Click OK.**

 5. **Click the Last Page control button to go to the last page of the report and see the result.**

   You may have to scroll the report using the vertical scroll bar at the right of the window. Figure 5-13 shows the result of grand totaling the numbers of records in a report.

Figure 5-13:
The grand
total of all
records in
the report.

XYZ Industries	Madison	$37,489
Ride 'Em Cowboy Co.	Madison	
	4	
59		1,715,611.16

Defining other calculations

The kind of summary operation you can perform depends upon the type of data in the field you have selected. Table 5-1 shows the types of calculations you can perform and their respective uses.

Table 5-1	Calculations You Can Perform on Fields
Calculation	*What It Does*
maximum	This summary works on text or numbers and prints the largest value in the field.
minimum	This summary works on text or numbers and prints the minimum value in the field.
count	This summary works on text or numbers and prints the number of entries in the field.
distinct count	This summary works on text or numbers and prints the number of unique records in the field. Ergo, if you have three records that are from Doug's Cycle Shop, Crystal Reports counts them as a single entry.
sum	This summary works only on numeric and currency fields and prints the total of the values in the field.
average	This summary works only on numeric and currency fields and prints the average of the values in the field.
sample variance	This summary works only on numeric and currency fields and prints the sample variance of a series of values.
sample standard deviation	This summary works only on numeric and currency fields and prints the standard deviation of the values in the field. If you have grouped data, then the standard deviation is printed by group.
population variance	This summary works only on numeric and currency fields and prints the population variance of the data.
population standard deviation	This summary works only on numeric and currency fields and prints the population standard deviation.

I must admit that the last four operations listed in Table 5-1 are out of my scope of knowledge. Consult your statistics textbook for explanations.

Changing a Group

If you have created a group, you can delete the group if you wish or you can modify the existing group. A modification is best made in the Design Tab, although it can be done in Preview. In this example, I show you how to fine-tune an existing group.

To modify an existing group:

1. **Click the Design Tab.**

2. **At the left edge of the Design Tab, locate the group you wish to modify. Right-click the group name.**

3. **From the menu that appears, choose the Change Group option.**

   The Change Group Options dialog box arrives (as in Figure 5-14).

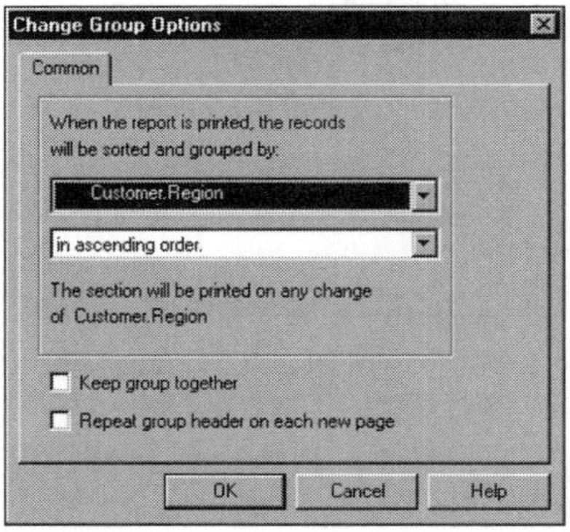

Figure 5-14: The Change Group Options dialog box awaits your command.

At this point, you can change the group by selecting a different field upon which to group and by changing the sort order. Two other options appear, which control the way the report prints. Table 5-2 shows these options.

Table 5-2	Options in the Change Group Options Dialog Box
Option	*What It Does*
Keep group together	Selecting this option causes Crystal Reports to print all the records in a group on the same page of the report. So if the group would start printing at the middle of the page and the page is not long enough for all the records to fit, Crystal Reports leaves a blank space at the end of the current page and begins printing the records at the beginning of a new page. A group of records may be longer than a single page. In that case, you can change the font size to reduce the amount of space used. See Chapter 3 for more information on text formatting.
Repeat group header on each new page	In the case where the group covers more than a single page or if you want to use the least number of pages for the report but want to be able to easily identify the groups, Crystal Reports prints the heading for the group at the beginning of each new page.

Doing a TopN Sort

A TopN Sort is a way to determine which groups of records are at the top. For example, if you wanted to determine which states are the top 5 for sales of your product, you would first group the records by state and then add the TopN Sort. The *N* in the heading of this topic refers to any number. Crystal Reports can sort the top 5, the top 10, the top 100, or whatever value you want to use. In the examples earlier in this chapter, the records have been sorted in ascending or descending order, whether as an entire report or within groups. This is a sort of a different kind, but one you will find very useful.

Note: Only fields with numbers are eligible for this type of sort.

To create a TopN Sort:

1. **Choose Report⇨TopN/Sort Group Expert.**

   The TopN/Sort Group Expert opens.

   You cannot use the TopN Sort if you have no groups in your report or if the group does not have a summary or subtotal, because you can always sort individual records in ascending or descending order. So the idea is that you have created groups and then want to see how the *groups* sort out in terms of sales or whatever criteria you have in mind.

2. **Enter the type of sort you want by clicking the down arrow.**

   You have three choices TopN, BottomN, or All. An example is shown in Figure 5-15. In this example, I indicate that I want to see the top 5 as the sort.

   Crystal Reports groups the top 5 or whatever number you designate and throws the remaining records into another Group labeled *Others*. Notice that each of the top 5 groups has its total printed by group, and, if you scroll down, the Others group then has a single total. Be aware that if you have included a grand total in your report for the number of records in the report or the total of a number field, Crystal Reports calculates those numbers based on *all* records in the report, not only the TopN group numbers.

   The other sorting options are Sort All, which rearranges all the groups in ascending or descending order, or BottomN, which allows you to arrange the number of groups using the smallest N records as the sort, such as show me the sales regions with the lowest 5 sales amounts.

3. **Select the field upon which you want the sort to occur. (It must be a summary field.)**

   In this example, only one field, Last Year's Sales, has numbers and therefore is the only field upon which Crystal Reports can perform this particular type of sort. You may have a report with several number fields. Figure 5-15 shows the completed dialog box.

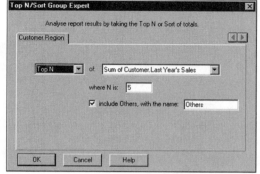

Figure 5-15:
The TopN/
Sort Group
Expert
dialog box
filled with
sort values.

4. Click OK.

The report is sorted as shown in Figure 5-16.

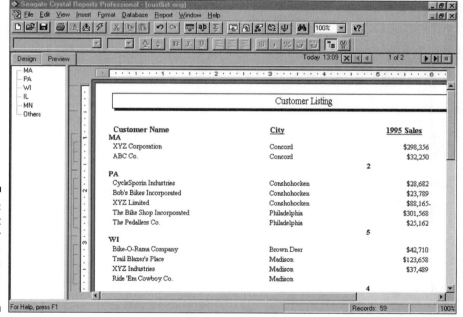

Figure 5-16:
A report
sorted for
the top 5 in
each of its
Region
groups.

Part III
Formatting and Formulas for Success

The 5th Wave — By Rich Tennant

THE COMMITTEE FOR THE PROLIFERATION OF CRYSTAL REPORTS FINALLY PAYS A VISIT TO LARRY, THE COMPANY'S LAST HOLD OUT.

In this part . . .

Time to add the dazzle and sizzle. A couple of charts and the boss will look good — and you will look even better. Add the company logo and a picture of the president of the company doing a rumba on the table at the company picnic and you really have hit the big time! And why not — you can link all kinds of graphics to a report using the techniques in this part. Every department will covet you as the person needed to get their reports just right. No, I am *not* going to repeat that tired cliché about a picture being worth a thousand words. I refuse to stoop so low.

Chapter 6

Graphing Data

● ●

● ●

*1*n this chapter I show you how to include a graph in your report.

I believe in clichés, because the truth is that a cliché almost always has a strong element of truth. So the cliché that a picture is worth a thousand words, to me is true. People can more easily understand relationships among numbers if the numbers are displayed in a graph. With this fact in mind, Seagate Crystal Reports includes a graphing function. Graphs can be drawn for any summary or subtotal field, detail or formula, or cross-tab data. As is true with other aspects of the report, a graph is considered to be an *object* in the report, making it amenable to being moved around.

The graph is dependent on the section of the report in which it is placed. For instance, placing the graph in the Report Header or Footer section means that the data for the entire report is represented. If the graph is in a Group Header or Footer, the data in that group is represented in the graph.

After you decide what to graph, the next decision is which kind of graph to use. Different graph types are better at displaying different kinds of information. For example, a pie graph is the best choice when you want to identify portions of a whole. Column graphs are preferable for representing data over a period of time, as in the amount of sales for a product, month by month over the course of a year.

By trying different graph types on your data, you can discern which graph best conveys the information. Fortunately, Crystal Reports makes creating a graph easy as pie.

Creating and Inserting a Graph

Crystal Reports includes a Chart/Graph Expert to walk you through the process of creating or editing a graph. Here are all the basic steps to inserting a graph into your report:

1. **Choose Insert⇨Graph/Chart Expert (or click the Insert Chart button on the toolbar).**

   The Graph/Chart Expert opens.

2. **In the Type tab, click the graph type you want.**

3. **Click the Data tab and choose the data to be graphed.**

   The remaining steps assume that you selected the Group graph options. These steps will vary slightly if you select the Detail, Formula or Cross-Tab option.

4. **Use the Put Graph setting to specify how many times the graph is to appear in the report.**

   With a report containing only one level of grouping, your choice is Once per report, by default (for details about groups, see Chapter 5).

5. **Use the On Change of box to pick the summary or subtotal information to be graphed.**

   Again, this option is where you would select the Detail, Formula or Cross-Tab data if you had selected those graph types.

Crystal Reports graphs

You can graph three types of data with Crystal Reports: Group; Detail, Formula; and Cross-Tab.

Group graphs: Use this option when you want to display one summary or subtotal in a graph. For example, when creating a Sales by Region report you may want to create a Group graph that shows the sales subtotals for each Region and place it at the beginning of your report. The next section of this chapter looks at creating a Group graph.

Detail, Formula: This graph option can be used to display database or formula field data from the detail section on a graph. Perhaps within each region on your sales report you want to show a bar chart of individual sales within the region. This option can also be used if you want to display two or more summaries or subtotals in one graph. Creating this type of graph will not be covered in this chapter; refer to the online help.

Cross-Tab: This graphing option allows you to show cross-tab data in a graph. This option is available only if you selected an existing cross-tab object on your report before selecting Insert⇨Graph/Chart Expert. This graphing option is not covered in this book.

6. **Use the Header and Footer radio buttons to determine whether the graph prints before or after the actual data.**

7. **Use the Show setting box to choose which field in the table the graph uses.**

   The On Change of setting and this setting work in concert to define the summary field to be graphed.

8. **Click the Text tab to determine what text is going to accompany the graph.**

   You can have a title, a subtitle, footnote, group title, series title, and the X, Y, and Z axis titles. At a minimum, you probably will want to enter a title.

9. **Click the Options tab to add a legend, show gridlines, show values on risers, direction of the bars, choose a font type, and specify the range of values.**

10. **Click the Graph Done button.**

    Crystal Reports inserts the graph into the section you indicated in Step 2.

Whew! Those steps are numerous and offer many choices, but the number of choices makes it easy to highly customize your graph. A real-life example is in order.

Creating a Group Graph

I have opened the CUSTLIST report as my example data. For simplicity in creating a graph, I have adjusted the report slightly to be a TopN report (see Chapter 5 for more information on TopN reports).

In this case, the report now contains the top five sales regions, with the remainder of the sales data not displayed in the report. You have decided to give STAR awards to the top five customers and to insert a graph in the report to show their proportion of the top sales.

If you do not have this report available, quickly create the report using the following instructions. Or you can use a report you have already created as long as it has one group and one subtotal.

1. **Create a new report using the Customer table within the CRAZE.MDB database.**

   See Chapter 2 for more information.

2. Insert the following fields into the detail section:

- The Customer Name field from the Customer table
- The City field from the Customer table
- The Last Year's Sales field from the Customer table

See "Inserting Fields" in Chapter 2 for more information.

While inserting fields you may want to resize the fields to make more room on your report.

3. Only include records on the report from USA (you would want to base the record selection on the Country field from the Customer table being equal to USA).

See Chapter 4 if you need further information.

4. Group on the Region field from the Customer table.

See Chapter 5 for more information on creating groups.

5. Create a total of Last Year's Sales for each Region using the Subtotal feature.

See Chapter 5 for more information.

6. Finally, use the TopN feature to look only at the top 5 regions.

See Chapter 5 (of course) for more information.

Your report should look similar to the report in Figure 6-1.

Customer Listing

Customer Name	City	1995 Sales
MA		
XYZ Corporation	Concord	$298,356.22
ABC Co.	Concord	$32,249.55
		$330,605.77
PA		
Bob's Bikes Incorporated	Conshohocken	$23,789.25
XYZ Limited	Conshohocken	($88,165.22)
The Pedallers Co.	Philadelphia	$25,162.05
CycleSporin Industries	Conshohocken	$28,681.53
The Bike Shop Incorporated	Philadelphia	$301,568.22
		$291,035.83
WI		
Trail Blazer's Place	Madison	$123,658.46
Bike-O-Rama Company	Brown Deer	$42,709.86
Ride 'Em Cowboy Co.	Madison	

Figure 6-1: Does your sample report look like this?

REMEMBER

A report must have a group and a summary or subtotal for that group in order for To create the Group graph. Now for the real-life example of inserting a graph:

1. **Choose Insert⇨Graph/Chart Expert (or just click the Insert Chart button).**

   The dialog box appears as in Figure 6-2. Across the top of the dialog box you see the tabs Type, Data, Text, and Options.

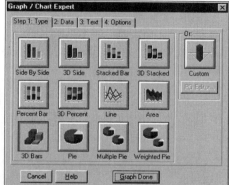

Figure 6-2:
The Graph/
Chart
Expert
dialog box.

2. **From the Type tab, choose the type of graph you want.**

   In this example, click Pie.

3. **Click the Data tab to choose the data you want to graph.**

   You can see the Data tab in Figure 6-3.

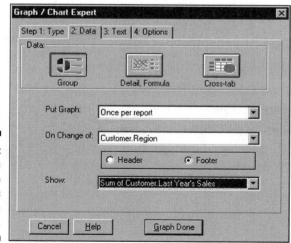

Figure 6-3:
The Data
tab
specifications
for a pie
graph.

4. **Click Group.**

   As mentioned earlier, you use the Group option when you want to graph one summary or subtotal.

5. **Click the down arrow next to the Put Graph box.**

   Based on the summary information in this report you have only one option.

6. **Click** `Once per report.`

   If you have group summaries in your report, you can have one pie graph to represent each group summary. Click the down arrow next to the Put Graph text box. Any groups in your report display here. Select the group after which you want to the graph to display.

7. **Click the down arrow next to the On Change of box.**

   Based on the data in this report, you have only one option.

8. **Click** `Customer.Region.`

9. **Click the Footer radio button.**

   This selection places the graph at the bottom of the report.

10. **Click the down arrow next to the Show box.**

    Only one field name displays, based on the data in this report.

11. **Click** `Sum of Customer.Last Year s Sales.`

12. **Click the Text tab.**

    From this tab, you may enter text to display in the report.

13. **Click the Title text box.**

    An insertion point is inserted there. It allows you to insert the text for the title of the report.

14. **For this example, enter** Last Year's STARS **as the title.**

    This text eventually displays centered at the top of the graph.

15. **Click the Subtitle text box.**

16. **For this example, type** The Top Five **as the subtitle.**

    This text displays in a smaller font just below the title. This graph is a pie graph, so it has no X and Y axes. You do not need to add text in these spots.

17. Click the Options tab.

At the top of this tab you have three check boxes. Crystal Reports will suggest the settings it thinks are appropriate for the type of graph you are creating, but you can override this if you wish.

The Options tab allows you to change a few basic settings for your graph. When you need to modify your graph over and above what you can do here, use the PGEditor option covered in a later section of this chapter.

18. Leave the check box checked to show the graph legend. Because this is a pie chart, do not show the gridlines. Because the chart contains no risers, don't show the values on the risers.

For a bar graph, you can choose a horizontal or vertical direction for the bars.

19. Click the down arrow button next to Font.

A list of available fonts for the graph displays.

20. Click a different font from this tab.

I chose Arial.

21. In the range of values box, you can enter a minimum or maximum.

22. Click G̲raph Done.

In the Design Tab, you can see the graph inserted in the report, as in Figure 6-4.

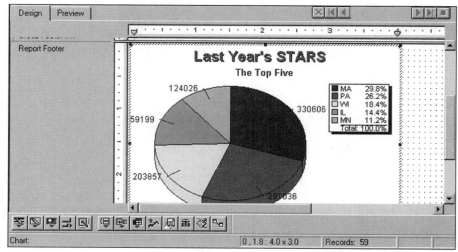

Figure 6-4: A pie chart inserted in the Report Footer as seen in the Design screen.

The graph will be inserted in the top-left edge of the specified section. You can move or resize the graph after it has been placed in the report.

Hint: Don't panic if your graph doesn't look as expected in the Design Tab. Check the Preview Tab first. Crystal Reports inserts the text titles you specified. It automatically creates a legend that designates a different color for every region, and it inserts the percentage for each region.

To view the graph in the Preview Tab, you have to move to the end of the report because the graph is in the Report Footer section.

Figure 6-5 shows how the report will look once you have previewed it.

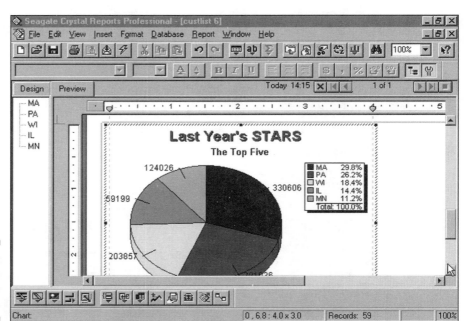

Figure 6-5:
Your graph
in the
Preview Tab.

Modifying a Graph

If you decide you want to make adjustments to your graph, you can modify a graph using the editing process. You have full formatting control of every graph element. Using any chart or graph you have inserted, make modifications to the graph.

Each graph becomes an object in a report. The graph object can be moved, resized, and reformatted just like any other object.

Moving the graph to the header (no change)

The easiest way to move a graph is to let the Graph/Chart Expert move it for you. Check out your graph and where it displays in the report. Using the Data tab and starting in either the Design or the Preview Tab, you can have Crystal Reports move the pie chart to the header or footer for you:

1. **Right-click anywhere on the graph object.**

   The Chart menu displays.

2. **Click Format Chart.**

   The Graph/Chart Expert displays.

3. **Click the Data tab.**

4. **Click the radio button next to** Header.

   This will tell Crystal to move the graph to the Report Header.

5. **Click <u>G</u>raph Done.**

Crystal Reports returns you to the graph Design or Preview Tab. The graph is now placed in the Report Header. When you preview the graph, you will notice that Crystal Reports placed it in the top-left corner of the Report Header, right on top of the title.

The next section shows you how to fine tune the positions of your graphs.

Where you place the graph determines where the graph prints in the report and which data is included in the graph. Use Table 6-1 to determine the best location for your chart or graph.

Table 6-1	Choosing a Location for a Graph	
Graph Location	*Prints*	*Includes Data*
Report Header	At the beginning of the report	For the entire report
Group Header	At the beginning of the group	For each group
Group Footer	At the end of the group	For each group
Report Footer	At the end of the report	For the entire report

Moving the graph

If you want to move a graph you have already placed in a report, be assured that it moves just like any other object.

Because the graph is an object, clicking on the graph displays the gray border with handles. The gray border shows you the outline of the object. The handles are the square boxes in the corners and in the middle of the lines. When the graph was placed in the header, it covered part of the report title that had been inserted. Move the graph so that the entire title displays:

1. **From the Preview Tab, click the graph so that the handles display.**

   While the pointer is over the object border, it turns into a magnifying glass. This pointer indicates that you can move this object.

2. **Click and drag the graph down the page, until the top line of the graph is even with the bottom of the title object.**

   You can also move the graph to the right to center it across the page.

3. **Release the mouse button.**

   The graph redraws in the new location, and the entire title is visible. See Figure 6-6.

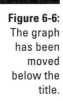

Figure 6-6:
The graph has been moved below the title.

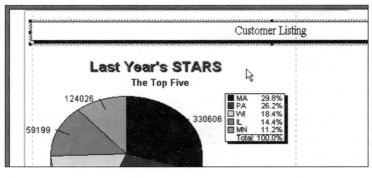

Note: Even though you moved the graph, it is still in the Report Header section, so it prints in the header of the report.

Resizing a graph

When you click an object, a gray outline and handles appear. You use the handles to resize a graph, or any object, for that matter.

1. **Click the graph so that the handles display.**

2. **Move the pointer over a handle until a two-headed arrow displays.**

3. **Click and drag the two-headed arrow until the graph or chart is the size you want.**

   If you click and drag a two-headed arrow in a corner of the object, you change the shape of the object in a diagonal direction. If you click and drag a two-headed arrow on one of the sides of the object, you move that side in or out.

Resizing and moving an object using the handles, the two-headed arrows, and the cross with arrows works the same way with every object.

Adding a border

The graph, like any object, can be formatted. You may want to add a border to enhance any graph by following these basic steps.

1. **Right-click the graph or chart.**

   The Chart menu displays.

2. **Click Change Border.**

   The Format Editor dialog box displays, with the Border tab chosen.

3. **Choose the border properties you want to display with the graph and click OK.**

For this example, add a navy single-line border with a drop shadow.

1. **In the Preview Tab, right-click anywhere on the graph.**

   The Chart menu displays.

2. **Click Change Border.**

   The Format Editor dialog box displays, with the Border tab chosen, as in Figure 6-7.

3. **Click the drop-down arrows to choose single borders for the Left, Right, Top, and Bottom of the chart.**

4. **Click in the check box next to Drop Shadow.**

   If a check already appears in the check box, skip to Step 5.

5. **Click the drop-down arrow in the Color box and choose** Navy **for the border color.**

6. **Click OK.**

   The graph has a border, as shown in Figure 6-8.

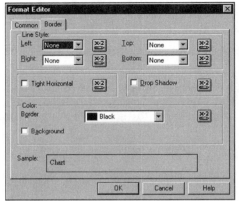

Figure 6-7:
The Format
Editor
dialog box,
with the
Border tab
on top.

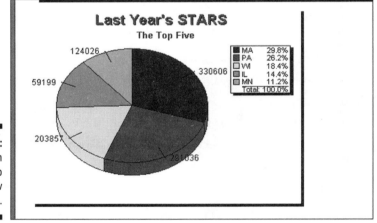

Figure 6-8:
The graph
with a drop
shadow
border.

Customizing your graph with PGEditor

Suppose that your company and your report have a preferred color scheme.
How do you make your graph match that color scheme? Well, you can
change the colors of each piece of the pie in the pie chart to make them
coordinate using the PGEditor option

The Custom option is very powerful, it will let you change colors; select
from more than 80 graph styles and modify pretty much any component of
your graph.

The following steps get you to a point where you can make those changes:

1. **Click the Design Tab.**
2. **Right-click anywhere on the graph.**

   The Chart menu opens.
3. **Click Format Chart.**

   The Graph/Chart Expert displays.
4. **From the Type tab, click Custom.**

   The PGEditor displays, as seen in Figure 6-9.

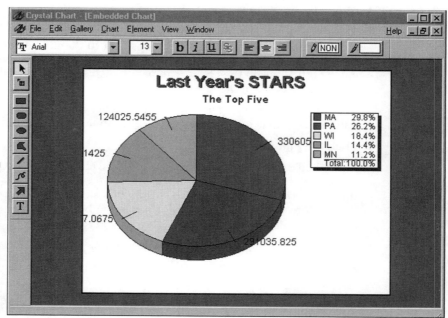

Figure 6-9:
The
PGEditor,
opened
from within
the Graph/
Chart
Expert
dialog box.

From this window, you can customize many aspects of the chart. The following sections of this chapter show you a few ways to customize this pie chart.

Using the PGEditor (Crystal Chart)

The Crystal Chart window is your window to the *PGEditor*. This is an add-on product to Crystal Reports that enhances your ability to customize any graph or chart. This tool offers you 80 graph types and formatting control of every graph object. The PGEditor and Crystal Chart are synonymous. In your documentation you will see references to the PGEditor.

A very popular feature of the PGEditor is creating graph templates. This topic is addressed at the end of this chapter. By using the PGEditor, you jump into graphing hyperspace.

In this chapter I show you some of the most popular editing capabilities of the PGEditor. Refer to the online help for more information.

Changing graph colors

Make this a bold colored pie chart!

With the PGEditor window on the screen, follow the steps to change the colors of a slice of pie:

1. **Click a slice of pie in the chart.**

   At the top of the window, below the menu, are a little pencil icon and a little paintbrush icon with color blocks next to them. The color block displays the current color of the selected item. The pencil tells you the color of the lines in the chart. The paintbrush tells you the color of the fill in that section of the chart or text.

   Note: If you are working in a 16-bit operating system, the pencil and paint brush icons may display in the bottom left of the window.

2. **Click the paintbrush.**

   A multi-colored box opens up just above the icon. On the left of this box are two boxes placed on top of one another. The top box tells you the color you have chosen. The bottom box shows the color where your pointer is located. Each color has a number, so you can identify that same color in any other objects you add to your report.

3. **Click the color you want for that slice of pie.**

4. **Repeat Steps 1 through 3 until you have changed the color for the entire pie.**

With the PGEditor window open, click the various objects. The numbers, the callout lines, the title, and subtitle are all small objects within the graph object. From this window, you can change the font, size, color, location, and other characteristics of these objects.

Depending on the company you keep, the numbered color scheme may be very important. I once worked for a company where the company logo had to appear in a particular green (number 86) or black, because that logo represented the company. No other color was acceptable. When a copy of your report displays on a company Intranet, be sure that the color of the logo is correct by defining the color number. Then use that number for your logo every time.

Changing a font size

The font size for the numbers that represent the percentage of sales is so small it makes it difficult to read. With a few clicks, you can change the font size of this or any text on the graph. The previous figure (Figure 6-9) shows the small font size for the numbers in the pie chart.

1. **Click the percentage numbers in the graph.**

2. **Look in the box just below the Element menu that shows the number of the font size. Click the down arrow to the right of that number.**

   The current font size is 9 points. A list drops down with various font sizes.

3. **Click 11.**

   All of the highlighted numbers change after you make the selection. Notice how Crystal Reports has changed all the percentages to the same size. You can also right-click to open the Number Format dialog box to make changes.

To select multiple objects in the graph, click the first object and then hold down the shift key while selecting the remaining objects.

Detaching a slice of pie

Often you see a piece of pie in a pie chart set apart for recognition. In this example, detach the piece of pie of the highest sales region:

1. **From the PGEditor window, click the slice of pie with the highest percentage of sales.**

2. **Choose Chart⇨Detach Slice.**

   From this menu you can make many adjustments to the pie chart, for the thickness of the chart, the rotation of the chart, and the size of the chart. After you do, the various detachment options are displayed.

3. **Click Minor.**

   The detached slice of pie appears in Figure 6-10.

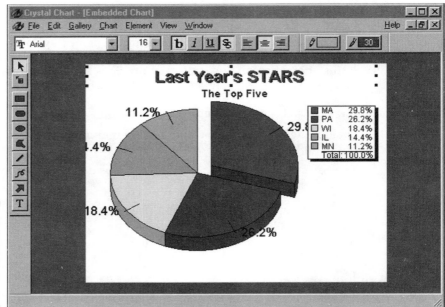

Figure 6-10:
The piece of pie with the highest sales region detached.

Undoing changes

Ooops! You made a big mistake. Say that you have spheres floating in your chart, but you don't want them. If you do something you do not want to do, you can undo the changes.

You must undo directly after doing something. The PGEditor only remembers one step back. You can't undo a mistake you made three tasks ago. Here's how to undo: After making a change in a chart that you don't like, choose Edit⇨Undo. This action undoes that last action you did.

Saving the pie chart

1. **Click the close button on the PGEditor window.**

   You are prompted to save the chart.

2. **Click Yes.**

3. **From the Graph/Chart Expert, click <u>G</u>raph Done.**

The changes you have made in the Crystal Chart window are applied to the graph in your Design or Preview Tab.

If you don't close and save the Crystal Chart Window and then click Graph Done, the changes you have made are not applied to the graph in your report.

Deleting a graph

After you delete a graph, that action cannot be undone!

1. **Begin in either the Design Tab or the Preview Tab.**
2. **Click the graph so that the gray border and handles display.**
3. **Press Delete on the keyboard, or right-click on the graph and choose Delete from the Chart menu that appears.**

   After you choose Delete, the Confirm Command displays.

4. **Click Yes to delete the chart. Click No to keep the chart in the report.**

Drilling Down on a Graph

Drill-down is a process that allows you to see the details of summary information in a report. The pie chart we have been working with holds the summary information of top sales by region. While viewing your graph, you can view the details of the summary information that *gave* you the graphed results.

Drilling down on reports is available from within Crystal Reports only. If you use the Crystal Reports Engine to distribute your reports with your application, the drill down feature is *not* available in those reports. In addition, drilling down is only available for group graphs.

The steps to follow to drill down to see more detailed information are:

1. **Click the Preview Tab to open it.**
2. **Move the pointer over a segment of the graph.**

   The pointer becomes a magnifying glass.

3. **Double-click a section of the graph.**

   The details of the summary information is displayed in a drill-down tab. The tab displays at the top of the Report window. Figure 6-11 shows a drill-down tab for the IL Region.

4. **To create a drill-down tab for each section, double-click all the sections in turn.**

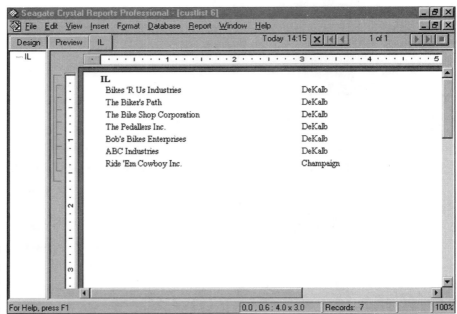

Figure 6-11:
Drill-down
into Illinois.

5. Close a drill-down tab by clicking the close tab button (the red X to the right of the date and time display in the Preview Tab).

Closing the drill-down tab does not close the report.

If you attempt to modify a report with a drill-down tab active, you will see the Drill-Down warning as shown in Figure 6-12.

Figure 6-12:
Read the
warning
and make
your
choice.

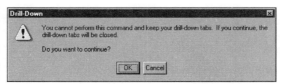

You cannot modify a report with drill-down tabs open. If you Select OK, Crystal Reports swill close all drill-down tabs and let you proceed. If you do not want to close the drill-downs, click Cancel.

Adding a special effect

For a classy finish to any graph, add a special effect (another feature available with the PGEditor). A special effect adds interesting backgrounds making the graph stand out. (You must open PGEditor, of course, to add an effect. See "Customizing your graph with PGEditor" earlier in this chapter for details.)

1. **Choose View⇨Special Effect Palette.**

   The Special Effect dialog box displays.

2. **Click Texture on the right side.**

3. **Click the drop down button at the top.**

4. **Click** 4 Blues.

5. **Click Apply.**

   The background of your graph displays the 4 Blues motif.

6. **Click the Close button (the X in the upper-right corner) to close the Special Effect palette.**

   Figure 6-13 shows how the special effect looks with the Special Effects palette still open.

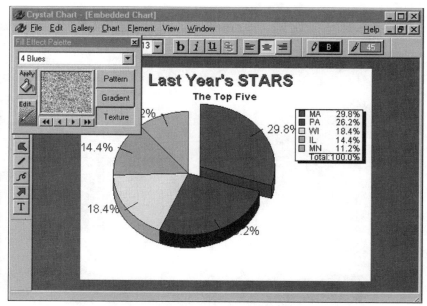

Figure 6-13: The Special Effects palette with applied special effects.

Note: Some of the special effects may look like good backgrounds for reports displayed on the World Wide Web.

Changing the Graph Type

Some types of data work better with different types of graphs. Earlier in this chapter, in "Creating and Inserting a Graph," you see how effective a pie chart is in showing the top five sales regions. When you are plotting percentages of a whole, pie charts show the proportion of each section to the whole very well. If you want to show monthly sales over the past year, a line graph is effective in showing the highs and lows.

Applying the graph gallery

Take a look at the graph in Figure 6-14. This is a side-by-side bar graph. If you want to change the graph type, apply the options in the Gallery menu to look at your graph type options. In the example that follows, you convert this side-by-side bar graph to a stacked bar graph.

While in the PGEditor window, choose the Gallery menu. Move your pointer to the various menu options. As the menu opens on the right, move your pointer to those options.

Each menu displays a picture of the graph type available on the gallery. Not all graph types work with every set of data.

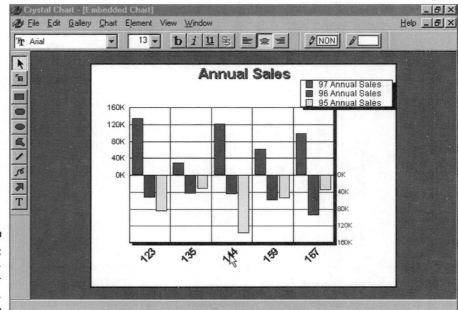

Figure 6-14: A side-by-side bar graph.

Now is when you can experiment with many kinds of graphs. Apply the changes to a graph by taking the following steps.

1. **From the Preview Tab, right-click the graph.**

   The Chart menu opens.

2. **Choose Format Chart.**

   The Graph/Chart Expert dialog box displays.

3. **Click PGEditor.**

   The PGEditor window opens.

4. **Choose the Gallery menu.**

5. **From the Gallery menu, click the type of graph you want.**

   Feel free to experiment with a variety of graphs.

6. **If you don't like how a graph looks, choose Edit⇨Undo.**

   The graph on the screen goes back to the original graph.

7. **Choose Gallery⇨Vertical Bar.**

8. **Choose Stacked.**

   Figure 6-15 shows a stacked bar graph with the same data used in the line graph in "Inserting a line graph," earlier in this chapter.

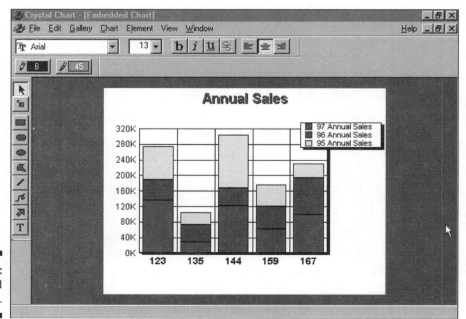

Figure 6-15:
A stacked bar graph.

This graph does a better job of representing the *total* sales of each customer. And you can easily discern the sales for each quarter of 1997, representing a portion of the total sales for that customer.

Looking at graph examples

Crystal Reports Professional comes with many report files for you to use. Some of those files I refer to throughout this book. If you want to see other examples of how a graph is used in a report, take a look at the following report files. (You can find these files in the Crystal Reports CRAZE folder. You will find the CRAZE folder under the Reports folder: \CRW\Reports\CRAZE. CRW is the directory in which Crystal Reports resides.)

- **Line Graph:** SPRODT1P.RPT
- **Bar Graph:** SPRODCAP.RPT
- **Bar Graph:** SEMPMO1.RPT
- **Pie Chart:** SCUSSA2P.RPT
- **Stacked Bar:** SEMPXTBP.RPT

Open any of these files to view a variety of graphs and how they are used in reports. Open the Graph/Chart Expert to look at how the data is graphed. Look at the PGEditor to view how the graph objects are formatted. Open one of the example files by following these steps.

1. **Choose File⇨Open.**

   The Crystal Reports folder displays in the Open dialog box.

2. **Double-click the Reports folder.**

3. **Double-click the CRAZE folder.**

4. **Move the pointer to one of the names of the files in the list that appeared earlier in this section.**

   You may have to use the scroll buttons to scroll to the right in the Open dialog box.

5. **Click the file you want to open so it is highlighted.**

6. **Click Open.**

   The report displays.

7. **View the graph in either the Design Tab or the Preview Tab.**

8. **From the Preview Tab, right-click the graph.**

   The Chart menu opens.

9. **Choose Format Chart.**

   The Graph/Chart Expert dialog box displays.

10. **Click PGEditor.**

Using a Graph Template

Refer to the earlier part of this chapter to create a graph and on how to move into and out of the PGEditor. After you have a graph created, you can save its format in the PGEditor and then apply that same graph as a template to other data.

A graph template is useful when you want to create a chart or graph that is consistent each time it appears. Each time you create a graph that represents the top five sales, you apply the graph template. Each top five sales graphs looks identical to the last, except for the changes in data. You can use this chart month after month, year after year, as a template so your reports have a consistent look.

Saving a graph as a template

With the graph you have created on screen, stay in the PGEditor window. When you have created the graph or chart to your liking, save the chart.

1. **From the PGEditor choose File⇨Save As.**

   The Save As dialog box displays.

2. **Type in the name of the file you want to save.**

   For this example, I will call this template TEMP01.

Crystal Reports will save the formatting of the graph in a separate file that you can reuse.

You should create one template for each graph type you commonly work with. For example, I have one template for bar charts and a separate one for pie charts.

Applying the template

To apply the template, open a completely new report with a pie chart in it. Or create a new pie chart. When you apply a template, the template must be of a similar nature to the chart in the file. Select a bar graph template to apply to a bar graph. Select a histogram template to apply to a histogram graph, and so on.

Open PGEditor with a new pie chart in it. First open a report (see Chapter 3 for how to open a report), and then open PGEditor. With a file open and with a graph in it:

1. **Right-click anywhere on the graph.**

2. **Choose the Format menu.**

   The Graph/Chart Expert displays.

3. **Click the Custom button.**

   The graph displays in the PGEditor window.

Apply the standard template you have created to this graph.

1. **Choose File⇨Apply Template.**

   The Apply Template Dialog box displays.

2. **Select** Temp01 **(or any graph you previously saved).**

3. **Click the Open button.**

   The template you created is applied to the graph in the Crystal Charts Window.

The chart now has the same color scheme and the same font size. It takes on the appearance of the applied template.

Applying Graph Templates Stored in PGEditor

Crystal Charts already has a myriad of chart templates created for your use. Instead of creating your own charts and graphs, you can apply the Crystal Chart templates. Here's how to apply a template.

Say, for example, that you have a hilo graph open and want to apply some Crystal Chart Graph templates to it.

1. **Choose File⇨Apply Template.**

   The Apply Template Dialog box opens.

2. **Double-click the Gallery folder within the CRW directory.**

3. Double-click the hilo folder or the folder that matches the graph type you are working with.

This screen lists all the Crystal Chart hilo templates available. Any of these can be applied to a hilo chart. Figure 6-16 shows the Apply Template dialog box with the hilo folder open.

4. Select a template.

When you see the names of the graph or chart templates, look for patterns. The names in Figure 6-16 have endings that tell you what the graph might look like. You can see a preview of the graph in the lower-left corner of the dialog box.

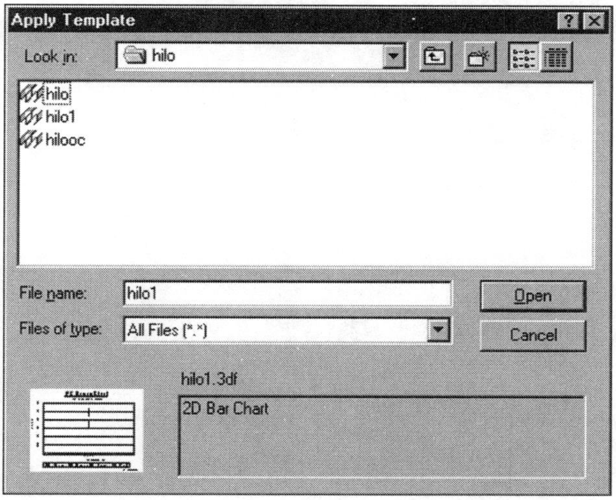

Figure 6-16:
The Apply
Template
dialog box
with hilo
templates.

Apply Template	? X
Look in: hilo	
hilo	
hilo1	
hilooc	
File name: hilo1	Open
Files of type: All Files (*.*)	Cancel
hilo1.3df	
2D Bar Chart	

5. Click the Open button.

Crystal Charts converts the original chart according to the template. Figure 6-17 shows the applied Crystal Chart Template.

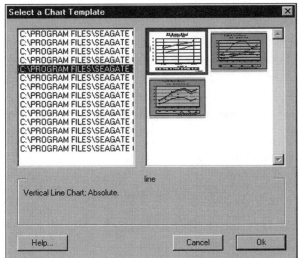

Figure 6-17:
The applied
Crystal
Chart
template.

Viewing Crystal Chart templates

From the PGEditor you can view many of the Graph and Chart options available. Simply choose File⇨New. PGEditor displays the Select a Chart Template dialog box.

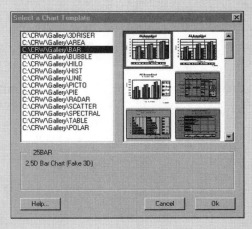

Chapter 7

Using the Crystal Formula Language

*I*f you hated algebra and dreaded calculus, do not skip this chapter because you think that math is what Seagate Crystal Reports formulas are. You can do many easy calculations without becoming a Hawking or a Newton.

What Is a Formula?

A formula is simply a *symbolic statement* that manipulates the data in your report. That is all it is. The tricky part is getting the formula to work with your data the way you want. But that tricky part is why you bought this book, isn't it? So you can have me show you how to get these things to work. Let's give it a whirl.

Chapter 6 helps you understand how to insert predefined summary calculations into a report using the built-in subtotal and *summary* operations. You do not have to type the particulars to make that happen; only indicate to Crystal Reports where and what field you want totaled and the total happens. In this chapter, you can see how to create mathematical and other calculations to suit your specifications.

A basic idea for a formula is to calculate the gross profit of products sold by your company. So to figure that number, you subtract the cost of the product from the sales price. A little more complicated formula is one that calculates the time elapsed between two dates. You may use this formula to determine whether a client is past due on a bill. This type of report is known as an *aging report.* Or suppose that the database has stored numbers as string values. In other words, the entries in the field look like numbers, but the database has designated the field as characters. Crystal Reports cannot perform a numeric calculation until you convert the characters to numeric, something you can do with formulas.

A really cool formula is a branching, or conditional formula, also known as an *if-then-else formula.* An example is a calculation that says that *if* the total amount owed is more than $1,000, *then* call your lawyer, or *else* call the client yourself. So the formula branches in two directions, depending upon the number generated. You do this kind of calculation every day while shopping. Computers are not as smart as you, and you have to create a precise formula for them to calculate what you do intuitively.

Acquainting Yourself with the Parts of a Formula

A formula consists of several distinct parts. First, you have to have database fields upon which the calculations are performed. Second, you have operators that perform calculations, and third, you have functions that are hybrid operators — meaning that a function performs an operation beyond simple + and – calculations.

Opening the Formula Editor

You can insert a formula into a report at any time when you want to perform a calculation beyond a simple sum on a field in your database. Before opening the database, these are the general steps that you undertake to insert a formula:

1. Open the report into which you want to insert a formula.

2. Choose Insert⇨Formula Field.

3. The Insert Fields dialog box appears, as in Figure 7-1.

If any formulas already exist in the report, they appear in the dialog box.

Figure 7-1:
The Insert
Fields
dialog box,
with the
Formula tab
selected.

4. **Click New.**

5. **In the Formula Name dialog box, enter a name for the formula.**

   This point is important because Crystal Reports uses the formula name as the field header in the report. It can contain spaces and special characters — and can contain as much text as you can fit in the text box. The name should be descriptive enough so that you can interpret what the formula does. In this example, I name the formula **TEST**.

6. **Click OK.**

   The Formula Editor dialog box appears, as in Figure 7-2.

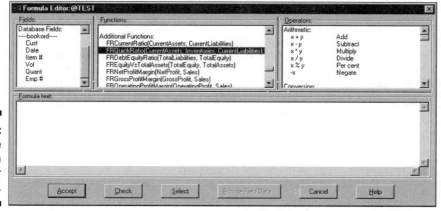

Figure 7-2:
The
Formula
Editor
dialog box.

In order to see more details in this dialog box, you can grab the border and expand the dialog box, and you can expand the size of each individual list box by positioning the pointer on the frames between the lists and dragging left or right.

This dialog box may be a little intimidating, but it is very approachable. At the left is the list of the Fields in the database that is open. In the middle is the list of Functions, and at the far right are the Operators.

The formula process consists of picking from each list, just like a menu, except you have no limits! That is, you could select six Fields, two Functions, and ten Operators — if you wish.

The Fields box

All fields in the table(s) used in the report are listed in the Fields box. If you have already inserted fields into the report, they are listed at the top of the list under the heading `Report Fields` (rather than `Database Fields` you see in Figure 7-2). Those fields are listed with the table name preceding them so that you can always tell where the fields are located. So if you have a report with fields from unique tables, you can identify the source of each field. Any formulas that have been inserted into the report have an @ sign preceding them.

You may notice that some fields appear in both the Reports field and the Database field section of the Fields box. Crystal Reports assumes that if you place a field on your report, you are likely to want to use it elsewhere in your report and includes it under Report Fields to make it easy to find. All fields will be listed under Database Fields.

Table names are listed, too, and you can double-click the table name to see each of the individual fields in the table. A second double-click closes the list. This feature allows you to easily surf the database for the table you want and then, in turn, surf the table for the exact field that you may need to create the formula. If you have created any groups, they, too, will be listed and can be used in formulas.

If you have groups on your report, all the information regarding the group (the Group Name field and any subtotals or summaries for the group) will also be listed in the fields box below report fields. If you want to reference this information within a formula, highlight it and select to save yourself time.

The Functions box

Functions are those exotic creatures that are *pre-built* formulas of a sort. Functions are hybrids in that they contain mathematical operations that are difficult to build for an average person, such as calculating the Quick Ratios for a business report. In other words, these are tools that exist for you to use instead of having to build them yourself.

You'll notice if you scroll through the functions box that there is a ton of information. How do you find what you're looking for? The functions are organized to make your life easier. The first category of functions is Arithmetic; look here when you're looking for functions to work with numbers. The next category is a Strings category that you can use to find functions when working with text or number fields. The remainder of the functions list is organized in the same manner.

The Operators box

Some of the arithmetic operators may be more familiar to you in that the symbols are mathematical symbols such as addition, subtraction and so on. There are also other categories of operators for use against other data types or in other situations. Notice that Crystal Reports shows you the correct way to use the operator by including an X and a Y as substitutes for the values.

The Formula text box

This is where you can do the work and create the formula. After you select a Field, Function, or Operator, it is inserted into the Formula text box. That way, you can see exactly what you are building as you go.

The Select button

Don't panic, you don't have to do a lot of typing in the Formula Editor. Simply highlight the Field, Function, or Operator you want to add to the formula, and click the Select button. The Field, Function, or Operator will be inserted into the Formula text box where your cursor is placed.

The Check button

After laboring mightily on a formula, have Crystal Reports check it for you. Simply click Check, and the formula is examined for any syntax problems. No, *syntax* is not a form of taxation on liquor or cigarettes (that is *sin tax*), but rather the proper placement of the parts of the formula. If a mistake is found, Crystal Reports moves the cursor to the area of the formula that it thinks is incorrect and prompts you with a dialog box message.

If you are working on a long or complicated formula, you can check it at any point. Simply click the Check button, and Crystal Reports will make sure it can understand what you have done to that point in the formula. You can then continue with the rest of the formula — confident that it's correct.

The Accept button

Click this button after you have created the formula, had Crystal Reports check it for you, and been given an okay. By the way, if you did not execute a check before clicking the Accept button, Crystal Reports does it anyway. If it finds a mistake, it gives you the option to correct the formula.

The Browse Field Data button — for accuracy

When you select a field that you think is the correct one for your formula, you can be sure that it is correct:

1. **Highlight the field name.**
2. **Click the Browse Field Data button to see the actual data in the field.**

Browsing also tells you the length of the field and the data type.

Syntax 101

What follows is a table of syntax that you use when creating formulas to make them as easy as possible. Table 7-1 lists them and explains their uses.

Table 7-1	Tools for Creating a Formula
Tool	**What It Does**
//	These two forward slashes can add a comment to the formula. Use comments to document your formulas and what the formula does — it will make modifying reports in the future much easier. So in any formula, you can type //; the text after // is not treated as part of the formula nor does it print.
()	The parentheses denote the arguments following a function. When you use a function in a formula, it may need information inside the parentheses in order to work. An example is the Trim(str) function. If you insert the Trim function in a formula, it has to have something inside the brackets to act upon.
{}	These are French braces, Oo La La! Not to get excited, they simply indicate that the information enclosed is a Database field or formula. You see them a lot.
" "	Any kind of character enclosed in quotation marks is called a *literal.* In a formula, a literal is text that you want to print at a certain point in the report. For example, if your formula calculates the length of time since your company has been paid by a customer, you can have Crystal Reports print PAST DUE by inserting it into the formula as a literal.

Crystal Reports ignores upper- or lowercase in the formula (except when looking at database values), as well as carriage returns (pressing Enter, for you post-typewriter types). Line breaks, too, are okay, as are spaces. Crystal reads the formula left to right, regardless.

Going Down the Road to Creating a Formula

The best way to understand how formulas work is to use real data in examples. The remainder of the chapter will add formulas to the Formula report (instruction follows on how to create it). In the following examples, you can create the formula report and follow exactly or try adding individual formulas to reports you may already have created against your own data.

If you'd like to work through the following examples, please take a moment to create the following report. If you need a bit of help, refer back to previous sections of the book as indicated.

1. **Create a new report utilizing all tables within the CRAZE.MDB database.**

   The linking suggested by Crystal Reports is correct. See "Accessing a Database" in Chapter 2 for more information.

2. **Insert the following fields into the detail section:**

   - The Customer Name field from the Customer table
   - The Product Name field from the Product table
   - The Unit Price field from Orders Detail table
   - The Quantity field from the Orders Detail table

   See Chapter 2 for details on inserting fields.

   While inserting fields you may want to resize the fields to make more room on your report. Only include records on the report from California (you would want to base the record selection on the Region field from the Customer table being equal to CA). See Chapter 4 if you need further information.

3. **Group on the Order ID field from the Orders table.**

   See Chapter 5 for more information on creating groups.

When you create this report, you'll notice that two of the records on the first page are blank. This happens because some of the records in the database don't have values in all fields. You may run into this situation when creating reports against your own data. The next section will discuss how to fix this problem.

Eliminating Blank Records

Welcome to the real world. You have a report that includes some data that is useless because it is only partially complete. In situations such as this, you will have to modify your record selection to exclude the partial data. In this situation, I only include records that have a quantity greater than zero.

1. **In the CRAZE report, click the Select Expert button.**

   The Select Expert dialog box appears, with the one condition, which is records from California only.

2. **Click the New tab.**

   The Choose Field dialog box opens.

3. **Select the Quantity field by double-clicking it.**

   The Choose field dialog box then closes.

4. **Back in the Select Expert dialog box, in the second drop-down box from the left, select the** Greater than **criteria.**

5. **In the third drop-down box from the left, type a zero (0).**

   The formula can be viewed by clicking the Show Formula button. The formula will extract only those records in California and with a Quantity greater than 0 (see Figure 7-3).

6. **Click OK to complete the record selection process.**

   Crystal Reports asks if you wish to refresh or use saved data.

7. **Select saved data.**

   No records with a zero quantity will remain.

Creating a Formula

With the report fields in place, the next step is to create the formula that multiplies the quantity by the number of units. Crystal Reports treats a formula as an object, and wherever you place the formula in the report is where the results of the formula are displayed. You can perform these steps in the Design Tab.

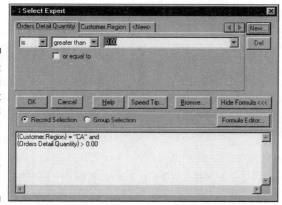

Figure 7-3:
Preparing
to select
records
from
California
that are
greater
than zero.

To create the price multiplication formula:

1. Click Insert Fields on the toolbar.

2. Click the Formula tab.

3. Click New.

Crystal Reports opens the Formula Name dialog box, into which you must enter a name for the formula.

4. Enter something original, such as Total.

Take a look at Figure 7-4 as an example.

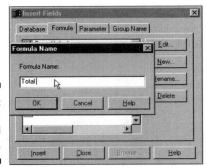

Figure 7-4:
The formula with a Total name.

5. Click OK.

The Formula Editor dialog box appears.

You are on the brink of becoming a *Smarty*. Everything that you have done in this book to this point has been pretty straightforward. Now, greatness has been thrust upon you — carpe diem!

Your goal is to multiply the unit cost by the quantity. In the Fields list of this dialog box is a list of the fields, formulas, and groups in the report. Your targets are the two fields Unit Price and Quantity.

6. In the Fields list, click Orders Detail.Unit Price.

7. Click Select.

The field name pops into the Formula text box in the bottom half of the dialog box, as you see in Figure 7-5.

Just in case you have forgotten, the name of the table in which the field is located — is part of the field name — in this case, Orders Detail.Unit Price.

The next step is to enter the mathematical operator that multiplies the numbers in this field by the numbers in the Quantity field.

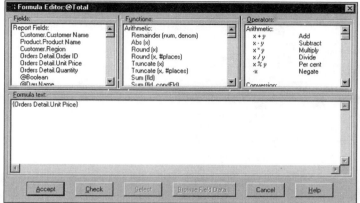

Figure 7-5:
The Unit
Price field
in the
Formula text
box.

8. **Click** x*y Multiply.

   The Operators are in the upper-right box of the dialog box. The arithmetic operators appear at the top of the list, and one of these is x*y Multiply, which is the one you want.

9. **Click** **S**elect.

   Crystal Reports inserts only the * symbol in the Formula text box, so it may be hard to see.

10. **In the F**i**elds list, click the next field in the formula,** Orders Detail.Quantity.

11. **Click** **S**elect.

    The second field is inserted into the Formula text box and looks like this:

    ```
    {Orders Detail.Unit Price} * {Orders Detail.Quantity}
    ```

Check please!

Although Crystal Reports checks the formula automatically after you click Accept, clicking Check is a good idea in order to confirm that your formula has the correct syntax.

1. **Click** **C**heck.

   The No Errors alert box appears, as in Figure 7-6.

2. **Click OK to close the dialog box.**

   If Crystal Reports found a mistake, it moved the cursor to the portion of the formula it recognized as being erroneous.

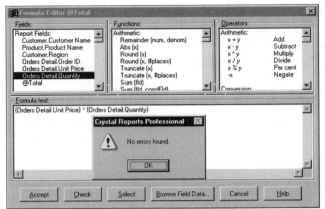

Figure 7-6:
Crystal
Reports
says that
the formula
checks out!

Accepting the formula

The final step is to accept the formula. A warning here: Just because Crystal Reports examined the formula and determined that it was properly constructed does not necessarily mean that the formula is correct. In the case of a simple formula such as this one, you can easily feel confident that the results of the formula are correct. But if you create highly intricate formulas, even if they are properly constructed, they can give the wrong results. Understand this difference, and use a common sense approach to the results you get when you check your formula. If you're sure that you're on the right track, continue on the road to completion:

1. **Click Accept.**

   The Insert Fields dialog box is still open with the newly created formula listed.

2. **Click the formula name, Total.**

3. **Click Insert.**

4. **In the Design Tab, insert the formula to the far right in the Details section of the report by clicking where you want the formula to go.**

   It appears, similar to Figure 7-7.

5. **In the Insert Fields dialog box, click Close.**

6. **Hold onto your hat, this is the moment of truth. Click the Preview Tab.**

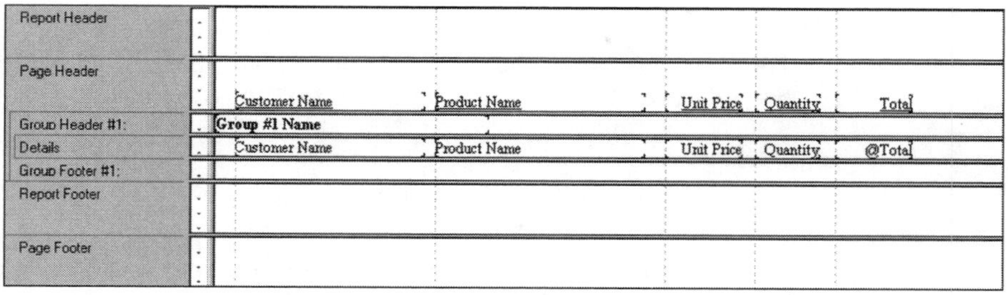

Figure 7-7: The formula name Total inserted into the Details section.

If everything went according to plan, your new report looks similar to the one in Figure 7-8.

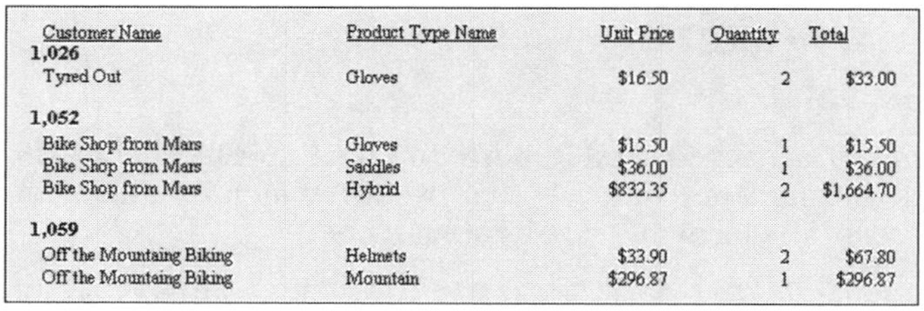

Customer Name	Product Type Name	Unit Price	Quantity	Total
1,026				
Tyred Out	Gloves	$16.50	2	$33.00
1,052				
Bike Shop from Mars	Gloves	$15.50	1	$15.50
Bike Shop from Mars	Saddles	$36.00	1	$36.00
Bike Shop from Mars	Hybrid	$832.35	2	$1,664.70
1,059				
Off the Mountaing Biking	Helmets	$33.90	2	$67.80
Off the Mountaing Biking	Mountain	$296.87	1	$296.87

Figure 7-8: A preview of the report with the new formula added!

Pretty exciting, I think! The ability to calculate all kinds of results is limited only by your ingenuity. In the rest of this chapter, I show you other terrific formulas using this same report.

Editing a Formula

Before moving to a new example formula, take a look at how easily you can edit a formula currently in a report. In this example, you add a calculation to compute the extended sales price *plus tax*.

1. **Click the Design Tab.**

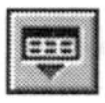

2. **Click the Insert Fields button on the toolbar.**
3. **Click the Formula tab.**
4. **Click the formula name** `Total`**.**

5. **Click Edit.**

   The Formula Editor dialog box appears, with the Total formula displayed in the Formula text box. The text for the formula currently is:

   ```
   {Orders Detail.Unit Price} * {Orders Detail.Quantity}
   ```

   In this example, the sales tax rate is 7 percent. All you need to do is edit the formula to add the percentage.

   Note: If you want to edit a formula, simply select it in the Design or Preview Tab, right-click, and select Edit Formula from the Shortcut menu.

6. **Click at the far right of the formula.**

7. **Click the Multiply operator.**

8. **Click Select.**

   The * is inserted.

9. **Type:** 1.07

   This edit causes Crystal Reports to take the results of the first portion of the formula and multiply that by 1.07, which is equivalent to adding 7 percent. The formula text should now be:

   ```
   {Orders Detail.Unit Price} * {Orders Detail.Quantity} *
   1.07
   ```

10. **Click Check and then OK to exit the dialog box.**

    The formula should check okay; Crystal Reports displays a small alert box indicating so.

11. **Click Accept.**

    You are back at the Insert Fields dialog box.

Adding a Formula That Totals by Group

With Crystal Reports, you can easily insert Subtotals, Summaries, and Grand Totals into a report automatically with built-in summary operations (see Chapter 5). There will also be times when you want to work with these summaries in the Formula Editor. Perhaps you want to calculate a percentage of total. In this section, I show you how to create these summaries within the formula language. Remember, let Crystal Reports do the work for you if you simply want to place the summary on the report. You only need to create a summary this way when you want to use it within a Formula. The report is grouped by order ID, and say that you have already created a total of the orders including sales tax. Therefore, the steps to create a formula that will total by the orders is as follows:

1. **Click the Design Tab.**

2. **Click the Insert Fields button on the toolbar and then click the Formula tab.**

3. **In the Formula tab, click New and enter a name, in the Formula Name dialog box, for the formula.**

   A suggestion is **Group Sum.**

4. **Click OK to open the Formula Editor dialog box.**

5. **Start the formula by clicking the Sum (fld, condFld) function.**

   You can find Sum (fld, condFld) in the Functions list of the Formula Editor dialog box.

6. **Click Select.**

   The function is inserted into the Formula text box.

7. **The first field to be summed is the one that gives you the extended price plus the sales tax, which is @Total. Click the formula name in the Fields list.**

8. **Click Select.**

   The first part of the formula is completed, as shown here:

   ```
   Sum({@Total},)
   ```

   Note that Crystal Reports automatically inserts a pair of French braces to enclose the formula name for you.

9. **Still in the Formula text box, move your cursor to the right of the comma.**

   You are now ready to enter the group field that will be subtotaled.

10. **Click** Orders Detail.Order ID **in the Fields list.**

Summing up

The two most often used summary functions are Sum (fld) and Sum (fld, condfld). You would use the Sum (fld) when you want to sum a field for the entire report. For example, if you wanted to create a total for Last Year's Sales for the entire report, your formula would be Sum ({Customer.Last Year's Sales}). This is equivalent to letting Crystal Reports automatically create a grand total for you.

You use the Sum (fld, condFld) function when you want to create a total for each group. The fld is the actual field you want to summarize, and the condFld is the group field for which you want a total.

11. Click Select.

The completed formula appears here:

```
Sum({@Total},{Orders Detail.Order ID})
```

12. Click Accept.

13. In the Insert Fields dialog box, click Group Sum.

14. Insert the formula in the Group Footer section of the report by moving the pointer to the Group Footer and clicking. (You probably want to insert it below the Total formula.)

This placement is important because you want the results to print after every group. Figure 7-9 shows the completed report in the Design Tab. The pointer indicates the location of the Group Sum formula.

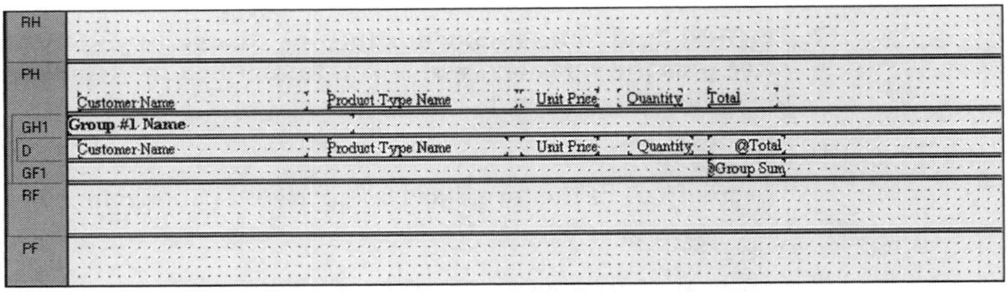

Figure 7-9: The Group Sum formula inserted in the Group Footer section of the report.

15. Click Close in the Insert Fields dialog box.

16. Click the Preview Tab.

Your report looks like the one in Figure 7-10.

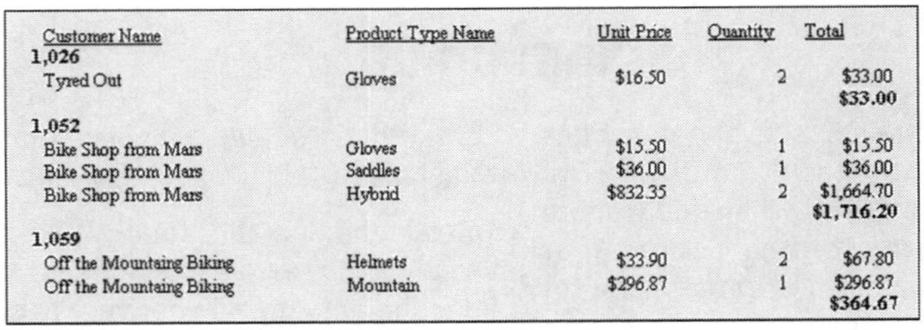

Figure 7-10: The Group Sum formula does its work!

Customer Name	Product Type Name	Unit Price	Quantity	Total
1,026				
Tyred Out	Gloves	$16.50	2	$33.00
				$33.00
1,052				
Bike Shop from Mars	Gloves	$15.50	1	$15.50
Bike Shop from Mars	Saddles	$36.00	1	$36.00
Bike Shop from Mars	Hybrid	$832.35	2	$1,664.70
				$1,716.20
1,059				
Off the Mountaing Biking	Helmets	$33.90	2	$67.80
Off the Mountaing Biking	Mountain	$296.87	1	$296.87
				$364.67

Adding a Formula That Calculates a Percentage of Total

You may want to create formulas to calculate percentage of totals. Perhaps you want to calculate the percentage a customer's sales represents as a percentage of the sales for the entire report. In this example, I show you how to create a calculation to determine what percentage the individual record represents of the total for the order.

When you want to calculate percentages, Crystal Reports has a percentage operator (%) that will quickly calculate the percentage.

1. **Click the Design Tab.**

 2. **Click the Insert Fields button on the toolbar.**

   The Insert Fields dialog box opens.

3. **Click the Formula tab, and then click Ṉew.**

4. **In the Formula Name dialog box, enter a name for the formula, such as** Percent of Order.

5. **Click OK.**

   The Formula Editor dialog box opens.

6. **In the Fields list, scroll down until you locate the** @Total **formula and click it.**

7. **Click Ṣelect.**

   The function is inserted into the Formula text box.

8. **Move to the Operators box and highlight the Percent Operator under the Arithmetic category.**

9. **Click Ṣelect.**

10. **Click** @Group Sum **in the Fields box** Order Detail.Order ID.

11. **Click Ṣelect.**

    The completed formula in formula text should look like this:

    ```
    {@Total} % {@Group Sum}
    ```

12. **Click Ạccept.**

13. **In the Insert fields dialog box, click the formula** Percent of Order.

14. **Click Ịnsert.**

15. **Insert the formula in the Details section to the right of the Total formula.**

16. **To close the Insert Fields dialog box, click <u>C</u>lose.**

17. **Click the Preview Tab to see the results, as in Figure 7-11.**

Figure 7-11:
With a
percent
formula
inserted,
you can
easily see
each item's
percentage
of the total
order.

Customer Name	Product Type Name	Unit Price	Quantity	Total	Percent of Order
1,026					
Tyred Out	Gloves	$16.50	2	$33.00	100.00
				$33.00	
1,052					
Bike Shop from Mars	Gloves	$15.50	1	$15.50	0.90
Bike Shop from Mars	Saddles	$36.00	1	$36.00	2.10
Bike Shop from Mars	Hybrid	$832.35	2	$1,664.70	97.00
				$1,716.20	
1,059					
Off the Mountaing Biking	Helmets	$33.90	2	$67.80	18.59
Off the Mountaing Biking	Mountain	$296.87	1	$296.87	81.41
				$364.67	

Working with Text Strings

Text strings are characters that can be numbers or letters, but the key is that they are considered to be text *even if* they look like numbers. Text strings can be manipulated to fit a variety of needs. Combining a first and last name in a report when the two pieces of information are in two distinct fields in a table is a common need. For the combination of multiple fields, Text Objects is the easy and powerful way to go (as described in Chapter 10).

Even though you will use text objects to combine fields, there will be certain situations where you need the additional power of the Formula Editor. Perhaps your report requires the display of a first initial only rather than the entire first name. You can use a formula to pull out a portion of a text entry and print it in the report.

In the CRAZE.MDB database, one table is named Customer. In that table is a field named First Name. The task is to use a formula to pull out the first letter of the first name of the customer. You could then create a text object to combine the first letter of First Name with the Last Name field to create a label that reads *D Wolf* instead of *Douglas Wolf.*

In this example, the first initial in the Contact First Name field is pulled out with a formula.

1. **Click the Design Tab.**

2. **Click the Insert Fields button on the toolbar.**

3. **In the Insert Fields dialog box, click the Formula tab.**

4. **Click New and enter a name for the formula in the Formula Name dialog box.**

   I suggest **First Initial** as the name.

5. **Click OK.**

6. **In the Formula Editor dialog box, select** Customer.Contact First Name.

   You have to scroll the Fields list to find this field.

7. **Click Select.**

   The field is inserted into the Formula text box.

8. **In the Operators list, choose an operator that allows you to use the first letter of the Contact First Name field.**

   Scroll the list of operators until you see Strings. Underneath that heading is an entry that reads x [y] Subscript. Click that operator.

   The way this operator works is that it pulls the character out of the field in front of it by counting from left to right. So the first letter of the first name is numbered 1, the second letter is 2, and so on.

9. **Click Select.**

   The operator is inserted into the Formula text box.

10. **Inside the brackets in the Formula text box, enter a 1.**

    The formula reads

    {Customer.Contact First Name} [1]

    Note that *no* comma appears between the field and the operator.

11. **Click Accept.**

    The Formula Editor dialog box closes.

12. **In the Insert Fields dialog box, click the formula name, First Initial, and then click Insert.**

13. **Insert the First Initial formula field in the Details section to the right of Percent of Order.**

    Figure 7-12 shows how the first initial formula will look in the Preview Tab.

Product Type Name	Unit Price	Quantity	Total	Percent of Order	First Initial
Gloves	$16.50	2	$33.00	100.00	T
			$33.00		
Gloves	$15.50	1	$15.50	0.90	B
Saddles	$36.00	1	$36.00	2.10	B
Hybrid	$832.35	2	$1,664.70	97.00	B
			$1,716.20		
Helmets	$33.90	2	$67.80	18.59	O
Mountain	$296.87	1	$296.87	81.41	O
			$364.67		

Figure 7-12:
The first
initial
added to
the report.

A text object is the quickest and simplest way to combine multiple fields. You can use text objects to combine a first and last name, but you can also use text objects to combine formula fields with other fields or text, as described in Chapter 10. You may want to take the First Initial formula field and insert it into a text object with the last name to create one field to display first initial and last name.

Changing Numbers to Words

You may have a report that has numbers in a field that you would prefer to display as words. The most common use of this formula is for check writing. In most checks, both the numbers and the words are included to indicate the amount of the check.

In the CRAZE.MDB database report, the Total/Tax field serves as the basis for this example of changing numbers to words:

1. Click the Design Tab.

2. Click the Insert fields button on the toolbar.

3. In the dialog box that opens, click the Formula tab.

4. Click New.

5. In the Formula Name dialog box, enter a name for the formula.

I suggest you use **Words.**

6. Click OK.

The Formula Editor dialog box opens.

7. In the Functions list, scroll the list until you find ToWords. (You will find it under the second category of functions — Strings.) Click it.

8. Click Select.

The insertion point is inside the parentheses; you are now ready for the next step.

9. In the Fields box, click @Total

10. Click Select.

11. Click Accept.

12. In the Insert Fields dialog box, click Words.

13. Insert it into the Details section to the right of the First Initial formula field, as shown in Figure 7-13.

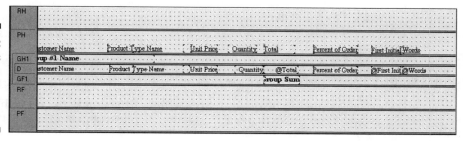

Figure 7-13:
The Words
formula
inserted
into the
report.

You may notice at this point that you are running out of room across your report. You could move and resize fields to try to make enough room for the Words formula. But if you are part way through a report and realize you will need to have more room to work across, you can change the page layout. From the File menu, Select Printer Setup. In this dialog box you can change the page orientation from Portrait to Landscape. Crystal Reports will immediately resize the page giving you more room to work. Be aware that changing the orientation changes the way the report prints, too.

14. Click the Preview Tab.

The report matches Figure 7-14.

Figure 7-14:
Words and
numbers
written out
as words in
the report.

Unit Price	Quantity	Total	Percent of Order	First Initial	Words
$16.50	2	$33.00	100.00	T	thirty-three and xx / 100
		$33.00			
$15.50	1	$15.50	0.90	B	fifteen and 50 / 100
$36.00	1	$36.00	2.10	B	thirty-six and xx / 100
$832.35	2	$1,664.70	97.00	B	one thousand six hundred sixty-ft
		$1,716.20			

You may have noticed that when you created the Words formula it wrote out the Total formula to two decimal places. If you would prefer to control how many decimal places are displayed, you can use the second ToWords option (ToWords, #places). For example, if you wanted to convert the Total formula to words but display it with zero decimal places, you would use the following formula:

```
ToWords({@Total},0)
```

Crystal Reports will convert the Total formula to words and also round and display to zero decimal places.

Going on a Date

Another popular type of formula determines the number of days that have passed between two dates. For example, if your company records the date a product is ordered and the date that it ships, you can determine how long processing the order takes.

If you have a report with date information of this sort, you can use it to create the formula by inserting the date fields into a report or use the CRAZE.MDB database example report from this chapter. The steps that follow begin by editing the report that has been used to this point in the chapter. You will delete a few fields to give you a little more room to work.

To delete fields and/or field names:

1. **Click the Design Tab.**

2. **Click the Quantity field, hold down the Control key, and then click the Total field, the Percent of Order field, the First Initial field, and the Words field.**

   Remember to click the column headers, too.

3. **Press the Delete key.**

   Both fields and column headers are deleted from the report.

In this example, you will be subtracting the Order Date from the Shipment date to determine the number of days it took to place the order. You could simply place the formula that calculates the number of days on the report, but you may want to place the Order.Ship Date and Order.Order Date field on the report so that you can check to see the formula is working correctly.

1. **Click the Insert Fields button on the toolbar.**

   The Insert Fields dialog box opens.

2. **Scroll the list until you see the table** Order.

3. **Click** Order.Order Date.

4. **Click** **I**nsert.

5. **Move the pointer to the Details section of the report and click to insert the field to the right of the other fields.**

6. **Repeat Steps 3–5 with the field Orders.Ship Date.**

7. **Click the Formula tab in the Insert Fields dialog box.**

8. **Click** **N**ew.

9. **When the Formula Name dialog box appears asking for a name, type:** Processing Days.

10. **Click OK.**

    The Formula Editor dialog box appears.

11. **In the F**ields list, locate Orders.Ship Date **and click it.**

12. **Click** **S**elect.

    The field name is inserted into the Formula text box.

13. **Because the formula is a subtraction, in the Operators field, click the Subtract operator** X-Y Subtract.

Undoing

Have you ever hit a button and then regretted it? Perhaps you deleted a field you actually want to keep on your report. Crystal Reports has an Undo feature that you should remember in just such instances. If you ever want to back up one step, use the Edit⇨Undo option.

Edit Undo will also let you undo multiple steps. So if you ever get into a jam, keep hitting Undo until you get back to where you want to be.

There are some steps that cannot be undone. When you see the confirm command, Crystal Reports is just reminding you to tread carefully — what you're about to do cannot be undone. If you don't want to proceed, simply click the No button.

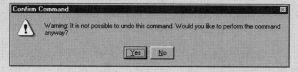

14. **Click Select to insert the subtraction operator.**

15. **In the Fields box, find** Orders.Order Date **and click it.**

16. **Click Select.**

    The text in the formula text should be:

    {Orders.Ship Date} - {Orders.Order Date}

17. **Click Accept. The Formula Editor dialog box closes.**

18. **From the Insert Fields dialog box, click the formula name** Processing Days.

19. **Click Insert.**

20. **Click in the Details section to insert the field placeholder of the report to the right of the date fields.**

21. **Click Close in the Insert Fields dialog box.**

22. **Click the Preview Tab.**

    The results appear in Figure 7-15. You can right-click the Processing Days field to format the results to 0 (zero) decimal places. Choose the Format Field option from the shortcut menu and select the number of decimal places you want displayed.

Figure 7-15: Two date fields and the results of subtracting the two.

Customer Name	Product Type Name	Unit Price	Order Date	Ship Date	Processing Days
1,026					
Tyred Out	Gloves	$16.50	12/7/95	12/11/95	4.00
1,052					
Bike Shop from Mars	Gloves	$15.50	12/12/95	12/12/95	0.00
Bike Shop from Mars	Saddles	$36.00	12/12/95	12/12/95	0.00
Bike Shop from Mars	Hybrid	$832.35	12/12/95	12/12/95	0.00

When you want to change the number of decimal places for a number field, you can use the Increase or Decrease decimals button from the format bar (see the Cheat Sheet). In this case, simply click the Decrease Decimals button twice with the Processing Days formula selected to remove two decimal places.

Using If-Then-Else Formulas

An *if-then-else formula* is a formula that you use to examine a value and then, depending on the value, execute one or more alternatives. A simple example is the case of someone owing your company money. The formula can look at the date and then either print *30 Days Past Due* or *60 Days Past Due,* depending on how long it has been since the last payment. The current date is the condition that determines the next action.

In Crystal Reports, both actions that may be taken after looking at the condition must be the same *type* of action. In other words, if the result is to print a text string (30 Days Past Due), the other option (60 Days Past Due) must be a text string also.

For those of you with a programming background, you do not have to include an else statement for these formulas to work. If the condition fails the if-then test, 0 is returned for numerics and " " (a blank text string) for text.

In this example, the CRAZE report is used with several fields that have been added earlier. If you are using your own database, all you need is a report that has a numeric field. Adjust the conditional values to fit your data.

In order for you to work this example, you'll want to modify your report a bit.

Make some room on the report by deleting the following fields: the Order Date field, the Ship Date field, and the Processing Days formula.

Then add back the Orders Detail.Quantity Field and the Total formula into the Details section. Your report should look similar to Figure 7-16 before continuing.

Figure 7-16:
Does your
report look
like this?

RH	
PH	
	Customer Name Product Type Name Unit Price Quantity Total
GH1	Group #1 Name
D	Customer Name Product Type Unit Price Quantity @Total
GF1	
RF	
PF	

Now begin the formula creation process. To become familiar with an if-then-else formula, you are going to create a formula that will display "Excellent" for any record that has a Total amount greater than 1,000. The formula looks at the value in the record and then prints the appropriate response based on that value. The formula is simple: If the value is less than or equal to a specific number, nothing is printed, but if it is greater than a specified value, the word Excellent is printed.

1. **Click the Formula tab of the Insert Fields dialog box. If it is not open, click the Insert Fields button.**

2. **Click New.**

3. **In the Formula name dialog box that appears, type:** Great Sales.

4. **To continue, click OK.**

   The Formula Editor dialog box opens.

5. **Scroll the Operators list until you see the operator that reads** If x then y else z. **(You will find it towards the bottom of the operator box under a category called Others.) Click the operator.**

6. **Click Select.**

   The if then else is inserted into the formula text. You will use this to start building a formula. Notice the cursor is positioned between if and then: This is where you normally start building your formula.

7. **In the Fields list, scroll the list to locate @Total. Click it.**

8. **Click Select.**

   The formula name is inserted. It will be inserted at the cursor between if and then.

   Your formula should appear as:

   if {@Total} then else

9. **Locate the greater than operator > in the Operators list by scrolling the list; it reads** x > y Greater than. **Click it.**

   It is under the heading Comparisons.

10. **Click Select.**

    The operator is inserted into the formula.

11. **The next step is to add the test,** Is total greater than 1000?.

    Your formula should now appear as:

    if {@Total} > 1000 then else

    Okay, 1,000 is now the condition (the if) in this formula. So if the result in the Total field is greater than 1,000 — then what? Well, you have to add the rest of the formula, that's what.

12. **Position the insertion point between the words** then **and** else.

13. **Type:** "Excellent"

    You must have quotation marks on either side of the word. With this part of the formula inserted, Crystal Reports prints the word *Excellent* whenever the value in Total/Tax is greater than 1,000.

    Note: A literal is the portion of a formula that is printed in the report exactly as you type it, depending on the result of the formula.

14. Delete the word else **by clicking on it and pressing the Delete key.**

You need to do this because only one literal is being printed.

At this point, the condition is either met or not, and if it is not, then a blank text string (it looks just like nothing) prints in the report. The finished formula looks like this:

```
if {@Total} > 1000 then  Excellent
```

15. Click Accept.

The Formula Editor dialog box closes.

16. In the Insert Fields dialog box, click Great Sales.

17. Click Insert.

18. Position the pointer in the Details section of the report to the right of the Total field, and click to insert the field.

Your report resembles the one in Figure 7-17.

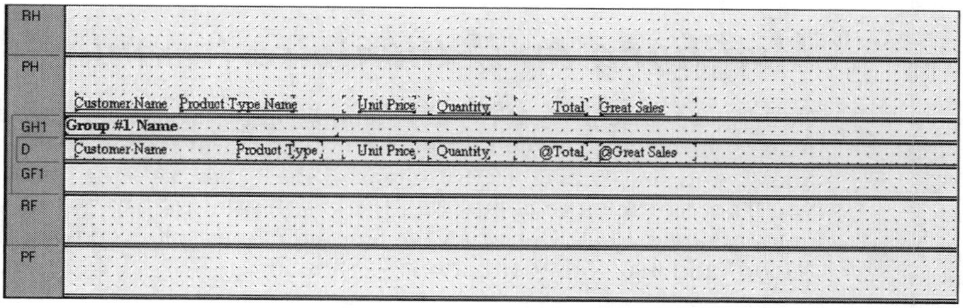

Figure 7-17:
An if-then-else formula inserted under the header Great Sales.

19. Click the Preview Tab.

This is the big moment. If it works for you, you have passed into the higher ranks of Crystal Report users. Hopefully your report looks like the one in Figure 7-18.

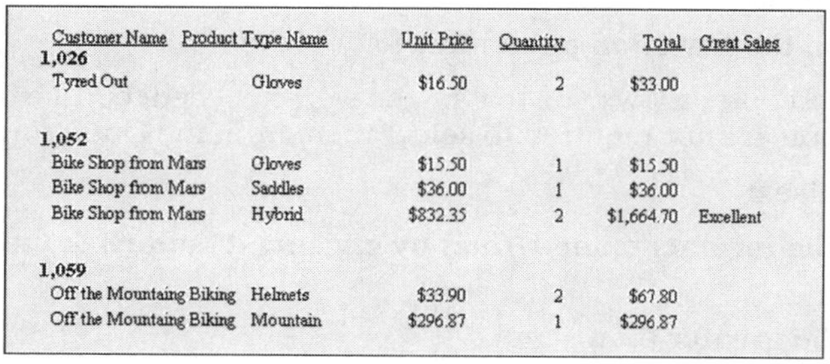

Figure 7-18:
An excellent report with a complex if-then-else formula.

Customer Name	Product Type Name	Unit Price	Quantity	Total	Great Sales
1,026					
Tyred Out	Gloves	$16.50	2	$33.00	
1,052					
Bike Shop from Mars	Gloves	$15.50	1	$15.50	
Bike Shop from Mars	Saddles	$36.00	1	$36.00	
Bike Shop from Mars	Hybrid	$832.35	2	$1,664.70	Excellent
1,059					
Off the Mountaing Biking	Helmets	$33.90	2	$67.80	
Off the Mountaing Biking	Mountain	$296.87	1	$296.87	

Figure 7-18 reveals the work of this formula in that only the records with sales in excess of $1,000 have any text printed. Although this formula works, it would be better if every record had a notation of some sort. The section "Modifying an if-then-else formula" next in this chapter helps you modify the formula to include several more text options.

In this example, we used an `if then` formula. It told the program what to do if the Total was over 1,000 and did nothing if the total was not over 1,000.

But how would you create a formula if you wanted to display "Excellent" when sales were greater than 1,000 and "Poor" in all other situations? You would use the following formula:

```
if {@Total} > 1000 then  Excellent
else  Poor
```

The `else  Poor` tells Crystal that if sales are less than or equal to 1,000 to display "Poor".

Modifying an if-then-else formula

Nothing is particularly tricky about modifying this kind of formula, but it may require a little careful formula building. In the preceding example above, you simply printed "Excellent" if the Total was over 1,000. This time, you'll get a little more complicated. You still want to display "Excellent" for amounts over 1,000. But when the amount is over 500, you want to display "Good" and in all other situations — "Stinko".

1. **Click the Design Tab.**

 2. **If the Insert Fields dialog box is not already open, click the Insert Fields button on the toolbar.**

3. **In the Insert Fields dialog box, click the Formula tab.**

4. **Click** `Great Sales`.

5. **Click** <u>E</u>**dit.**

6. **Position the insertion point after** `Excellent`.

   Crystal Reports allows you to type the words needed to make the formula work; you are not required to select them from the <u>O</u>perators list.

7. **Type:** else if

8. **Enter the formula name @Total by clicking it, and click the Select button.**

9. **Type the greater than sign:** >

10. **Type:** 500

11. **Type:** then

12. Type: "Good"

13. Type: else

14. Type: "Stinko"

The completed three-condition formula text should look like this:

```
if {@Total} > 1000 then  Excellent
else if {@Total} > 500 then  Good
else  Stinko
```

Notice that I've broken the formula over three lines. Crystal does not care where you insert line breaks. Simply place them where it makes sense to you.

To get the three different comments, I used an *if-then-else-if* formula. The first line asks Crystal Reports to check if sales were greater than 1,000 and if they are to display "Excellent". The next line then tells Crystal Reports when sales were not greater than 1,000 to continue to check to see if sales were greater than 500 and when they are to display "Good". Think of the else "Stinko" as just saying: If it's not greater than 1,000 or greater than 500, then display "Stinko".

15. Click Accept.

16. Click the Preview Tab to see the results in the report, as in Figure 7-19.

Customer Name	Product Type Name	Unit Price	Quantity	Total	Great Sales
1,026					
Tyred Out	Gloves	$16.50	2	$33.00	Stinko
1,052					
Bike Shop from Mars	Gloves	$15.50	1	$15.50	Stinko
Bike Shop from Mars	Saddles	$36.00	1	$36.00	Stinko
Bike Shop from Mars	Hybrid	$832.35	2	$1,664.70	Excellent
1,059					
Off the Mountaing Biking	Helmets	$33.90	2	$67.80	Stinko
Off the Mountaing Biking	Mountain	$296.87	1	$296.87	Stinko
1,065					
Tyred Out	Gloves	$15.50	2	$31.00	Stinko
Tyred Out	Mountain	$764.85	1	$764.85	Good
Tyred Out	Mountain	$479.85	1	$479.85	Stinko

Figure 7-19: A preview of a report and if-then-else-if formula.

Nested if-then-else formulas

You just looked at two variations of working with fairly simple *if-then-else* formulas. If you need to, you can get quite complicated with these types of formulas. You can create very powerful, multi-condition formulas. This procedure is known as *nesting formulas*. A nested if-then-else formula can evaluate two conditions and then print a text string as in the previous example or whatever you designate.

This formula looks at the country and the sales amount to determine a discount percentage.

```
if Country = USA then
        if Sales > 1000000 then .25
        else .2
else if Sales > 1000000 then .15
        else .10
```

Now try to work your way through what this formula is showing. First of all, it checks to see which country the record deals with. If it is the USA, it continues to check the amount of that American sale. If the American sale is greater than 1 million, the formula sets the discount rate at 25 percent. If the American sale is not greater than 1 million, the formula sets the discount rate to 20 percent. However, if the country is *not* USA, the formula skips the test completely. It assumes this is a foreign sale. The formula then checks the foreign sale to see if it is greater than 1 million. If it is, the discount rate gets set to 15 percent. Otherwise, it gets set to 10 percent.

Understanding Boolean Formulas

A Boolean formula is not anything esoteric. (Ahh ha! I have not slipped one of these exotic words in lately, have I?! *Esoteric* means knowledge for the highly intelligent or for the privileged.) It is simply a formula that returns one of two possible answers: True or False.

You may use a Boolean formula if you have a field that has numbers in it and you want the formula to print whether or not the numbers meet a condition. Usually, you use Boolean formulas as a basis for another action in Crystal Reports, such as record section as described in Chapter 4 or conditional formatting as described in Chapter 8.

To get familiar with Boolean formulas, just create a formula that displays True if Total is greater than 1,000 and False when not. To create a Boolean formula:

1. **In the Design Tab, open the Insert Fields dialog box by clicking the Insert Fields button on the toolbar.**

2. **Click the Formula tab.**

3. **Click <u>N</u>ew, and type a formula name in the Formula Name dialog box.**

   I suggest you use **Boolean.**

4. **Click OK.**

   The Formula Editor dialog box opens.

5. **In the Fields list, click** `Total/`

6. **Click Select.**

   The formula name is inserted into the Formula text box.

7. **Type a greater than sign:** `>`

8. **Type** 1000

   The completed formula reads: `{@Total}>1000`

9. **Press Accept.**

10. **From the Insert Fields dialog box, click the formula name** `Boolean.`

11. **Click Insert.**

12. **Position the pointer to the right of the existing fields in the Details section and click to insert the formula.**

    The result appears in Figure 7-20. Values greater than $1,000 are True, and values smaller than $1,000 are False.

Customer Name	Product Type Name	Unit Price	Quantity	Total	Great Sales	Boolean
1,026						
Tyred Out	Gloves	$16.50	2	$33.00	Stinko	False
1,052						
Bike Shop from Mars	Gloves	$15.50	1	$15.50	Stinko	False
Bike Shop from Mars	Saddles	$36.00	1	$36.00	Stinko	False
Bike Shop from Mars	Hybrid	$832.35	2	$1,664.70	Excellent	True
1,059						
Off the Mountaing Biking	Helmets	$33.90	2	$67.80	Stinko	False
Off the Mountaing Biking	Mountain	$296.87	1	$296.87	Stinko	False

Figure 7-20: Boolean logic applied to the Total field.

Creating a Record Selection Formula

When you select a database and its table to be part of a report, you may want the entire set of records to be included in the report. Many times you will not, and Crystal Reports provides a way to select specific records for the report, as described in Chapter 4. Formulas can be incorporated into the selection process to add precision to the selection process. If you are creating a report, you may want to add numeric ranges to capture records in certain sales volumes, transactions occurring in specific date ranges, or records that pertain to a certain area of the country. The simple selection criteria are handled easily via the Select Expert. But, there will come a time when you need more advanced selections to create the report. You can simulate the following example with any database you have that includes state as a field. Otherwise, follow the steps in this example to understand how to create a formula for record selection.

In the example report used in this chapter, the records were selected by using the Region field and CA as the match. But suppose that the records are entered into the underlying database in an inconsistent manner. Some records are entered with the region as *CA* and some with the region as *ca*. In Crystal Reports, record selection is dependent on the case sensitivity in the source database and must be precise. So any records that have *ca* in them when you indicate that you want records with *CA*, are not included in a report. You can try this potential pitfall yourself with the CRAZE database, using Region as the selection field, by replacing CA with ca in the Select Record dialog box.

To overcome this obstacle and to make certain that all records are included in the selection, uppercase or not, you can create a Record Selection formula using Boolean logic.

Use the Select Expert as much as possible to get Crystal Reports to create your record selection easily. In the Select Expert, you simply use the drop-down boxes to build a record selection criteria. Crystal Reports, behind the scenes, creates a Boolean formula given what you have entered. It compares the Boolean formula against each record in the report, and when it returns True, the record will be included. If it returns False, the record will not be included in your report.

Keep this in mind when modifying the Record Selection formula. You need to ensure you are creating a Boolean formula that returns True when you want to include the record in the report. To show you how this works, assume that the Region field can be stored as ca, CA, Ca or cA. You want to include all occurrences of ca in the report, regardless of what case they are in. To do this, we will convert the text in the Region field to uppercase and then search for an uppercase CA.

1. **Click the Select Expert button.**

   The Select Expert dialog box appears. In this example report, the previous selection criteria, *Region equal to CA and Quantity greater than 0,* is still in effect. If you are using your own database, the Choose Field dialog box opens first. Choose state as the field upon which to make the selection (assuming that you have state as a field in your database); the Select Expert dialog box then appears. Click the down arrow in the second box from the left, and select the *equal to* setting. Next, a third box opens to the right, and in that box enter the state from which you want records. At this point, you can follow the remaining steps.

2. **Click Show Formula.**

   The underlying formula for record selection appears at the bottom of the dialog box, as in Figure 7-21.

   Remember, you added Quantity greater than 0 to exclude records with only partial data.

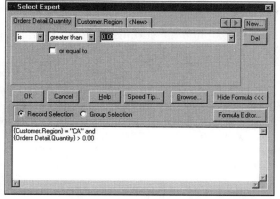

Figure 7-21:
The Select
Expert
dialog box
with the
formula
exposed!

3. Click Formula Editor.

The Formula Editor dialog box opens.

4. Place your cursor before the {Customer.Region} field.

This is where you want to insert the UpperCase function.

5. In the Functions list, click UpperCase (), **which is listed under the String heading.**

Headings are listed within the Functions list that designate what kind of function follows. This feature makes finding the function easier for you.

6. Click Select.

Crystal Reports inserts the formula, but the close parenthesis (the one on the right) is not enclosing the Customer.Region portion of the formula.

7. Delete the close parenthesis at its current location, and type it after Customer.Region **and before the** =.

8. Click Accept.

The completed formula now appears in the Select Expert dialog box. Your formula should look like this:

```
UpperCase ({Customer.Region}) = CA and
{Orders Detail.Quantity} > 0.00
```

9. Click OK to close the Select Expert dialog box.

To see the changes, if any, click the Preview Tab. After you do, Crystal Reports asks if you want to use saved or refreshed data. Currently the saved records are only records that have CA as region, so click Refresh Data. Crystal Reports seeks out the database tables and finds any records that meet the new criteria.

See Chapter 4 for a full description of Saved versus Refresh data.

In this chapter, you have scratched the surface of what Crystal Reports can do with formulas. A complete listing of every function and operator is found in the Seagate Crystal Reports User's Guide.

If you are trying to create a report from a database such as ACT!, you may encounter a problem when you try to access a field which in ACT! is supposed to be a currency or number field. The problem is that the field in ACT! is not truly formatted as currency or number. So, in order to use the data, you must insert a formula to convert the data from text to numbers. The function is listed under Strings and is listed as ToNumber(X).

If you're not sure if your field is coming into Crystal Reports as a currency or number, just choose Browse Field Data — on that field. The Browse dialog box will show you what Crystal Reports believes it is seeing for a datatype.

Chapter 8
Using Conditional Formatting

In This Chapter

▶ Absolute versus conditional formatting

▶ Setting a conditional format for fields and objects

*T*he idea of *conditional formatting* is that objects such as numbers, are displayed a certain way if the number is of certain value. So, you can create formulas that determine the format of your report depending on the data within the report. The same idea applies to sections of a report. You will probably get much more out of this chapter if you read Chapter 7 on formulas first.

Absolute versus Conditional Formatting

When you add a format to an object in Crystal Reports (see Chapter 10 for more on formatting), whether it be a text object or a field of numbers, that object is displayed and printed per your formatting. This type of formatting is considered to be *absolute* in that it stays the same despite what numbers or values are being printed.

But, if you want to add intelligence to your report, Crystal Reports can evaluate the number and, based on the value, print the number in different formats. A simple example is to print every negative number in red ink. Or you can have Crystal Reports look at a text string, and if that string matches a string that you designate, Crystal Reports can then execute an action for you.

Another idea is to add conditional formatting to your company invoices. Suppose a customer has not paid their invoice for 90 days. By printing the amount owed in red, that invoice would be easy to identify in a report.

Using On or Off Properties

An on or off property is identical to a formula that returns True or False. Either the condition is met or it is not — and if it is, the format is turned on. Simple enough.

Using Attribute Properties

Attribute Properties are identical to if-then-else formulas in that several types of formatting can occur depending on the result of the formula you have created. For example, the Attribute Property can print a number in red if the value is less than 0 (zero) or print in black if the value is greater than 100 and print in blue if the value is greater than 500. See Chapter 7 on formulas for more information on this technique.

Crystal Reports tests each record and determines which format should be used, per your formula. A good start on learning conditional formatting is printing numbers in red if they are less than zero.

Figure 8-1 is a report that shows sales figures for a series of stores.

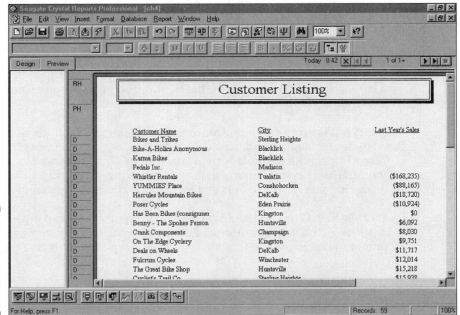

Figure 8-1:
A sample report with some negative numbers.

The report includes several figures that are negative numbers. They are identified in this report by being displayed in parentheses. Identifying the negative numbers would be much easier if they were more prominent in the report. You can use the following steps to add conditional formatting to any report:

1. Right-click the field that you wish to format.

A menu appears, as shown in Figure 8-2.

Figure 8-2:
Right-clicking the field you want to format reveals the format menu.

2. Click the Format Field option.

The Format Editor dialog box appears as shown in Figure 8-3.

Because the mouse pointer was on a number field when you right-clicked, Crystal Reports assumes that you want to modify the number format. Not quite!

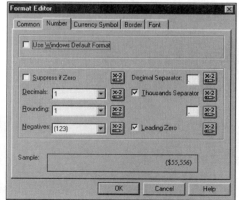

Figure 8-3:
The Format Editor dialog box.

3. Click the Font tab at the top of the dialog box.

Figure 8-4 shows the dialog box that is displayed.

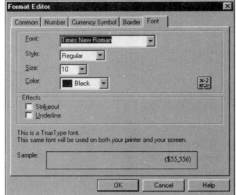

Figure 8-4:
The Font
tab clicked
in the
Format
Editor
dialog box.

4. Click the Conditional Formatting button.

When you click this icon, the Format Formula Editor dialog box opens
as shown in Figure 8-5.

Wherever you see the Conditional Formatting button (X+2), you
have the opportunity to add conditions to that particular portion of
the report.

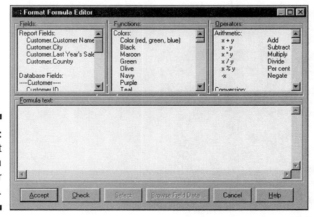

Figure 8-5:
The Format
Formula
Editor
dialog box.

This dialog box has four main components:

- The Fields box, which lists the fields in the report, the Groups, formulas, and report source database tables.
- The Functions that are prebuilt formulas that perform specific calculations.
- The last box has arithmetic operators and is named Operators.
- The final box is the Formula text box in which the actual formula is created.

5. **Because this formula requires two variables, you need to use an if-then-else formula.**

   To do so, scroll the Operators to find the `if x then y else z` operator. Click the operator, and then click the Select button. The `if then else` operator is inserted into the Formula text box.

   Note that the blinking insertion point is located inside the current formula, between the `if` and `then`, right where it should be.

6. **Click the field to which you want to apply conditional formatting.**

   In this example, the field you want formatted is Last Year's Sales.

7. **Click the Select button.**

   The formula name is inserted into the Field text box, like this:

   ```
   if {Customer.Last Year s Sales} then else
   ```

   The insertion point moves to the end of the field name outside the bracket. The next step is to indicate the calculation Crystal Reports is to perform. In this case, you want to format values that are less than zero in a different color. So, you need to insert the less than (<) sign.

8. **Scroll the Operators box until you find the** `x < y less than` **operator, and click it.**

9. **Click the Select button.**

   The < appears in the formula.

10. **Type a zero:** 0

11. **Move the insertion point so that it is after the word** `then` **and type:** Red

12. **Move the insertion point after the word** `else` **and type:** Black

    The completed formula appears as:

    ```
    if {Customer.Last Year s Sales} < 0 then Red else Black
    ```

13. **Click the Accept button.**

    If the formula contains any errors, Crystal Reports will not accept it and displays a dialog box with a warning and the most likely cause of the error.

Because this is an exercise that uses color to define the output, I cannot show you how it will look. You can see the effect of the red color if you have entered the formula on your reports, provided they contain negative numbers. If you have a color printer, you can share this wonderful format with your colleagues.

Another conditional format

You can also use a conditional format on a Summary field. Suppose that you wanted to highlight a value that is less than the average of the other values in the field. Using the data from the prior example report, the formula would look like this

```
if {Customer.Last Year s Sales} < Average({Customer.Last
Year s Sales},{Customer.Region}) then Red else Black
```

Still another conditional format

When you create a report, you will often want to print a Report Footer that gives the name of the author, the report date, or describes what is contained in the report. But you may want the front page of the report to be free of any footer. You may want a page number to print on every page except the first, for example. To accomplish this task, you must add a conditional format after inserting the field into the Page Footer section, as follows:

1. **In the Design window, choose Insert⇨Special fields.**

   The sub-menu appears as shown in Figure 8-6.

2. **Select the special field you want to insert.**

   In this case, the choice is Page Number. When you make the selection, the pointer changes to a grayed box, allowing you to insert the Page Number field anywhere in the report.

3. **Move the mouse pointer to the Page Footer section of the report.**

   Be careful that you position the field in the Page Footer section — it appears beneath the Report Footer and so it can be confusing.

Figure 8-6:
The Special
Field sub-
menu.

4. **Click the mouse button to insert the field.**

5. **Right-click the inserted field and choose Format Field.**

The Format Editor dialog box appears as shown in Figure 8-7.

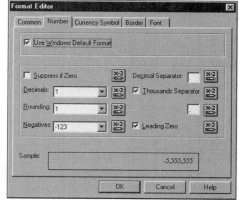

Figure 8-7:
The Format
Editor
dialog box.

6. **Click the Common tab.**

7. **Click the Suppress box so that a check mark is inserted.**

8. **Click the Conditional Formatting button.**

The Format Formula Editor dialog box appears.

9. **Scroll the Function box, until you see the function named
PageNumber.**

10. **Click the PageNumber Function.**

11. **Click the Select button.**

12. **After the function, type** = 1

    The completed PageNumber formula thus appears in the Formula text box:

    PageNumber = 1

13. **Click the Accept button.**

14. **Click OK to close the Format Editor dialog box.**

You are looking at the Design window and should see no discernible changes. The only way to see if the formula worked is to go to Preview and look at the first page of the report, at the bottom, and then go to the next page and see if the page number has printed.

Note: More information on this kind of formatting is covered in Chapter 10.

Deleting a conditional format

The only way to delete a conditional format is to erase the text in the Formula text box in the Formula Editor.

1. **Right-click the field upon which you have applied a conditional format.**

2. **Click Format Field from the shortcut menu that appears.**

    The Format Editor dialog box appears.

3. **Click the Font tab.**

 4. **Click the Conditional Formatting button.**

5. **The Format Formula Editor dialog box appears.**

6. **Click the formula, and drag the mouse over it until the formula is completely highlighted.**

7. **Press the Delete key, or right-click and choose Cut.**

8. **Click the Accept button.**

Conditional formatting is a tool that can be exploited throughout a report. Anywhere you see the Conditional Formatting button is a place where you can tweak your report to get it just right. If you are an obsessive-compulsive when it comes to perfecting reports, keep your Valium handy.

Part IV
Putting On Some Finishing Touches

The 5th Wave   By Rich Tennant

DAVE GETS READY TO RUN HIS FIRST REPORT.

In this part . . .

Many great artists are not recognized as such in their lifetimes. In this part, you cannot be ignored. Great honors await those who read this part. Your reports will show the talents known only to a gifted few — at least until this book arrived. Polishing the chrome, a slight adjustment of the carburetor, and your report is ready for the Indy 500. As they say, 10 percent of the job takes 90 percent of the time. Well, with the information in this part, you will be taking a long lunch and heading home early — while everyone is convinced that you slaved for hours over your reports. Ha! If only they knew your secret!

Chapter 9

Formatting Sections of a Report

● ●

In This Chapter

▶ Resizing a section

▶ Formatting sections with the Section Expert

● ●

The way a report prints is highly dependent upon the format of the individual sections in a report. This chapter deals with making your report look just right. (Chapter 10 shows you how you can add real pizzazz by combining the section formatting with other objects.)

In this chapter, I am going to show you how to change the layout of sections of the report. These techniques make reading your reports and highlighting certain aspects of the report much easier.

Changing the Size of a Section

Each report you create in Crystal Reports has a minimum of five sections: the Report Header, the Page Header, the Details, the Report Footer, and the Page Footer. Crystal Reports allocates space for each section. You can modify the space for any and all sections; however, judging what adjustments may be necessary to the different sections is difficult until you print the report. The Preview Tab gives an excellent representation of what the printed report will look like, but with the huge number of printers, each with its own quirks, the best way to test your formatting is to actually make a hard copy.

The Design Tab is the place to be if you want to make changes in the size of a section. On the left side of the window, in the gray area, each of the sections is labeled. Between the section labels are thin horizontal lines, representing the boundaries between the sections. The lines are the key to eyeball adjustments in that you can move your pointer to a line, click and hold the left mouse button, and drag the line to adjust the height of the section. A simple example follows.

To change the height of a section:

1. **In any report, click the Design Tab.**

   A typical report appears in Figure 9-1.

2. **Click and hold down the left mouse button, on the line dividing the section.**

   Click in the design area, not in the left margin. When you do, the mouse pointer changes to a double-horizontal line. You will be resizing the section above the mouse pointer.

3. **Drag the line up or down.**

   The entire line will move with your pointer.

4. **Release the mouse button where you want the line to be redrawn.**

In Figure 9-2, the Report Footer line has been dragged up to decrease the size of the Report Footer.

To see what effect the changing of a Report Footer has, or any other change you make, click the Preview Tab, as shown in Figure 9-3.

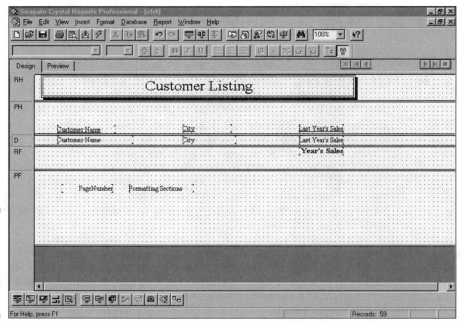

Figure 9-1:
A typical report, from the Design Tab point of view.

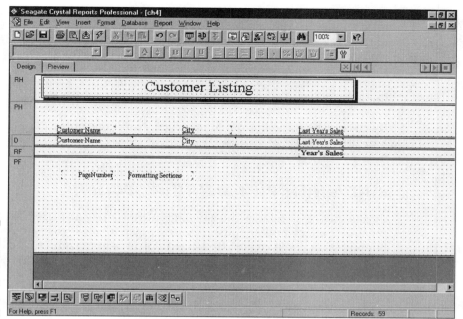

Figure 9-2:
The Report
Footer
border now
resized.

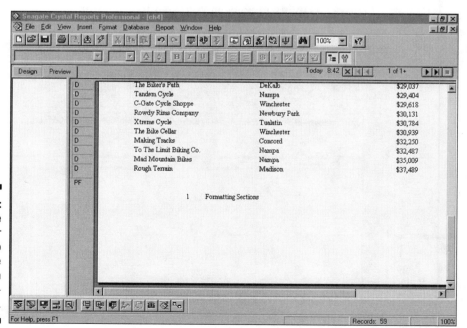

Figure 9-3:
The Page
Footer
higher up
on the
page in
the Pre-
view Tab.

You can also squeeze the Report Footer to a smaller size. First, drag the Page Footer line down the page; then, drag the line that indicates the bottom of the page itself up. Crystal Reports will not allow you to draw the line so closely that any object inserted into a section will be hidden. In Figure 9-4, the Page Footer is reduced to a very small size.

Click the Preview Tab to see the results, as shown in Figure 9-5.

By clicking near the bottom of the page, the outline of the Page Footer appears.

Automatically sizing a section

Crystal Reports includes the capability to automatically size a section for you. After all, computer software is supposed to make your job easier. Suppose that you have inserted a text object, a graph, and a Special field into a section, and you want Crystal Reports to best fit the objects to the section. Crystal Reports will also eliminate any white space that would be wasted when printing the report.

To automatically size a section:

1. Insert as many objects as you wish in a section.

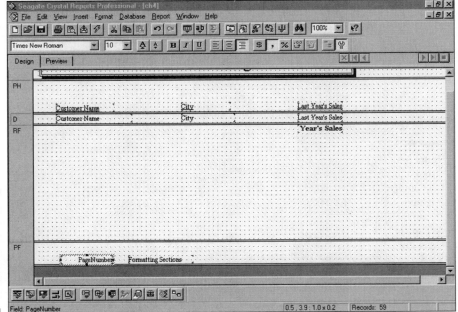

Figure 9-4:
The Page Footer section squeezed to a small space.

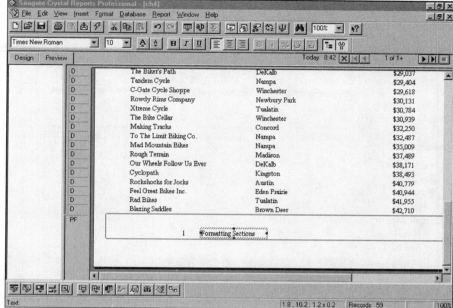

Figure 9-5:
The
reduced
size of
Page
Footer in
the Pre-
view Tab.

2. Move the mouse pointer to the left margin space corresponding to the section you want to modify.

3. Right-click in the margin.

A menu appears as shown in Figure 9-6.

In this example, the space for the Page Footer has been increased and several objects are present.

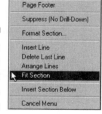

Figure 9-6:
The section
shortcut
menu.

4. Click the Fit Section option.

Figure 9-7 shows that the bottom of the page line has been drawn up against the text object, Making a Section Fit, so as to eliminate any unneeded space in the printed report.

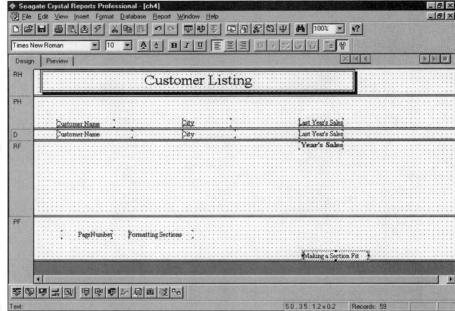

Figure 9-7:
The Page
Footer is
resized
automatically
to make the
best use of
the
available
space.

Looking at the shortcut menu

In the previous section, the right mouse button was clicked on the left margin of the Design Tab. When that happened, a menu appeared that lists, among other things, the Fit Section option, which automatically arranged the size of a section with several objects. But there are also several other options that you need to know about. Figure 9-8 shows the opened menu.

Figure 9-8:
The
shortcut
menu
appears
when right-
clicking
the margin
in the
Design Tab.

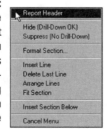

If you are ever in doubt about what you can do to or on a particular object in Crystal Reports, just right-click on the object. A shortcut menu will come up with a concise list of what you are able to do.

The key point of a shortcut menu is the fact that it provides a quick list of relevant actions available for the object or objects currently selected.

> ✔ At the top of the menu is the name of the section with which the menu is associated. In this case, the mouse pointer was on the Report Header and so that is the name at the top.

> ✔ The next option listed has to do with drill-downs. A *drill-down* is simply a means to hide and then display underlying information, as required, on a report. For example, if your report is grouped by Region, you can see the record details for a particular region by double-clicking the Group Name in the Preview Tab. Rather than seeing all the detailed information, you can hide the detail and just see the summary information for the region. Crystal Reports adds a tab at the top of the report window indicating the individual group (see Figure 9-9). You can also drill-down on a graph, as described in Chapter 6.

> ✔ If you do not want the drill-down capability available for a particular section, right-click that section, and you have two options. You can hide the section so that it does not print but can be drilled-down, or you can suppress the section so that it is hidden from print and cannot be drilled-down.

For example, you may use this capability if you are doing a report on salaries. You can do the summary calculations, but the report won't print the underlying contents of the section, thus preserving confidentiality.

Drill-down is not available at run-time in either case.

> ✔ When you hide or suppress a section in the Design Tab, the left margin changes to reflect the new format. In Figure 9-10, the Report Header has been suppressed and therefore is no longer listed in the margin.

Note: Drill-down is not available in run-time versions of reports, as described in Chapter 14.

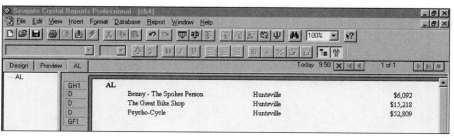

Figure 9-9:
The drill-down tab beside the Preview Tab.

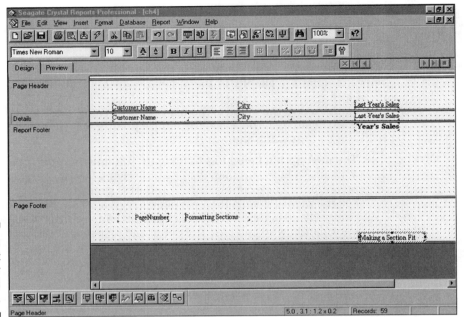

Figure 9-10:
The Report
Header
suppressed
in Design.

✔ The next item on the list, after the Format Section option, which opens the dialog box, is the Insert Line option. This option works in conjunction with the next two options, Delete Last Line and Arrange Lines. Crystal Reports includes line formatting options to enable you to precisely size the sections in the report. You already know how to click and drag the sections to resize them, but with the line-by-line format, you can get the sections just right. Notice that red marks indicate that an object is attached to a guideline.

✔ If you want the section to grow by a single line, you choose the Insert Line option.

✔ If you want to make the section smaller by a single line, you can do so by right-clicking and choosing Delete Last Line.

✔ The final option on this menu is the Insert Section Below option. When you select this option, a subsection is inserted under the section that you clicked upon. A *subsection* is used when you want a report that has distinct information included in the report that is a subset of the section. You may never need to use this concept in your dealings with Crystal Reports, but if you do, at least you'll know how.

Cool stuff about subsections

All of the work with subsections can be done by just using the mouse, too. Subsections are used for multi-section or multi-detail reports, which are very popular in Crystal Reports. When necessary, subsections allow you to create very powerful tools.

The best way to understand the Insert Line feature is to click on a section and insert the lines themselves.

1. Right-click a section of the report.

In this example, the Page Header section is chosen.

2. Choose the Arrange Lines option.

Horizontal lines are inserted into the section as shown in Figure 9-11.

Figure 9-11:
A series of horizontal formatting lines in the Page Header section of the report design.

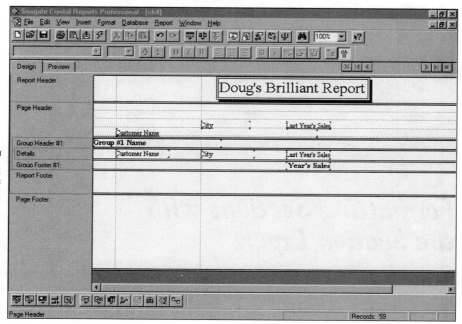

Suppose that you want the Detail section to print each record with more space between each record.

1. Right-click in the left margin on the Detail section of the report.

2. Choose Insert Line.

3. Repeat the procedure two more times.

The Details section now looks like the one shown in Figure 9-12.

Of course, you could have added the space simply by dragging the line between the Details section and the Group Footer section, but the foregoing method is more exact. Figure 9-13 shows the results (in the Preview Tab) of adding lines to the Details section, resulting in more room between each record.

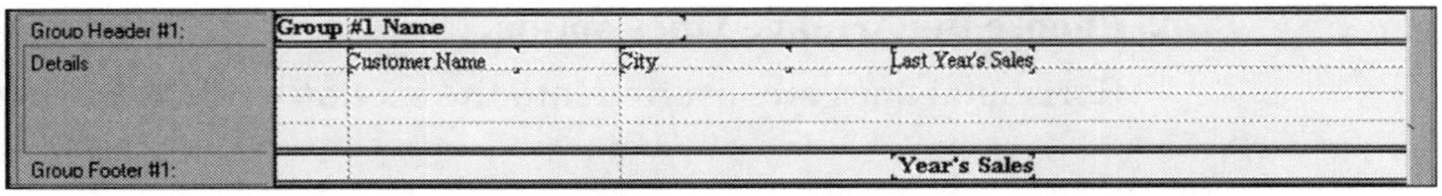

Figure 9-12: Three lines inserted in the Details section.

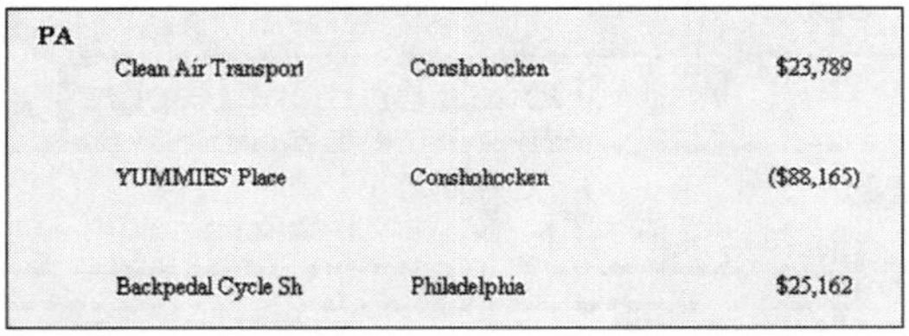

Figure 9-13: A preview with spaces added between records.

Formatting Sections with the Section Expert

Because so many options exist in terms of formatting sections, Crystal Reports includes a handy Section Expert to show you the way.

You can open the Section Expert in three ways:

✔ Right-click on the section that you wish to format and choose Format Section.

✔ Click the Section Expert button.

✔ Choose Format⇨Section.

Figure 9-14 shows the Section Expert dialog box.

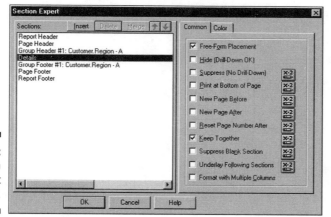

Figure 9-14:
The Section
Expert
dialog box.

This dialog box is a busy one! You can make several choices, so I'm going to take the dialog box a bit at a time to help you better understand your options.

On the left side of the dialog box is a listing of all the sections in your report. At the bottom of the Section list is a horizontal scroll bar that enables you to move left and right so as to read the entire section name if necessary. When you open this dialog box, the highlight is automatically positioned on the name of the section where your mouse pointer was when you opened the dialog box.

The top of the dialog box contains a series of buttons. The Insert button is used to insert subsections in the report. For example, Crystal Reports allows for several Page Footer sections, enabling you to print different page footers at certain pages of the report. These added sections can be formatted so that they are conditional, in the same way as the standard section, and therefore print based on a formula you have entered into this dialog box as explained in a moment. In Figure 9-15, a subdetail section has been added by clicking the Details Section listing and then clicking the Insert button.

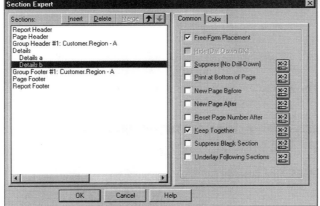

Figure 9-15:
The Section
Expert with
a new
Detail
section
inserted.

When you click OK to close the dialog box, the new section is inserted into the report as shown in Figure 9-16.

The section can be deleted as easily as it was added. Open the Section Expert, click the section you want to delete, and click the Delete button. *Note:* The Delete button was not active — it was grayed out — when this dialog box was opened, because you cannot delete the five basic components of a report design, the Report Header and Footer, the Details, and so on.

Figure 9-16:
The Details
b section is
added to
the report
design.

You cannot delete sections from the Section Expert if only one section is left, even if that includes a Group Header or Footer.

The other two buttons at the top of the Sections box are for promoting or demoting sections that you have added. By clicking a subsection, you can move it up or down in the report layout. You are unlikely to ever use this feature unless you become the Crystal Reports maven for your company and need to keep a few tricks up your sleeve to justify your bonus, but it never hurts to know what these features do.

Using the Common tab

The Common tab deals with options that are generalized to most sections. If you need to set something related to labels or colors, you use the other tabs. Basically, the Common tab combines all the options that don't fit the other tabs — the Common tab is a catch-all tab.

The list of formatting options on the right side of the dialog box corresponds to the section selected in the left side.

Free-Form Placement

With Free-Form Placement, Crystal Reports lets you place objects anywhere in your report. Most of the time, you want this option turned on. Turning off Free-Form Placement causes Crystal Reports to create an underlying grid in the Design Tab, which, in turn, causes objects to line up with the grid as you insert them.

You may make an exception if you have a paper form that you are trying to match in a report and you can use the grid lines to align the objects to the paper form. Free-Form Placement only goes so far, however; Crystal Reports will not allow you to place a graph or a Cross-Tab object (see Chapter 11) in the Page Header, Page Footer, or the Details section because Cross-Tabs and graphs represent a grouped set of data that may span multiple pages.

Hide (Drill-Down OK)

This option is designed to stop the section from printing but not stop drilling down. So, you can still double-click a summary field and get a Drill-down tab in Preview.

Suppress (No Drill-Down)

This option stops the section from being printed and stops a summary field from being drilled down. You can enter a formula to make this option conditional. That is, in some cases the drill-down would be available, and in others it wouldn't. This feature is also formula driven, offering different detail sections in different situations.

Print at Bottom of Page

You can use this option to print sections as far down a page as possible. The genesis for this alternative is the good old invoice. Obviously, you want the total to an invoice to print at the very bottom of the page, leaving the rest of the page for the invoice details. This option can be turned on or off by using a formula.

New Page Before

If you want a new page to begin before the section starts printing, click this option. You may use this feature when you have inserted groups into the reports (listings by state, for example) and you want each group to print on a separate page. You can use a formula to turn this option on or off.

New Page After

Select this option if you want a new page to start after the section is printed. This option is most often used with groups and can be turned off or on by a formula. The ideal use of this option is for a report's cover page. You can put all the information you need in the Report Header section, and then force a new page to print after the header, ensuring that just the information you want is on the cover page.

Reset Page Number After

If you are using page numbering in your report, and you should be, you can adjust the count by turning this option on. A good example of using this option is groups. A group may very well span several pages of a report; if the pages are numbered by group, the report is easier to read. To achieve this numbering, you would set the option to on and insert the special field page numbering into the Group Footer section. Again, you can switch this option off or on by using a formula.

Keep Together

This option prevents Crystal Reports from printing a record on more than one page. If a full record with multiple lines does not fit at the bottom of a page, none of that record will print on that page — the entire record will be written on the next page.

Say that a page can show 64 lines. Each detail record is three lines long, so 21 full records (21 x 3 = 63) will print on the first page. The last record (line 64) would print without its counterparts if it could, but Crystal Reports has told the section to stay together. So instead of the first line of record 22 printing on the first page, all three lines are printed at the top of the second page. This feature avoids having records split across pages, which is known as *widow/orphan protection.* (When used with a group section, this option keeps the group together.)

Suppress Blank Section

If a section contains no objects, this option prevents Crystal Reports from printing white space. Have you ever created mailing labels from a database where some addresses have a suite number and others do not? The labels without the suite numbers have a gap when printed. This option prevents that from happening and can be turned on or off by using a formula.

Underlay Following Sections

This option creates a special effect in the report. The option's purpose is to print graphic objects such as a logo underneath the sections that follow.

Format Groups with multiple column

This option is only available in the Details section, which you get to by highlighting it in the dialog box. You use this option when you want the report to print in a multi-column format. Instead of having the data print straight down the page, you can set up multiple columns and have the data flow from column to column. You can also have your data print across and then down the page, printing one record in each column, and then printing a second record in the next column, then a third, and so on.

Click this option, and a new tab called Layout appears at the top right of the dialog box. This tab is divided into four smaller boxes: Width, Height, Horizontal, and Vertical. The Layout tab is selected in Figure 9-17.

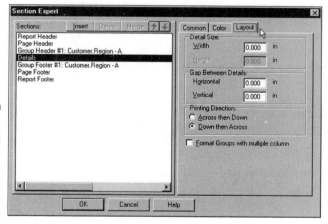

Figure 9-17:
The Layout tab in the Section Expert dialog box.

The measurements in the smaller boxes determine the position and spacing of each of the record details. At a minimum, you must enter a width measurement. Most likely, you would use this option for name- and address-type reports (like mailing labels).

Using the Color tab

After formatting each of the sections with the settings I just mentioned, you can add color to the section as an absolute format or as a conditional format. If you have skipped all the other chapters in this book in order to figure out how to use conditional formatting, your best bet is to read Chapter 7 on formulas and Chapter 8 on conditional formatting. You do not have to be expert on either, but these chapters give you some ideas as to how to construct formulas for this purpose.

In Figure 9-18, the Section Expert is open and the Color tab has been clicked.

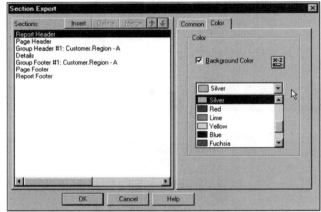

Figure 9-18:
The Section
Expert
dialog box
with the
Color tab
selected.

The colors work in conjunction with the section you have highlighted. In other words, to set the background color for the Report Header, click Report Header in the Sections list and then click the Color Tab.

To add an absolute color to any section, follow these steps:

1. **Choose Format⇨Section (or press the Section Expert button).**

   The Section Expert dialog box appears.

2. **Click the section you want to format with a background color.**

3. **Click the Color tab.**

4. **Click the Background color setting so that a check mark appears in the box.**

5. **Click the pull-down arrow to see the color options, and then click the color you want.**

6. **Click OK.**

In Figure 9-19, the Detail section has been colored red, so the records' background are in a darker hue than the rest of the report. I know the background may look gray to you, but trust me, it's red.

An example of a conditional format formula

Suppose that you want to color every other record in the Details section, making the report easier to read. Here are the steps to creating this formula:

1. **Open the report that you wish to format.**

2. **Choose Format⇨Section.**

3. **Click the Details section of the report.**

4. **Click the Color tab.**

5. **Click the Background Color box.**

 6. **Click the Conditional Format button.**

When you click this icon, the Format Formula Editor dialog box appears as shown in Figure 9-20.

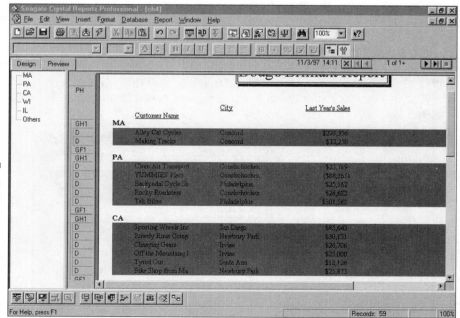

Figure 9-19:
The Details
section is a
darker hue
because
red is
applied
in the
background.

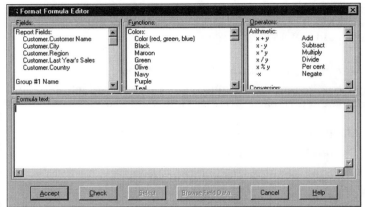

Figure 9-20:
The Format
Formula
Editor
dialog box.

I could go into all the details on entering a formula, but I won't here. See Chapter 7 for more information. Enter the formula exactly as follows:

```
if Remainder (RecordNumber,2) <> 0 then red else white
```

How does this formula work, you ask? The remainder (RecordNumber, 2) takes the record number and divides it by two. If a remainder other than zero is present, then the row will print in red (`then red`). Otherwise, the row color will be white (`else white`). Figure 9-21 shows the formula properly entered in the Format Formula editor text box.

For a complete tutorial that explains this whole effect, look up Green Bar Paper Effect in the Seagate Crystal Reports User's Guide.

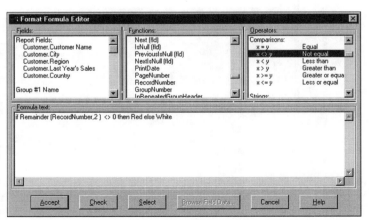

Figure 9-21:
The every
other
record
coloring
formula in
the Format
Formula
Editor
dialog box.

7. Click Accept to enter the formula.

8. Click OK to close the dialog box.

To see the results of using the formula, click the Preview Tab. The records are colored in every other fashion as shown in Figure 9-22. Very cool.

A conditional formula to color group results

Another use of color is to format certain group totals in a distinguishing color from other totals based on a conditional formula. If you have grouped your records by state or region and have added a subtotal by group, you can enter a formula that changes the color based on the value in the sum.

To add a conditional coloring formula to a group total:

1. Open the report to which you want to add a conditional color.

In this example, the CUSTLIST report I created for this example is used. The report has been grouped by region (which in this report is the same as state), and a sum has been added to each group by using the field Last Year's Sales.

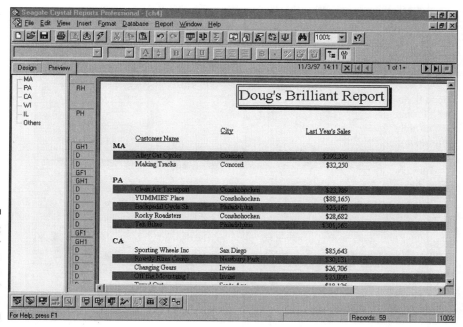

Figure 9-22: Every other record colored in the Preview Tab.

2. **In the Design Tab, choose Format➪Section.**

   The Section Expert dialog box appears.

3. **Click the Group Footer section of the report.**

4. **Click the Color tab.**

5. **Click the Background Color option.**

6. **Click the Conditional Formula icon.**

   When you do, the Format Formula Editor dialog box appears.

7. **Enter:**

   ```
   if
   ```

8. **Go to the Fields list.**

9. **Find the Sum of Last Year's Sales under your Group Footer on Region and double-click it.**

   The following text is inserted:

   ```
   Sum ({Customer.Last Year s Sales}, {Customer.Region})
   ```

10. **Then type:**

    ```
    > 90000 then Red else White
    ```

    The result looks like the formula shown in Figure 9-23.

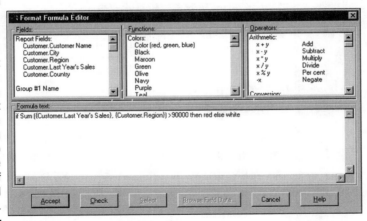

Figure 9-23:
The Conditional format formula entered into the Format Formula Editor dialog box to change the color of specified group totals.

In plain English, what this formula says is that if the total of the values in the Last Year's Sales field by Region is greater than 90000, the total will be printed in red. If not, then the total will be printed in white.

11. **Click <u>A</u>ccept to enter the formula.**

12. **Click OK to close the dialog box.**

13. **Click the Preview Tab to see the results, as shown in Figure 9-24.**

The coloring options are limited only by your imagination. However, if you get too wild with colors, you'll distract from the report itself. I suggest that you set a color scheme for your company so that every report has identifiable qualities, such as coloring groups sums that fall below the company average and/or a color for those groups with negative values.

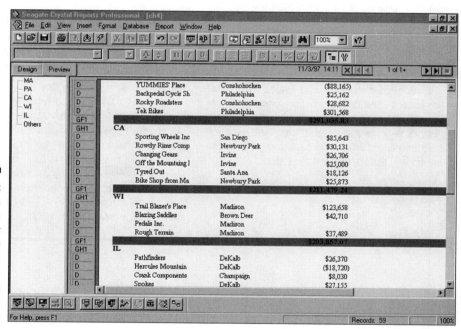

Figure 9-24: Groups with sales greater than 90,000 are printed in a different color.

A brief look at subreports

Crystal Reports produces very exquisite reports, which are more than adequate for most folks. But some people wanted the capability of subreports: a report that is inserted inside another report. The uses of such a capability are many. An example would be a situation in which you wanted the primary report to have data related to the company in its entirety, and the subreport would detail a particular division. So, if you work for a conglomerate, you could create reports that show both how the organization is doing and then insert a subreport detailing each individual operating division. The organization report would be the primary report and the division would be the subreport. Conversely, you could show your division as the primary report and the whole company's results as a subreport. Another example is a primary report that shows each customer and the subreport then shows the individual orders for that customer.

A subreport differs from a primary report in a few ways:

✔ A subreport is considered to be an object that is inserted into a primary report.

✔ A subreport can be placed in any section of the primary report, and the entire subreport then prints in that section.

✔ A subreport cannot in turn contain a subreport.

The next obvious question is: Does the data in the primary report and the subreport have to be linked? The answer is it does *not*. It can be linked or unlinked depending upon your needs. And both reports can use that same source database or entirely distinct databases.

Obviously, creating a report that includes a subreport is an advanced topic in the sense that you must first master creating a report before deciding why and how to insert a subreport. But I would be remiss in not mentioning that Crystal Reports 5.0 has this capability. The Crystal Report User's Guide has an excellent example of how to insert a subreport and how to make the linking between the primary and subreport process work.

Chapter 10
Creating Presentation-Quality Reports

● ●

In This Chapter

▶ Using quick format options

▶ Adding special fields

▶ Inserting lines and boxes

▶ Inserting a picture file

▶ Using Can Grow

▶ Inserting an OLE object

▶ Using Auto Arrange

● ●

*I*f you are not a very creative person when it comes to formatting and designing report layouts, never fear! Seagate Crystal Reports includes ten predefined formats that you can apply to your report for eye-pleasing effects. If none of these formats turns you on, you can read the rest of this chapter to learn how to apply formats yourself.

Quickly Formatting a Report

Your report is done, complete with groups, as in Chapter 5, and totals, as in Chapter 7. Now that the substance is finished, you're ready to add some veneer to the report.

With a report open and ready, follow these steps to apply a quick format:

1. **Open a report that you want to format using the Style Expert. (See Chapter 9 for the lowdown on the Style Expert.)**

   Figure 10-1 shows a report with little formatting.

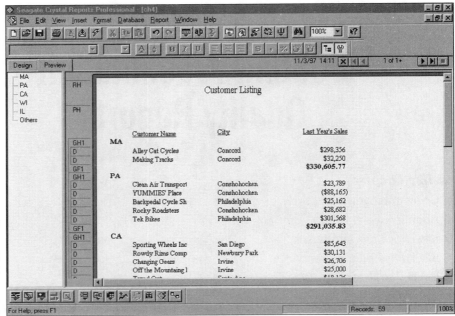

Figure 10-1:
A report
without
much
formatting.

2. Choose Format⇨Report Style Expert.

Before the dialog box opens, Crystal Reports displays a warning dialog box alerting you to the fact that applying a style is not reversible with the Undo command. Do not worry, you can always remove a format that is not what you want on a case by case basis. The Report Style Expert dialog box is shown in Figure 10-2.

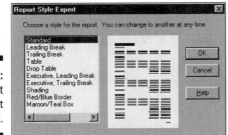

Figure 10-2:
The Report
Style Expert
dialog box.

You can choose a style from this dialog box, apply it, and if you do not like it, re-open the Report Style Expert and apply a new format. You do not have to worry about removing the previously applied format; the new format replaces it. As a preview of the format, click the format name and Crystal Reports shows you a representation of the format on the right side of the dialog box.

3. **Click a style that you want to apply to your report.**

   Figure 10-3 shows the results of applying the Standard report style.

4. **If you want to try another style, select Format⊅Report Style Expert.**

   In Figure 10-4, the Leading Break style has been applied to the report.

   One more time! This next style is called Drop Table, as shown in Figure 10-5.

Try the rest of the formats yourself on a report and see which appeals to you. If you try them all without satisfaction, you can return to the original formatting by choosing File⊅Close. Crystal Reports will ask if you want to save the report with the changes. By selecting No, the report is closed without any changes from the time you first opened it.

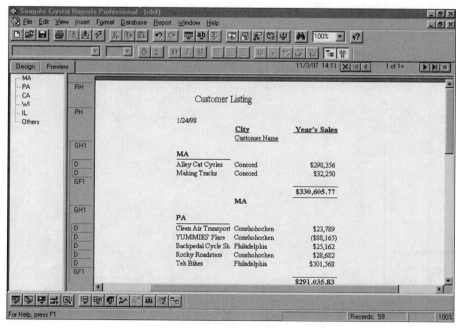

Figure 10-3:
The Standard report style added to a report.

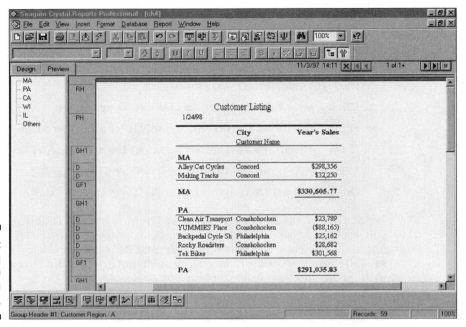

Figure 10-4:
The Leading
Break style
applied to a
report.

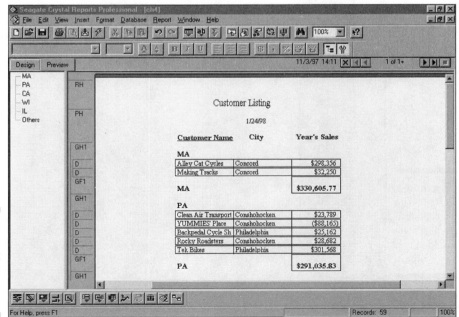

Figure 10-5:
The Drop
Table report
style
applied to a
report.

Zooming In on the Report

When you are working hard to get a report to look just right, Crystal Reports gives you a tool to save your eyes from straining. The Zoom function enables you to take a close-up look at the formatting you have applied and to zoom out to see how the report looks in full-page view.

The Zoom feature works best in the Preview Tab, because you are looking at live data. However, if you are working to get spacing just right, the Design Tab, when zoomed, gives you an easy way to see exactly where an object is on the layout. Formatting in the Design Tab is easier because every time you make a change, the screen does not have to be refreshed, as it does in the Preview Tab.

There are two ways to adjust the zoom factor:

✔ Choose <u>V</u>iew➪<u>Z</u>oom.

✔ Click the downward-pointing arrow near the right end of the toolbar to use the Zoom Control drop-down list.

In the first case, the Magnification Factor dialog box appears, as shown in Figure 10-6. If you use the drop-down list, you choose from several predetermined percentages.

Figure 10-6:
The
Magnification
Factor
dialog box.

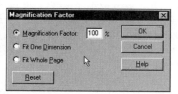

The first setting that you can adjust with the Magnification Factor dialog box is the magnification factor, by typing a new value into the box. The valid zoom range is 25 to 400 percent. To see the report at twice the default magnification, type **200** in the box, which is exactly what's been done in Figure 10-7.

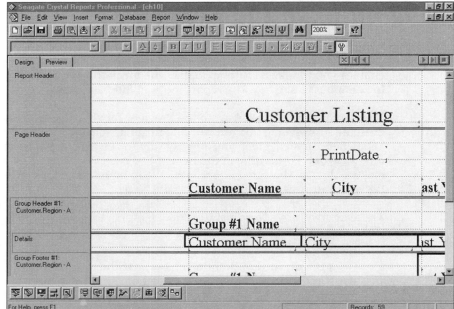

Figure 10-7:
The Design
Tab zoomed
by a factor
of 200
percent.

You may suppose that if you change the magnification factor in one window, the magnification carries over when you switch to the other window. It does not. Crystal Reports does not assume that you want the Preview magnified. This approach makes sense because you may be changing the formatting in the Design Tab and then desire to see the change in the Preview Tab at a static magnification. In this way, you can more easily compare apples to apples, so to speak.

The other options are Fit One Dimension and Fit Whole Page. When you toggle on the Fit One Dimension option, Crystal Reports fits the page according to the width of the report in the Design or Preview Tabs. In other words, the report dimensions are controlled by the report objects and not by margin settings. The Fit Whole Page option causes Crystal Reports to adjust the report so that all the objects can be seen on the screen. Or in Preview, it shows one whole page.

In Figure 10-8, the Fit Whole Page option has been selected in the Preview Tab. (If you use the Fit Whole Page option in the Design Tab, the effect is not very noticeable.)

To return the report view to the default setting, click the Reset button. The 100 percent magnification factor returns. Now that you know how to adjust the view of the report in order to better judge the effect of formatting, a discussion of the special fields is in order.

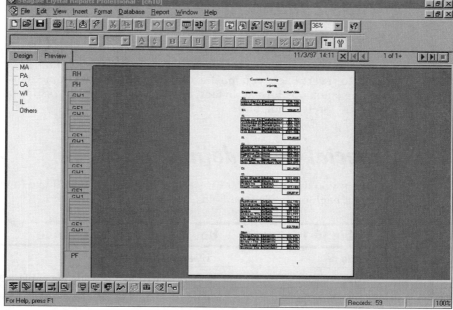

Figure 10-8:
The
Fit Whole
Page
option
selected
in the
Preview
Tab.

Working with Special Fields

A presentation-quality report requires types of information that are not automatically part of a report. The reason is that not every report requires the same Special fields, and you need to decide what fields to include. Special fields are used to insert information into a report that is not derived from an underlying database table or from a report formula. To insert a Special field:

1. **Choose Insert⇨Special field.**

   The list of Special fields appears.

2. **Click the Special field you want to insert into the report.**

   The frame cursor is attached to the mouse pointer. When you move the mouse to a position where the field can be properly inserted, the placeholder appears as a grayed rectangle, and if it cannot be inserted at the location of the mouse, the placeholder appears as a circle with a line drawn through it.

3. **Position the mouse pointer in the section of the report where you want the Special field information to be displayed.**

4. **Click the left mouse button to insert the field.**

Undo command

With any format that you add (except the Style Expert), you can always revert to the original report status by choosing Edit⇔Undo. The Undo command is dynamic in that it will reflect the last action taken. So, if you want to revert back, you must execute this command immediately after adding a noxious format. In fact, the Undo command works for multiple levels — pretty cool, huh?

Special fields defined

To help you decide which of the Special fields you would like to include in a report, each of the Special fields is described in Table 10-1.

Table 10-1	How Special Fields Operate
Field	**What It Does**
Page Number	Prints the current page number of the report.
Total Page Count	Prints the total number of pages in the report. This field is usually inserted in the Report Footer. This can also be useful on each page within a Text Object. For example, "Page 1 of 10."
Record Number	Prints the current record number. This is usually used in the Details section of a report.
Group Number	Prints the current group number. This feature could be used in the Group Header or Group Footer.
Print Date	Prints the current date based on the clock in your computer. (You can change the date by using Report⇔Set Print Date.)
Print Time	Prints the current time based on the clock in your computer when the report was last refreshed.
Data Date	Prints the date when the data in the report was last refreshed. This field works only with a report that has saved data.
Data Time	Prints the time when the data in the report was last refreshed. This field works only with a report that has saved data.
Last Modification Date	Prints the date on which the report was last modified.

Field	What It Does
Last Modification Time	Prints the time at which the report was last modified.
Report Title	Prints the contents of the Title field in the Document Properties dialog box. You can use this dialog box to enter summary information such as the title of the report, the subject, and the author. Chapter 18 covers the File Options and this topic.
Report Comments	Prints the contents of the Comments field from the Document Properties dialog box. You can use this dialog box to enter summary information such as the title of the report, the subject, and the author. Chapter 18 covers the File Options and this topic.

Inserting a Special Field

Before you actually insert a Special field into a report, consider where you want the information generated by the Special field to print. For example, the date field probably belongs in the Report Header section or perhaps in the Page Footer. Report information such as the last modification date, report comments, and report title (not of the report itself, but of the computer file name) may belong in the Report Footer. As with most formatting in Crystal Reports, trying different locations and combinations is the best way to determine what works for your reports.

A further consideration is that you can condition the printing of the Special field information and the way it displays by using a formula. See Chapter 5 on formulas for more information.

Following is an example of inserting the current date:

1. **Open the report into which you want a Date field inserted.**
2. **Click the Design Tab if you are looking at the Preview.**
3. **Choose Insert⇨Special Field.**
4. **From the list of Special fields that appears, choose Print Date Field.**

   The menu closes and the mouse pointer is transformed, so that a gray box is attached to it. This box indicates that the field placeholder is ready for insertion, as shown in Figure 10-9.

Figure 10-9:
The mouse
pointer with
a Special
field box
attached.

5. **Move the pointer to the section of the report in which you want the Special field to print.**

In this case, the pointer is positioned in the Report Header section.

If you move the pointer over an existing text field, the placeholder may disappear for a moment. Be patient, move the pointer to another area of the report, and wait for the pointer to reappear.

6. **Click the left mouse button.**

The field is inserted at that point. Figure 10-10 shows the Date field inserted above the report title in the Report Header section of the report.

Figure 10-10:
A Date field
inserted
into the
Report
Header.

Previewing the report with the new field inserted yields the result shown in Figure 10-11.

Adding a Record Number field

The *Record Number field* simply lists the number of the record in sequential order as it is printed on the report. Because this field generates a number for each record, the best place to insert this field is in the Details section of the report. In Figure 10-12, the field has been inserted to the right of the Last Year's Sales field. This feature is used quite often in legacy reports (mainframe-style reports) usually in control breaks. That way, even though the records have been split across many groups, the record numbering remains the same.

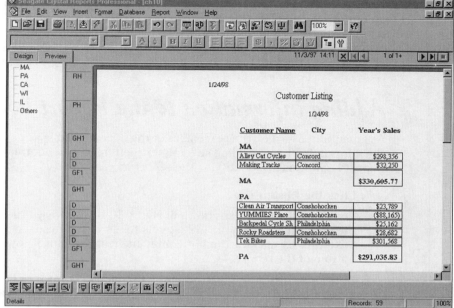

Figure 10-11:
The Print Date field is visible in the top-left corner of the report in the Preview Tab.

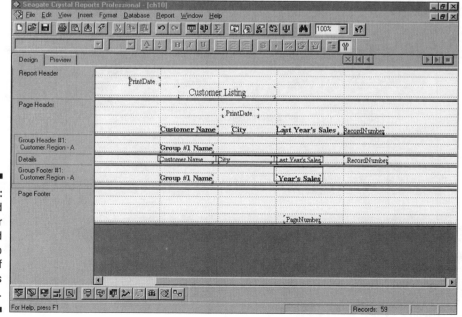

Figure 10-12:
The Record Number field inserted to the right of Last Year's Sales field.

The *Group Number special field* counts the number of groups in the report and prints the number where you specify. So, the first group printed on the report is Group Number 1 and so on. In Figure 10-13 the Group Number special field has been inserted into the Group Footer section of the report and is seen in the Preview Tab.

Adding information to the Report Footer

As I mentioned earlier, the placement of the Special field is as important as the information itself. Adding several pertinent pieces of information to the Report Footer makes identifying the report an easy task:

1. **Click the Design Tab.**

   The example report, as shown in Figure 10-14, has very little room for the Report Footer. So the first step is to increase the space allotted to the footer by clicking the horizontal line and dragging it toward the bottom of the report.

2. **To see the formatting better, move the mouse pointer to the left margin of the report and right-click to open the shortcut menu.**

3. **Choose the Arrange Lines option from the shortcut menu, to insert horizontal guidelines, as shown in Figure 10-15.**

   Now, add the Special fields.

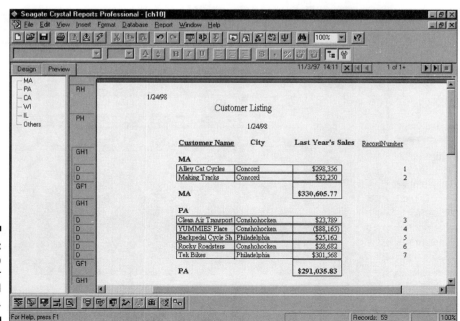

Figure 10-13: The Group Number field inserted.

The Group Number special field in action

Joe is the manager of the Craze Mountain Bikes Sales Force. He has a report that shows him all of the sales reps sorted into their regions (NE, SE, and West) and then sorted by descending order on their sales so that the top sellers are at the top. But, this report is *pages* long because Joe has a sales force of 1,000 people. Yikes. What he is really interested in is giving a bonus to the top five reps in each region. So, Joe goes into the report and selects Report⇨TopN/Sort Group Expert. After he gets in there, he chooses the grouping related to their sales figures. Where the Sort All is selected in the drop-down list, Joe selects TopN. Crystal Reports automatically grabs the most logical summarized field. In this case, Joe is looking for Sum of the Sales Forces Last Year's Sales. Then he realizes that he wants a descending order because he wants to reward his hard-working staff. (Of course, if he wants more than 5 records for this group, he would just change the N from 5 to any other number.) So he hits the OK button and then clicks the Refresh button. Wow! A potentially 32-page report to get 15 names has been reduced to a page or two. And now Joe realizes that with the change from TopN to BottomN, he can find out who his delinquent reps are. What a product!

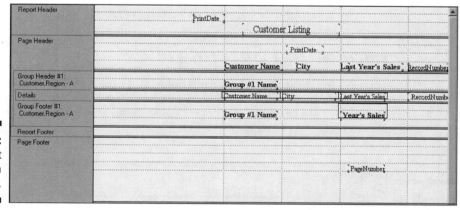

Figure 10-14: The Report Footer with little space.

4. Select Insert⇨Special field.

5. Select the Total Page Count field.

6. Insert the placeholder into the Report Footer section by moving the mouse pointer to that section and clicking.

7. Select Insert⇨Special field.

8. Select the Last Modification Date field.

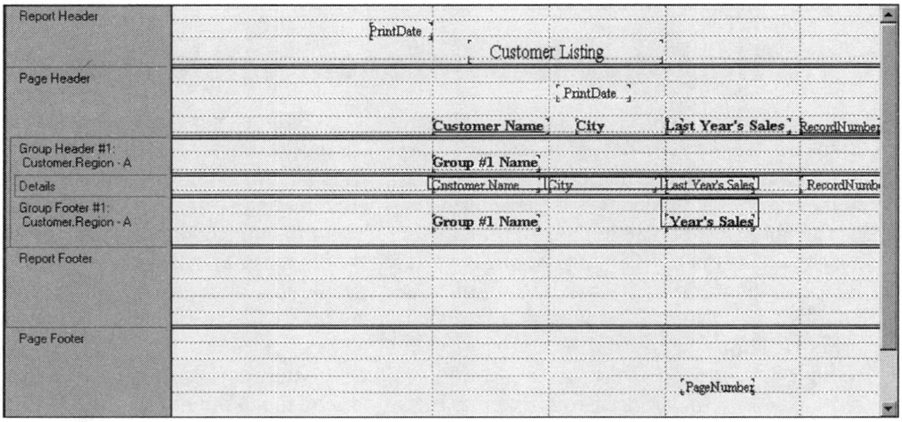

Figure 10-15:
Horizontal
lines
inserted in
to the
Report
Footer
section of
the report.

9. **Insert the placeholder into the Report Footer section.**

   The results are shown in Figure 10-16.

 10. **Click the Preview Tab, and click the Page Movement button that takes you to the last page in the report.**

   The inserted fields appear, as shown in Figure 10-17.

Formatting Special fields

You may find that the default font, color, and other format attributes are fine as presented, but that's not likely. To make changes, simply right-click the particular field or on the particular value in the Preview Tab. Figure 10-18 shows the shortcut menu.

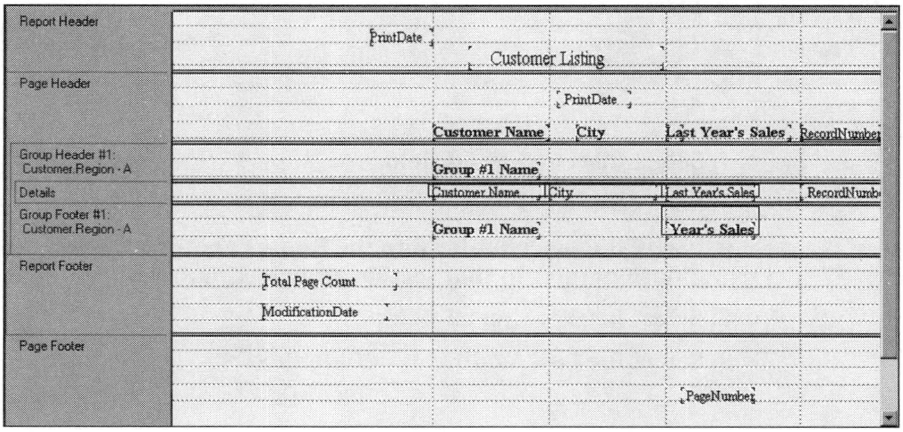

Figure 10-16:
The last
modification
date and
the total
page count
are inserted
into the
Report
Footer
section of
the report.

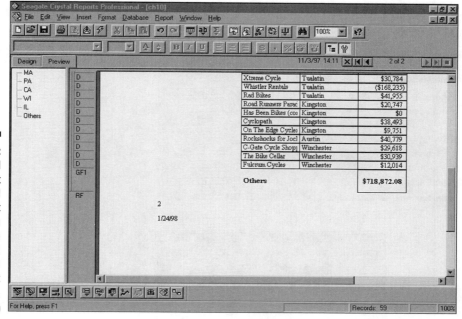

Figure 10-17:
The Total
Page Count
(3) field and
the Last
Modification
Date are
inserted
into the
Report
Footer.

Figure 10-18:
Right-click
to open the
Format Field
shortcut
menu.

Choose the Format Field option, and the Format Editor dialog box appears, as shown in Figure 10-19.

Note: If you are on a String field or a Date field when the Format Field option is chosen, the tab that is highlighted will be called String or Date, respectively. The information in the tab will be slightly different as Crystal Reports displays relevant information to the field.

The formatting possibilities are seemingly endless! The abundance of adjustments you can make to a field make exposing them all nearly impossible. But, just for the fun of it, click the Font tab to adjust the size of the number, as in Figure 10-20.

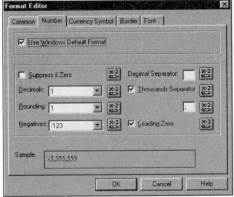

Figure 10-19:
The Format
Editor
dialog box,
opened
on the
Number tab.

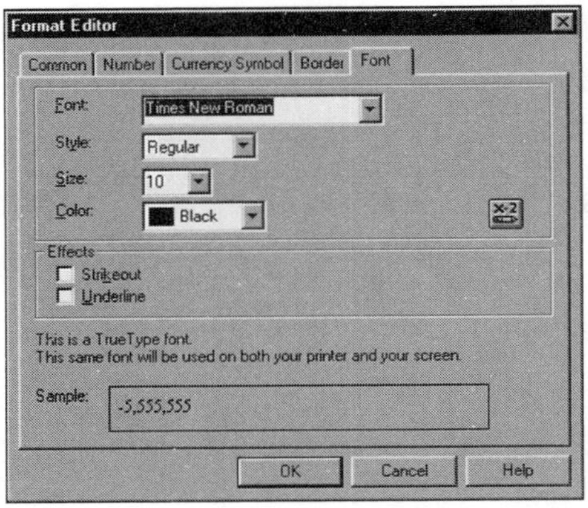

Figure 10-20:
The Font
tab
selected in
the Format
Editor
dialog box.

When you adjust the size, Crystal Reports shows you the effect in the
Sample box at the bottom of the dialog box. If you increase the size too
much for the space allotted in the Sample box, the numbers appear cut off.
But, not to fear, the numbers will look okay in the report.

A point to consider is that the Underline option in this dialog box works
together with the Border options (which I discuss later). In other words, you
can have an underline and a border at the same time.

As is true with most format settings, the application of the particular format
can be conditioned by a formula. Click the Conditional Formatting button to
open the Formula Editor dialog box and enter the conditions. For more on
formulas, see Chapter 5.

Formatting a Date field

A Date field can be formatted in a variety of ways, too. To see the formatting options, right-click the Date field that you have inserted, in the Design Tab, or on the date itself in the Preview Tab. Figure 10-21 shows the date after it has been right-clicked and the Format Field option has been selected.

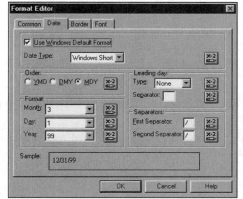

Figure 10-21: The Format Field dialog box for a Date field.

This dialog box includes a sample box at the bottom that reflects the changes you make as you make them. The default setting that Crystal Reports uses is derived from the date setting established by the Windows operating system, as indicated by the check mark. However, if you prefer to have your own format, you can certainly do so. An easy change is to select the Windows Long format, which changes the date to something like Tuesday, March 16th, 1998, instead of a numerical format. To choose this format, click the down arrow on Date Type and select it, or go wild and select Custom. With Custom as the selection, you can change the Order of the date numbers, the exact Format of each of the components — Month, Day, and Year — and so on.

If you change the date format from short to long, you must reformat the field by stretching it in order for the entire date to display.

Combining a text object with a Special field

Knowing how to execute this next bit of formatting really sets you apart from a novice Crystal Reports user. So far, you have seen how easy popping a Special field into a report is. But, what if the person reading the report does not know what the Special field numbers represent? For example, the Total Page number field can be mistaken for just about anything, so you, the report creator, have the duty to include explanatory text for each Special field entry.

When the Record Number field was added, Crystal Reports included the name of the field because the field was added by itself in an open column. The other Special field that you added to the report did not have the luxury of the space to include a field name. Yet, knowing the identity of each object is crucial for everyone dealing with the report.

You may be thinking that you can simply add a text object preceding or following the Special field and enter the description of the field. Crystal Reports has a much more elegant solution: combining the Special field and a text object.

In order to demonstrate this technique with the sample report, the Page Number must be deleted and reinserted. You cannot drag a Special field into a text object and get the correct result, so starting over is easier.

1. **In the Design Tab, right-click on the Total Page field, and from the shortcut menu, select Delete.**

2. **Click the Text Object button on the toolbar, and insert a text box into the Report Footer section of the report.**

   The best location is where the Total Page Number field used to be, before being deleted. The Text Object Edit field appears with a ruler line, as in Figure 10-22.

Figure 10-22:
A new text
object
being
inserted.

3. **Type** Total Number of Pages:

   Do not forget to add a space after the colon! Now, the pièce de résistance . . .

4. **With the text object still open, choose Insert⇨Special Field.**

5. **Choose the Total Page Count field.**

6. **Move the mouse pointer inside the text object, and click.**

   The Special field is inserted in the Text Object box, as shown in Figure 10-23.

7. **To see this very esoteric formatting trick in action, click the Preview Tab.**

   The report appears as shown in Figure 10-24. The Preview Tab has been zoomed to 200 percent in order to better see the result.

Figure 10-23:
The Total
Page Count
special field
inserted in
the Text
Object box.

This combination of a Special field and a text box gives you much more
flexibility in terms of options than creating two separate objects ever could.
You can even combine two database fields together rather painlessly. Just
drag and drop them into a text object and off you go.

Inserting Lines and Boxes

Lines and boxes can enhance particular values in the report and are a snap
to add to the layout. If you add a line object in a group summary, Crystal
Reports assumes that you want the line inserted in every group summary in
the report.

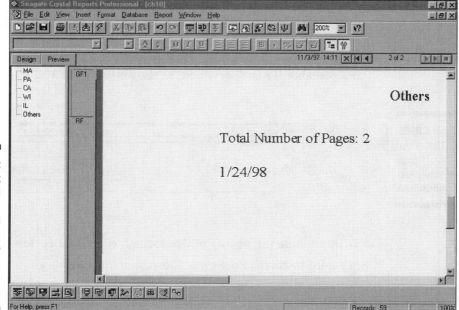

Figure 10-24:
A text box
combined
with a
Special
field in the
Preview
Tab,
zoomed to
200 percent.

If you are really looking to underline the contents of just *one* field, click the Underline button.

You can insert a line in three ways:

- ✔ Click the Insert Line button on the supplementary toolbar.

- ✔ Choose Insert⇨Line.

- ✔ Highlight the object you want underlined, and then hit the Underline button.

In either case, the mouse pointer is transformed to look like a small pencil on the screen. You then use your mouse to draw the line by holding down the left mouse button and dragging the mouse. Use the Design Tab to add these formats.

To add a line to a group summary:

1. **Click the Design Tab.**

2. **Right-click the mouse, choose Change Zoom, and then increase the magnification to 200 percent.**

3. **Click the Insert Line button on the tool bar.**

    The mouse is transformed into a pencil.

4. **Position the pencil tip underneath and to the left of the object you want to underline.**

    In this example, the placeholder for the Last Year's Sales group total is the target.

5. **Click the left mouse button, and drag the pencil to the right so that the placeholder is underlined, as shown in Figure 10-25.**

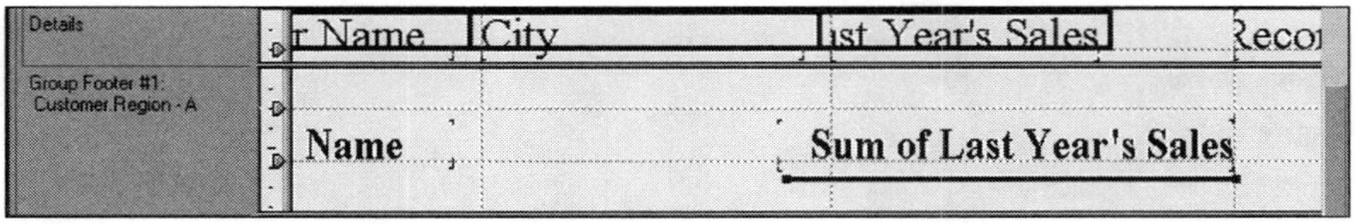

Figure 10-25:
The group total placeholder underlined.

Details	r Name	City	ıst Year's Sales	₹eco⌐
Group Footer #1: Customer.Region - A	Name		Sum of Last Year's Sales	

6. **To appreciate the beauty of this format, click the Preview Tab.**

    In Figure 10-26, the Preview is shown and the magnification is 200 percent

Using the Supplementary toolbar

New to Version 6.0 is an additional toolbar just for adding enhancements to your reports. To see the new toolbar, click the icon at the far right of the second toolbar from the top of the screen. It is directly under the Zoom button, and the icon has a yellow wrench-like figure on it. With the mouse on the icon, the popup reads "Toggle Supplementary Toolbar". Clicking the icon causes the toolbar to display in the lower-left corner of the screen, just

above the Windows Start button. Move your mouse pointer over each of the icons, and Crystal Reports displays the popup description of each.

All the toolbars are at your command. Choosing View⇨Toolbars displays a dialog box from which you can toggle off and on any or all of the three toolbars.

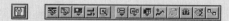

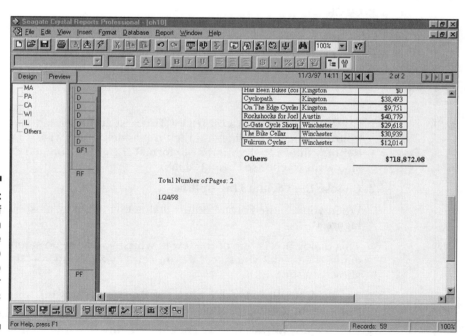

Figure 10-26: Preview of an underline added to the group total for Last Year's Sales.

The advantage of adding a line this way is that you can choose exactly what you want to emphasize. Whereas, the Field Format options regarding borders are drawn where Crystal Reports thinks they should go.

A drawn line can only be horizontal or vertical. Angled lines are not possible. The benefit is that you can be certain that any lines you draw are perfectly aligned.

Formatting a line

Lines can be adjusted once they are in place. You begin any line object with the original line, as demonstrated in the preceding example, and then build from there.

To change the format of a line in a report:

1. Right-click the line to open the shortcut menu, as in Figure 10-27.

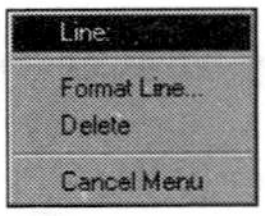

Figure 10-27:
The
shortcut
menu for
line
formatting.

Opening this menu is a bit tricky. The best approach is to move the pointer beneath the line and then right-click. Otherwise, Crystal Reports thinks that you want to format the group summary. You may also want to choose Format⇨Line.

2. Choose the Format Line option.

When you do, the Format Editor dialog box appears, as shown in Figure 10-28.

This dialog box is one of the few in which you have no sample field to gauge the format you select before actually applying it — the buttons show you the width.

3. To check the line density, click the line size you want, and the number, in points, displays at the right.

4. Add a color preference by clicking the down arrow, and if you want the line to print at the bottom of the section, like an accounting statement, you can have it do that.

5. Click OK to close the dialog box.

One other thing you can do, and the magnification makes it easy, is grab the handles at either end of the line and lengthen or shorten the line to match the length of the field if you have misdrawn the line.

Figure 10-28:
The Format
Editor
dialog box
for line
formatting.

Boxing records in a group

What if you want to add a border around every record in a report? Simply use the following instructions. To add a border around individual records in a report:

1. **Click the Design Tab in your report.**

2. **Click the placeholder in the Details section of the report.**

3. **Right-click to open the shortcut menu.**

   The shortcut menu is shown in Figure 10-29.

Figure 10-29:
The
shortcut
menu to
format a
field.

4. **Choose Change Border.**

   The Format Editor dialog box appears.

   Crystal Reports, being the flexible tool that it is, gives you a choice of exactly which lines should be included in the border: top, left, right, bottom, all, or some. On top of that, each of the border lines can be conditional! Set a formula to determine which line prints when — a little much in my opinion, but some folks undoubtedly will use this feature.

5. Click the down arrow next to the border that you want to include and select the kind of line.

6. Click OK to close the dialog box and apply the new format.

The Tight Horizontal option trims the border to the size of the field. When this check box is toggled off, the border will be the same size for each record. When this check box is toggled on, the border will be trimmed to the size of each individual record.

The Drop Shadow option adds a façade of depth to the border. Check this box if you want that effect. In this case, where the border is going around each individual record, the shadow would be an over-format — all it would do is add clutter.

The color of the border lines can be selected, as well as a background color inside the border lines.

Figure 10-30 shows the report with each of the individual records with a border drawn.

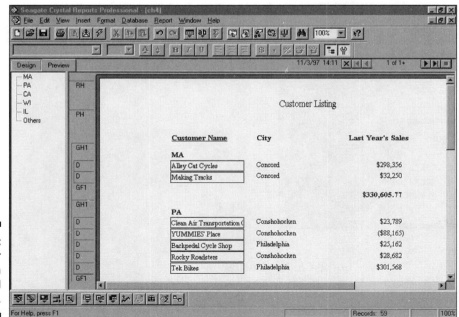

Figure 10-30:
A border drawn on individual records.

Adding a drop shadow to the title

A great place to use the drop shadow effect is on the title to the report. The effect is easy to create and adds a classy, professional look to your report.

1. **Click the title of your report, or any text object, so that the border is outlined.**

2. **Right-click to open the shortcut menu.**

3. **Choose the Format Border option.**

   The Format Editor dialog box appears.

4. **Add borders on all sides of the text object.**

5. **Click the Drop shadow check box.**

6. **Click OK.**

   The title displays, as shown in Figure 10-31.

Figure 10-31: A border and drop shadow added to the title of the report.

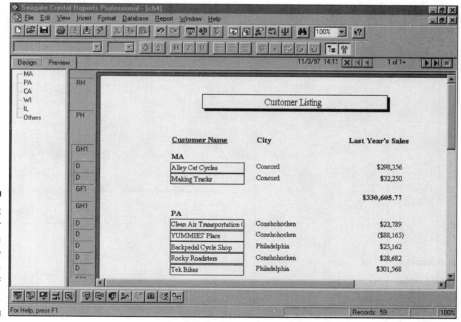

Drawing a Box around an Object

Drawing a box around a group of records can be especially tricky if you try to draw a box that crosses sections of the report. Drawing a box involves a little planning. The best way to draw it is to select the point where the upper- left corner will be and then draw the box by dragging the lines across and down to the point where the lower-right corner will be.

To draw a box around an object or objects:

1. **Open the report, in the Design window, as it is easier to see the lines that define sections in the report.**

2. **Click the Insert Box tool button.**

   The mouse pointer is transformed into a pencil shape.

3. **At the point where the upper-left corner of the box is to start, click the left mouse button and hold it.**

4. **Drag the mouse across and to the right to the point where you want the lower-right corner to be drawn.**

5. **Release the mouse button.**

You may format the box by clicking it to show the handles and then right-clicking to open the shortcut menu. Choose Format Box to select the line type, color, and thickness. You my even add a drop shadow. In Figure 10-32, a box has been drawn around the Group Header, which includes the names of the fields in the report.

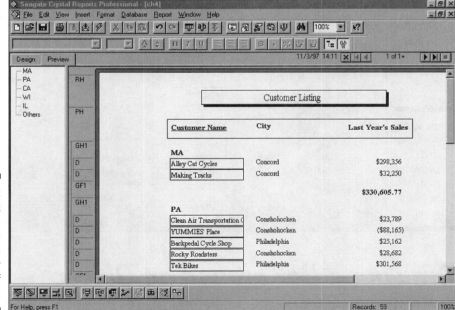

Figure 10-32:
A box
drawn
around the
Group
Header
section of
the report.

Text Objects Extra

If you have read the rest of this chapter, you already know how to insert a text object and then type the text you want in the object. You know how to right-click to add formatting. You know how to combine a text object with a Special field. This next example shows you how to insert database fields into a text object and then to format the field so that no matter how long the information in the database is, it will print properly.

The example report file has a list of customers, their respective cities, and their last year's sales. Adding the name of the owner enhances the report.

1. **From the Design Tab, choose Insert⇨Text object.**

2. **Insert the text object above the placeholder in the Details section.**

   You may have to resize the section in order to fit the new field.

3. **Type some explanatory text such as:** Owner's name:

   Add a space after the word name:.

4. **Choose Insert⇨Database field.**

   The field placeholder is attached to the mouse pointer. In this example, the first field to insert would be the Contact First Name.

5. **Position the mouse pointer right behind the text that you just typed in the text object box.**

   The field placeholder becomes a small insertion point when it is inside the text box.

6. **Left-click the mouse button to insert the Database field.**

   The text box appears, as shown in Figure 10-33.

7. **Choose Insert⇨Database field.**

   Don't forget to add a space before adding the second field.

8. **In this example, the next field to insert is the Contact Last Name, so that field is selected.**

Because the fields are long, the XXXs wrap around to another line, but the printed output will look different, as shown in Figure 10-34.

The XXXs signify a text field, and Crystal Reports inserts as many Xs as the longest entry into the field. The great thing about this process is that Crystal Reports automatically trims the field information so that the format is correct. Without this capability, your report would have significant gaps between the first and last names.

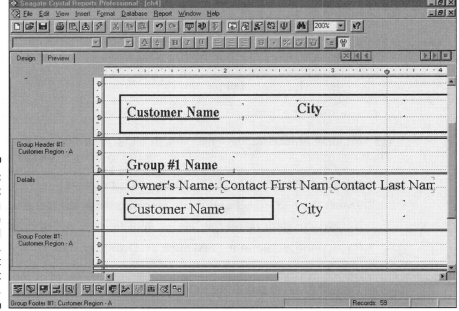

Figure 10-33:
The text box with a Database field inserted, shown at 200 percent zoom.

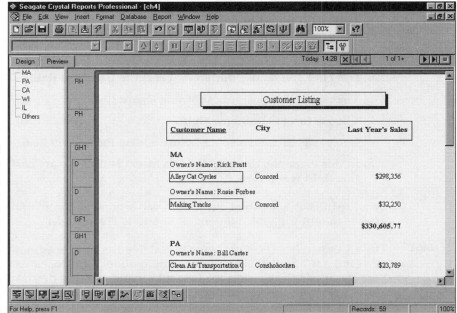

Figure 10-34:
Two Database fields inserted into a text box, shown in the Preview Tab.

Rather than look at XXXs every time you insert a Database field, wouldn't you rather see the field name itself? Of course you would, and I know you are thinking: Why did he wait so long to tell me this? Because it opens a whole new set of options that are going to be covered in Chapter 18 on file options. But, digress I will. Select File⇨Options. On the Layout Tab, search around to find the option Show Field Names. From that point on, instead of X, you will get the actual field names from the database.

Adding the Can Grow option

Although the report printed properly in the foregoing example, you can take another step to make sure that the text box is the correct size to contain the fields you insert.

1. **Right-click the text object.**

   The shortcut menu appears.

2. **Choose the Format text menu item.**

3. **In the Format Editor dialog box, click the check box in front of the Can Grow option.**

With this option on, the text object grows vertically, not horizontally. That is, the text object gets taller, not longer.

As soon as a field (any type) is dropped into a text object, Can Grow is automatically turned on (so you don't have to go and find it). Cool, huh?

Editing text within a text object

A text object may not be perfect after you insert it into a report, so you may need to make some changes.

1. **Double-click the text object that you want to edit.**

   The text editor ruler appears above the object, and you can edit the text inside the box.

2. **If you would like to change options for the whole text object, choose the appropriate option, such as Font, Border, or Format Text to open the Format Editor dialog box by right-clicking on the text object.**

Inserting a Picture or Logo into the Report

Your boss will ask for this capability as soon as she sees the other nifty formats that you have added. By the time you have added all of the other attributes, that finishing touch will be the company graphic. And why not? The big deal with Windows is the ability to bitmap throughout all applications. Before you can insert a picture or logo, it must exist in a format Crystal Reports can accept, such as BMP (a bitmap), PCX, TIF, JPG, or TGA. The Paint program included with Windows creates files in the BMP format. So to insert your company logo into a report, follow these steps:

1. **Open the report into which you want to insert a picture or logo.**

2. **Click the Design Tab.**

   Depending on where you want the picture inserted, you may have to resize the section to accommodate the new picture object. However, Crystal Reports will adjust the size of the section for you if you position the picture beneath an existing object and the section border. For example, if you want the picture to be in the Report Header, beneath the title, position the pointer just underneath the title and click. Figure 10-35 shows the picture outline at the point where Crystal Reports will adjust the section size to make the fit.

    3. **Choose Insert⬩Picture (or press the Insert Picture button on the toolbar).**

   The Open dialog box appears. You may have to switch folders or drivers in order to locate the file you want to insert. Crystal Reports includes a bitmap of the Craze Mountain Bike Company logo in the Crystal Reports folder named CRAZEC, making this file easy to use as an example.

4. **Click the file you want to insert.**

Linking versus embedding

Linking: When a linked object (let's say a company logo) is added to a report, if the logo changes, the next time the report is run, the *new* logo will be on the report.

Embedding: When an embedded object is added to a report, even if the object (file) changes (someone goes out and nukes the logo file . . .ooops), those changes would not be made in the refreshed report.

5. Click the Open button.

The Open dialog box closes, and the mouse pointer has a gray outlined box attached, indicating the size of the picture or logo. The outline of the logo is shown in Figure 10-35.

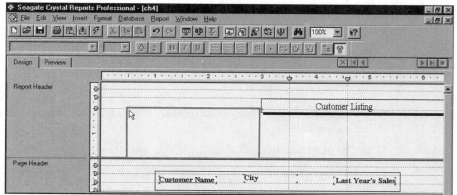

Figure 10-35: The logo outline attached to the mouse pointer.

6. Position the box at the point where you want the logo inserted.

7. Click the left mouse button to insert the picture.

See Figure 10-36. Notice that Crystal Reports has pushed the Page Header down to make room for the logo.

Figure 10-36: The CRAZE logo inserted as a picture into the Report Header section.

Inserting an OLE Object

An OLE (Greek — or is it geek speak? — for Object Linking and Embedding) object is different from any ordinary picture or logo file in that it is an active file. That is, an OLE object is usually a file that was created in another application such as MS Paint. If the object needs editing, you normally have to go to the trouble of making the edit in MS Paint, delete the old object from your report, and then reinsert it. Whew! Too much like work. So, to make life easier, using OLE, you can click the object, and the application that created the object starts so that you can make changes directly.

To insert an OLE object:

1. **Open the report you want to insert the OLE into, and click the Design Tab.**

2. **Choose Insert⇨OLE.**

   At this point, you can use an existing object or create a new one.

   You can embed a wide variety of OLE objects in a report. The range is from a picture to a spreadsheet.

3. **For an existing object, click the Browse button to locate the file.**

4. **Click the Link box if you want the object automatically updated. This means that if you change the object in its native program, like Excel, the changes are automatically reflected in Crystal Reports.**

   The OLE can be identified in the report by an icon created by Crystal Reports or by an icon you select.

5. **Move the mouse pointer to the position in the report where you want the OLE inserted and click.**

To activate the OLE, double-click it. If you have inserted a spreadsheet, Excel then starts within Crystal Reports. Very cool.

Using Auto Arrange to Format Reports

When you place a field from a database into your report, Crystal Reports allocates space in the report based on the length of the field as designated in the database table. So, if the designer of the database allocated 50 character spaces for the Product Name field, that is the length of the field set aside in Crystal Reports. Often, the space allocated is far too long. The Auto Arrange command resizes the field length by finding the longest entry in the Database field and adjusting the length in the report based on that.

The second thing that Auto Arrange does is to reposition the field to better use the space freed up by the resizing. Auto Arrange also centers the report on the page.

To use the Auto Arrange command:

1. **Insert the fields you want into the report, and add groups and other formatting.**

2. **Select Format⇨Auto Arrange.**

   Crystal Reports warns you that this command cannot be undone.

It seems that every aspect of Crystal Reports can be modified in some way. The key idea may be that you should be careful not to overdo the formatting. If the report is too busy, it takes away the message you are trying to convey. Of course, if *obfuscation* is your goal, you can accomplish it easily with the formatting options.

Part V

Creating Specific Types of Reports

The 5th Wave   By Rich Tennant

CRYSTAL REPORTS HAS REALLY MADE THE JOB A LOT LESS COMPLICATED...

In this part . . .

*V*ariety is the spice of life, and in reporting, it is no different. So, in this part, the thyme, sage, saffron, curry, and fenugreek all become a part of your flavorful report repertoire, metaphorically, at least. Seagate Crystal Reports has a wide variety of report types from which you can choose. This part is devoted to helping you cook a report that will cure the common cold and land you that corner office with a key to the executive washroom. By matching the report type with the needs of those in your organization you will gain the reputation of a master report chef. Stand aside Wolfgang Puck, there is a new report maker in town.

Chapter 11

Creating a Cross-Tab Report

. . . .

In This Chapter

▶ Creating a new Cross-Tab

▶ Inserting a Cross-Tab into an existing report

▶ Using the Cross-Tab Expert

. . . .

A Cross-Tab object turns the fields on their side, so to speak, so that you can see different relationships between and among fields, much like a spreadsheet. It can be a great analytical tool and a way to identify trends. In this chapter, I create a simple Cross-Tab report for your perusal.

Identifying the "By" Word

A Cross-Tab is an arrangement of fields in such a way that the data in the fields can be compared in order to identify trends. Pollsters, those best friends of politicians, use cross tabulations of voter interviews to see which issues are creating a response *by* age, *by* location, or *by* whatever demographic or psycho-graphic category the respondent fits. Then campaign directors design TV and direct mail ads to target those respondents in a way that their candidate's image is acceptable to those respondents. If they are good at reading Cross-Tabs, they get their candidate elected.

In using Cross-Tabs, the operative word is *by,* in that the genesis of a Cross-Tab is sales *by* region, products *by* customer, votes *by* precinct, and so on. Whenever you think that a report would be more valuable if it included a set of data that can be defined as something *by* something else, you are in Cross-Tab land.

In business, the same principle applies. With an existing or new product, the survey research can be cross tabulated to determine which customer profile is most likely to purchase the product. You can even determine the price range acceptable to the customer. In the example in this chapter, a Cross-Tab is created to determine which suppliers sold in which regions.

A Cross-Tab is hard for people to handle conceptually. Think of something like this:

	Beer	Wine	Total
Males	100	20	120
Females	15	75	90
Total	115	95	210

For example, the preceding diagram is actually a Cross-Tab analyzing sales by sex and alcohol type. You can learn a lot by taking a quick look at a Cross-Tab.

In Crystal Reports, a Cross-Tab is an object, not the entire report. So, a Cross-Tab can be inserted at a particular place in the report or combined with a summary report (see Chapter 12 on summary reports). The Cross-Tab can be inserted into the Report Header or Report Footer or the Group Header or Group Footer. Where the Cross-Tab object is placed is crucial in this respect: If you insert the Cross-Tab into the Report Header or Footer, the Cross-Tab object is displayed only once and will include every record in the report. The other option, inserting the Cross-Tab in the Group Header or Footer, causes the Cross-Tab to consider only the records in that particular Group and the Cross-Tab displays before or after every Group of records.

Creating a Cross-Tab Object in a New Report

A Cross-Tab object is arranged by rows and columns. If you have worked with a spreadsheet, then you have seen the concept. When you select a Database field for inclusion in the Cross-Tab, each value in the Database field is accorded its own row or column. The column or row header is the name of the field.

Before discussing adding a Cross-Tab to an existing report, start with a new report to see the entire process. In this example, the CRAZE database is used.

1. **Choose File⇨New.**

2. **From the Report Gallery dialog box select Custom.**

3. **At the bottom of the dialog box, click Data File.**

4. **In the Choose Database File dialog box, click CRAZE.MDB.**

5. **Click OK.**

   The Select Tables dialog box appears (see Figure 11-1).

6. **Click the Select All button to include all tables.**

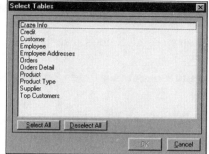

Figure 11-1:
The Select
Tables
dialog box.

7. Click OK.

The Visual Linking Expert dialog box opens, as shown in Figure 11-2.

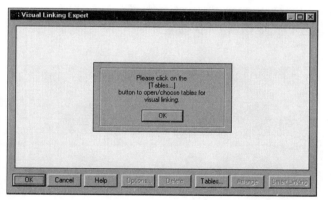

Figure 11-2:
The Visual
Linking
Expert
dialog box.

8. Click OK.

9. Click OK, again.

You now have the opportunity to insert fields into the report. The Insert Fields dialog box appears in the Design window.

In order to follow this example, insert the following tables in the Details section of the report:

- Customer name from the Customer table
- Order ID and Order Amount from the Orders table

1. **From the Insert Fields dialog box, click the field name Customer Name, and then click the Insert button.**

2. **Position the mouse pointer so that the field is inserted into the Details section of the report.**

3. **Repeat the process to insert the remaining fields, Order ID and Order Amount.**

   You may want to resize the Customer Name field.

   Figure 11-3 shows the report with the fields inserted.

Group the report by Product Name by following these formatting steps:

1. **Choose Insert⇨Group.**

   The Insert Group dialog box opens.

2. **In the Insert Group dialog box, select Product Name from the Product table.**

3. **Click OK to close the dialog box.**

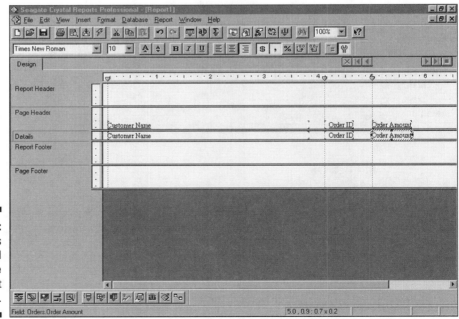

Figure 11-3:
Fields inserted into the report design.

This example database contains many records, so the next step is to use the Select Record Expert to select records from the regions of IA, MN, and TX. (Because Crystal Reports is a Canadian product, the generic term *region* is used for states and provinces.) For more detailed information on creating a record selection, see Chapter 4.

1. **Click the Select Records button on the toolbar.**

2. **From the Choose Field dialog box, select the Region field from the Customer table (as shown in Figure 11-4) and click OK.**

   The Select Expert dialog box appears.

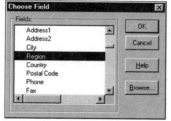

Figure 11-4:
The Choose
Field
dialog box.

3. **From the second box of the Select Export dialog box, select the** one of **option.**

   A third box appears to the right.

4. **Click the pull-down list from the third box, and individually select IA, MN, and TX.**

   The CRAZE database contains some records with incomplete information. You do not want to include them on your report, so you need to fine-tune your record selection. To eliminate partial records, only include records if they are from one of the regions selected and the Order Amount is greater than zero.

   Remember this step. It is not uncommon for databases in the real world to contain some records with partial or incomplete information. You may need to fine-tune your record selection to remove this incomplete data from your reports (assuming you do not want it displayed on the report).

5. **Click the New tab in the Select Expert (shown in Figure 11-5).**

6. **Select the Order Amount field from the Choose Field dialog box.**

7. **Press OK.**

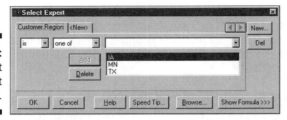

Figure 11-5:
The Select
Expert
dialog box.

8. **From the second drop-down box, select** greater than.

9. **Enter** 0 **(the number zero) in the third drop-down box.**

10. **Click OK.**

Finally, add a subtotal to the Order Amount field by taking the following steps:

1. **Right-click on the Order Amount field, opening the short cut menu.**

2. **Choose the Insert Subtotal option, as shown in Figure 11-6.**

Figure 11-6:
The Insert
Subtotal
dialog box.

3. **Press OK**

 4. **Click the Preview button to see the report with a summary added, as shown in Figure 11-7.**

5. **Click the Design Tab.**

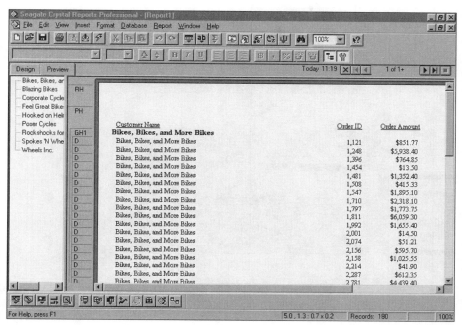

Figure 11-7:
The report
previewed.

Inserting a Cross-Tab into an Existing Report

At this point, the report is ready for the Cross-Tab object. You can open the Cross-Tab dialog box in two ways:

✔ Click the Insert Cross-Tab button on the toolbar.

✔ Choose Insert menu⇨Cross-Tab.

Take a look at the Cross-Tab dialog box, as presented in Figure 11-8.

This Cross-Tab is designed to show the quantity of sales by supplier in each region. You have added several fields to the report; the Cross-Tab is created with several fields that are not in the report.

1. **From the Fields box within this dialog box, click the Customer.Region.**

2. **Click the Add Column button.**

   The field name is inserted into the Columns box. Next, a row is needed.

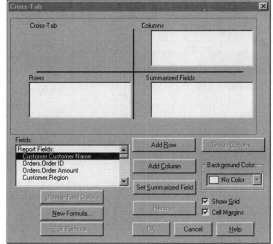

Figure 11-8:
The
Cross-Tab
dialog box.

3. Scroll through the Fields box until you find the table named Supplier.

4. Click the Supplier Name field name.

5. Click the Add Row button.

When adding fields to the Cross-Tab, you can use the Add Column, Add Row, or Set Summarized Fields button, but a shortcut is to just drag and drop the field from the Fields list to Rows, Columns, or Summarized Fields.

The field name is inserted into the Rows field.

The final step is to add a summarized field in order to see the quantity of each product ordered from each supplier by region.

6. Scroll through the Fields box and locate the Orders Detail table.

7. Click the Quantity field.

8. Click the Set Summarized field button.

The completed Cross-Tab dialog box is shown in Figure 11-9.

9. Click OK.

The Cross-Tab is attached to the mouse pointer as a rectangle; you insert the Cross-Tab in the same way as you insert a field.

10. Insert the Cross-Tab object into the Report Header section of the report by moving the mouse pointer to that section and clicking the left mouse button.

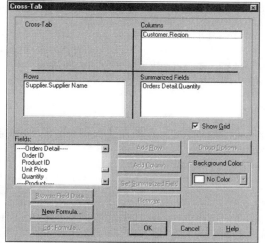

Figure 11-9:
The
completed
Cross-Tab
report
dialog box.

11. Click the Preview Tab to see the report.

In Figure 11-10, the Cross-Tab object in the Preview Tab.

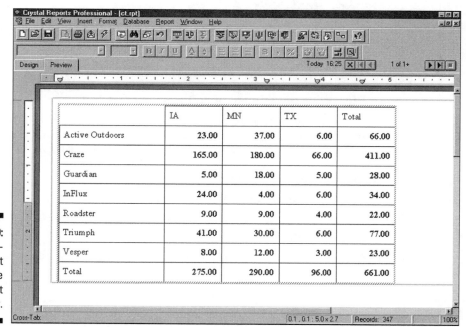

Figure 11-10:
The Cross-
Tab object
in the
Report
Header.

	IA	MN	TX	Total
Active Outdoors	23.00	37.00	6.00	66.00
Craze	165.00	180.00	66.00	411.00
Guardian	5.00	18.00	5.00	28.00
InFlux	24.00	4.00	6.00	34.00
Roadster	9.00	9.00	4.00	22.00
Triumph	41.00	30.00	6.00	77.00
Vesper	8.00	12.00	3.00	23.00
Total	275.00	290.00	96.00	661.00

Crystal Reports is quite smart when it comes to Cross-Tabs. The program automatically takes care of generating the appropriate rows and columns. In this case, we see one column for each region and one row for each supplier. But if you have incomplete data, you may end up with blank rows or columns. If this happens, you will need to fine-tune your record selection so that the report does not contain records with partial information. This is just like what we did earlier in the chapter when we got rid of partial data by adding `And Order Amount greater than 0` to the record selection.

Figure 11-10 reveals the results of a Cross-Tab. At the left is a list of the suppliers to the stores, at the tops of the columns are each of the region locations, and in the intersections of the rows and columns, you find the number that represents the quantity of product purchased by each region and supplier.

You can reformat the layout of the Cross-Tab tab by clicking and dragging. To resize a column, simply resize any field in the column. By shortening the intersection cells, you obscure the column headings, so you have to adjust prudently. You can reformat the numbers by right-clicking them and choosing a format option from the shortcut menu.

Removing the grid

Besides formatting the individual numbers in the table or resizing the columns, you can turn off the grid outline that defines the table.

To remove the table grid:

1. **Right-click the table to open the shortcut menu.**

   The shortcut menu should be headed by the name Cross-Tab. ***Note:*** You may find that when you right-click over the Cross-Tab, Crystal Reports thinks you are trying to modify a single field rather than the entire Cross-Tab. To select the entire Cross-Tab for editing, try right-clicking over the top-left corner of the Cross-Tab.

2. **From the menu, select Format Cross-Tab.**

   The Cross-Tab dialog box appears, as shown in Figure 11-11, with the Show Grid option checked.

3. **Click the Show Grid option to turn off the grid around the Cross-Tab.**

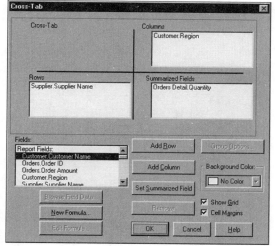

Figure 11-11:
The
Cross-Tab
dialog box.

Adding a second summary field to the example Cross-Tab

Perhaps you want to know the quantity ordered as well as the dollar amount of the orders. Adding this second summary operation is easy. You can accomplish this task by using the shortcut menu and Format Cross-Tab option.

To add a second summary field to a Cross-Tab:

1. **Right-click the Cross-Tab object in either the Design or Preview window.**

2. **From the shortcut menu, choose the Format Cross-Tab option.**

   The Cross-Tab dialog box opens.

3. **Scroll the Fields list to locate the field you want to add.**

   In this example, the Order Amount field from the Orders table is selected.

   Cross-Tabs are very powerful. You can insert multiple fields for summarized fields, for rows, and for columns. You can insert formula fields into your Cross-Tab as summarized fields, rows, or columns.

4. **Click the Set Summary Operation button.**

5. **Click OK.**

   The newly reformatted Cross-Tab appears, as shown in Figure 11-12.

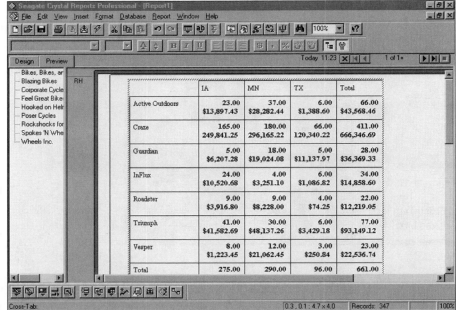

Figure 11-12:
The second
summary
operation
added to
Cross-Tab
in Preview.

In order to make any changes to the Cross-Tab, such as adding rows or columns directly in the report, you must use the Cross-Tab dialog box.

Creating a Cross-Tab Using the Cross-Tab Expert

The earlier example in this chapter showed you how to add a Cross-Tab object to an existing report. But you may want to have a report that only contains a Cross-Tab. The easiest way to do this is to create a Cross-Tab using the Cross-Tab Expert and then follow the prompts that are offered by Crystal Reports to complete the Cross-Tab. When you create a Cross-Tab this way, the report contains a Cross-Tab only to start with. You could then go back and add other data to the report over and above the Cross-Tab object. In this example, walk through the steps using the CRAZE database to create a Cross-Tab using a Cross-Tab Expert. (For a brief introduction to using the Experts, refer to Chapter 2.)

1. Choose File⇨New.

The Report Gallery dialog box appears, as shown in Figure 11-13. Because you want to use a Report Expert to create your report, find the expert that most closely matches the type of report you want to create — in this case the Cross-Tab option.

Figure 11-13:
The Report
Gallery
dialog box.

2. Click the Cross-Tab icon.

When you do, the Create Report Expert dialog box appears, as shown in Figure 11-14.

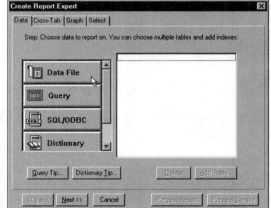

Figure 11-14:
The Create
Report
Expert
dialog box.

3. Your first step is to tell the program what data you want to use for your report. Click the Data File button.

The Choose Database File dialog box opens, as shown in Figure 11-15.

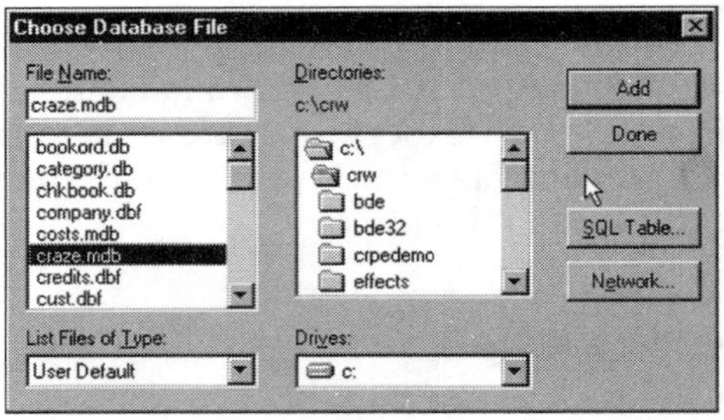

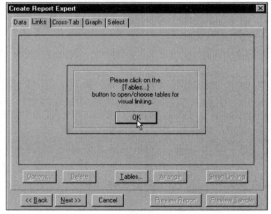

Figure 11-15:
The Choose
Database
File
dialog box.

4. Click the CRAZE.MDB file name, and click the Add button.

5. Click Select All.

The Create Report Expert dialog box appears, with the Links tab selected, as shown in Figure 11-16.

Figure 11-16:
The Create
Report
Expert
dialog box
with the
Links tab
selected.

6. Click OK.

Crystal Reports gives you an opportunity to select another database to add to the Cross-Tab. If you need to use several different databases, you can continue adding the databases you need. In this example, the CRAZE database is enough.

7. Click Done.

8. Click the Tables button at the bottom of the dialog box.

The Choose Tables To Use In Visual Linking dialog box appears, as shown in Figure 11-17.

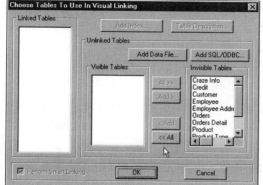

Figure 11-17:
The Choose
Tables To
Use In
Visual
Linking
dialog box.

9. **Click the All button.**

10. **Click OK.**

The field links are represented graphically in the dialog box.

11. **Click the Next button, unless you want to add or delete links at this point.**

See Chapter 13 for more information on linking.

After clicking Next, the Create Report Expert dialog box appears with the Cross-Tab tab selected. The layout of this dialog box is slightly different from the Cross-Tab dialog box you see when you create a Cross-Tab from inside a report. But it works exactly the same way. Figure 11-18 reveals the new arrangement.

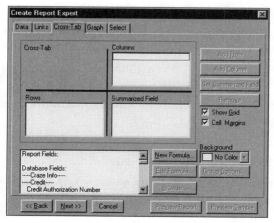

Figure 11-18:
The Create
Report
Expert
dialog box,
Cross-Tab
tab
selected.

12. Insert the rows, columns, and summary operations you want.

In Figure 11-19, the same fields that were used in the Cross-Tab that you inserted into a report are selected.

Insert the following fields:

- Supplier Name from the Supplier table as Row
- Region and then City as Columns (both from the Customer table)
- Quantity from Orders Detail as Summarized Field

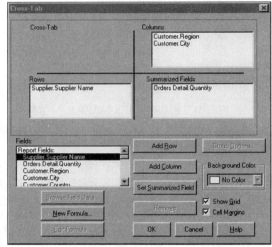

Figure 11-19:
The Create
Report
Expert
dialog box
filled with
fields.

13. Click the Select tab.

Notice I skipped the graphing tab or step. When working with experts, you can miss steps if you don't want to use the functionality.

Here I build our record selection using the Select Expert to include only records if the customer is Canadian.

14. In the Report Fields box, scroll down and highlight the Country field in the Customer table.

15. Click Add.

16. In the second drop-down box, select Equal to.

17. In the third drop-down box, drop down and select Canada (see Figure 11-20).

18. Click Preview Report.

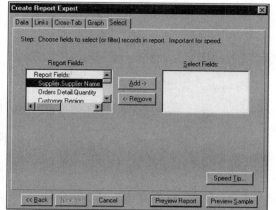

The Cross-Tab is shown, as in Figure 11-21. Notice that you may want to adjust your record selection to eliminate the blank row.

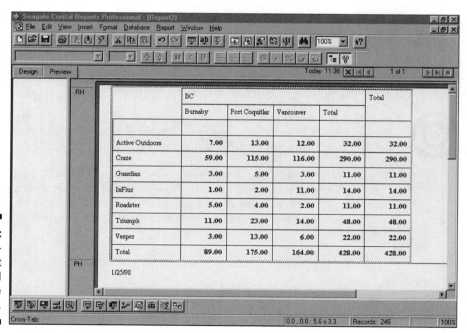

Figure 11-21:
A Cross-
Tab object
created
using the
Expert.

Preview Report versus Preview Sample

What's the difference between Preview Report and Preview Sample in the Expert? Preview Report generates the report including all data that meets your record selection. Preview Sample allows you to tell Crystal how much data to include in the report. Do you want to show 100 records, 500 records, or 1,000 records?

Preview Sample is great to use when you are creating a report that will include tons of data. Maybe it's a quarterly transaction report of all orders and easily contains 100,000 records. You can speed up the report design process by using Preview Sample and designing the report against a smaller number of records.

If you want to use this feature, click Preview Sample. The Preview Sample dialog box is displayed.

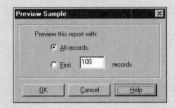

If you want to preview the report with all records, press OK. If you want to limit the number of records, click the First 100 records radio button, enter the sample number you want, and click OK.

After you have finished designing the report and want to show all records, simply click the Refresh Report Data button on the toolbar or choose Report⇨Refresh Report Data.

At this point if you want to modify the Cross-Tab, you can return to the Report Expert to make any changes. Simply click on the Report Expert Button, or choose Report⇨Report Expert.

A Cross-Tab is one of the more obscure aspects of Crystal Reports but extremely useful when you identify the kind of information you want to compare with other information in a report. Remember it and what it can do, and you'll wow and amaze co-workers, friends, and bosses alike.

Chapter 12

Creating a Summary Report

● ●

In This Chapter

▶ Creating a summary report

▶ Suppressing data

● ●

After you complete a report, you sometimes want to condense the report information. For example, if you have hundreds of records in the Details section, the individual records may not be as important as the summary operations that you have created — but maybe someone else wants to delve in and see them. No need to create two reports; all you need to do is use drill-down on the summary information to get the details. So, in this chapter, I show you the best ways to present the report in a summarized fashion.

Creating a Summary Report

You cannot create a summary report without first having a, for lack of a better word, full report that includes records in the Details section and, this is important, a Group and a Summary field.

You can consider a *summary report* to be the opposite of the drill-down, in which you double-click a summary operation to see the underlying individual records.

To create a summary report:

1. Open the report you want to modify.

Make sure that the report has at least one group already created. If not, you must create one, as described in Chapters 2 and 5. Figure 12-1 shows a sample report.

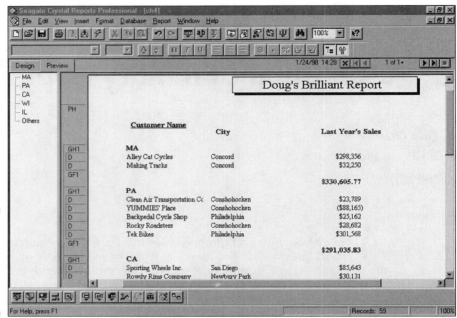

Figure 12-1:
A sample report with a Group and a Summary field.

2. **Click the Design Tab.**

   Open the Section Expert in one of the following three ways:

   - Click the Section Expert button.

   - Choose Format➪Section.

   - Move the mouse pointer to the left margin, right-click to open the shortcut menu, and then choose Format Section. The Section Expert dialog box appears as shown in Figure 12-2.

   If you have read Chapter 9 on formatting sections, you have some familiarity with the options in this dialog box.

3. **Click the Details section, which is listed in the left side of the dialog box.**

   The options listed on the right side of the dialog box, on the Common tab, pertain to the particular section that is selected on the left. Having already selected Details, the next step is to choose the option.

4. **Click the option listed as** Hide (Drill-Down OK).

5. **Click OK.**

6. **Click the Preview Tab to see the result of choosing this option, as shown in Figure 12-3.**

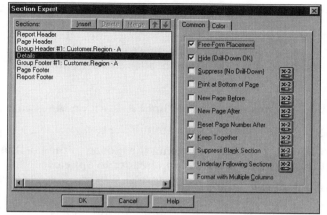

Figure 12-2:
The Section
Expert
dialog box.

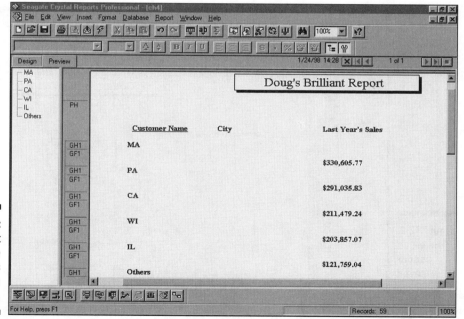

Figure 12-3:
A report
with the
Details
section
hidden.

The report has only two reappearing entries, the group name, which in this example is the name of the state (region in Crystal Reports jargon) and the summary fields for each group. The first thing I noticed was that identifying the correct group name with its respective total may be difficult. One solution would be to move the group header closer to the totals. To do so, follow these steps:

1. **Click the left mouse button and hold it down on the group header.**

   When you do so, a box appears around the text.

2. **Move the group header by moving the mouse to the position in the report where you want the group header to appear.**

3. **Release the mouse button.**

Figure 12-4 shows the report with the group header moved.

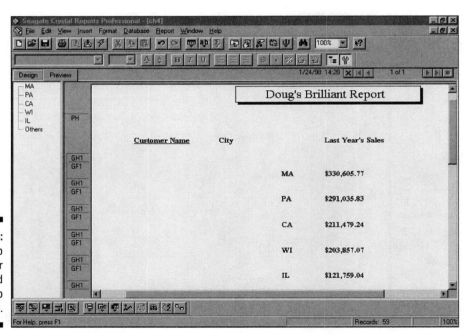

Figure 12-4:
The group header moved closer to the totals.

To Drill or Not to Drill, That Is the Question

Forgive the bad allusion to Shakespeare, but I cannot help but show off my liberal arts education. When you opened the Section Expert dialog box, you had two options regarding the way Crystal Reports should format the section. In the example above, the option chosen was Hide, and the rest of the option read, Drill-Down OK. That means that anyone looking at the summary report can double-click on the summary number and get the underlying records to display in a new Preview window. Try this trick yourself.

Double-click a total in your report. The new Preview window appears as in Figure 12-5. With the Summary set to Hide, by allowing drill-down, you can see the underlying records as you wish.

Figure 12-5: Double-click a summary and the drill-down tab appears.

If you do not want anyone to see the underlying records, you can select the Suppress (No Drill-Down) option in the Section Expert dialog box. An example where this option comes in handy may be a report with payroll, in which each record lists the salary of employees. Other people may need the summary data but not the individual record data. With this option, you can hide the information and make it somewhat inaccessible.

The Suppress option overrides the Hide option, so if you mistakenly have them both set to on, the Suppress option is in charge.

Figure 12-6 shows an example of what happens when you try to drill down with suppression set to on.

Figure 12-6:
An
attempted
drill-down
on a report
summary
with the
Suppress
option on.

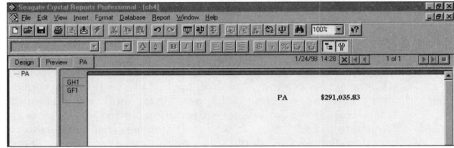

Crystal Reports gives you the same summary information, albeit in a new tab.

As you move the mouse pointer over the various components in a previewed report, you may see the mouse pointer transformed into a magnifying glass. The magnifying glass is your clue that the object underneath the pointer can be drilled down. By the way, the drill-down feature works on graphs, but it is not available in the run-time version of reports. Drill-down is only available in the Designer itself; it is not currently available as a run-time feature.

If the drill-down mouse pointer is active, only the data in drill-down is exported or printed.

Chapter 13
Linking to Other Databases

In This Chapter

▶ Linking concepts
▶ Working with links
▶ Using SQL Joins

*I*n the esoteric world of database design, one table does not a database make. (*Esoteric*, in this usage, means understood by a chosen few, which now includes you!) While you can make a database with one table, most databases are made from collections of tables and these tables have links between them. The links are made from fields in one table that are similar, perhaps even identical, to fields in another table. In this chapter I will explore the ins and outs of linking database tables and files.

Linking Concepts

The simple answer is that if you don't link, your reports won't work. But much more is involved in linking than that simple answer implies. Following is an example. In Tables 13-1 and 13-2, you have an order table and a customer table.

Table 13-1	Order Table	
Order #	**Customer #**	**Product**
055	467	Pupas
056	258	Butterflies
057	333	Pupas
058	258	Caterpillars
059	467	Moths

Table 13-2	Customer Table	
Customer #	*Address*	*City*
258	5050 Parkland Road	Indianapolis
333	657 Maple Plain	Pittsburgh
467	95443 High Hills Plaza	Tucson

When customer number 258 places an order, you could enter all the information about 258 in the order table. You could take an order, complete the customer's address, add the phone number, and so on. But by using links, you save yourself unnecessary steps by simply inserting the customer number. The database then goes to the customer table, finds the matching number 258, and then finds the address for you. You enter 258, and the database finds 5050 Parkland Road. By using this technique you only type the address one time, not on every order, every invoice, or every letter.

Normalizing a database

The process of making a database as efficient as possible, by not storing redundant data, is called *normalizing* a database. A well-designed database is normal. (Our only hope is that we can all be somewhat normal.)

Having a normalized database means that the person who enters certain types of data enters that type only one time, in one table. When that data is needed in conjunction with other information, the database goes out and looks it up. This is where the links come in.

The two preceding tables, the Customer table and the Order table, are linked by a common field. The common field is the customer number. The linking field usually has the same kind of data in it, in this case a number. The data is usually the same length, in this case three digits. The linking field usually is a primary key in a table.

Keying primarily

A *primary key* is a field in a database that serves as a unique identifier for each record. You have a primary key. If someone wants to find information about you, they would look up your social security number. This is a unique number for each individual. (Hopefully, no two people have the same social security number.) In the preceding examples, you would look up a customer based on the customer number. The customer number is the primary key for the customer table.

Usually a primary key has an index or is an indexed field. That means that a database, by using a number of techniques, can look up a record very quickly on an indexed field. Using primary keys to link tables with indexed fields makes your database fast and efficient.

How does an index work? The name gives the secret away. Just as an index in a book makes looking up specific information easier for you, a database index makes looking up data faster and easier. An index may organize the same data in several different ways, allowing you to easily find matches among hundreds of records.

Some of the databases on which you will do reports automatically index a primary key. Other databases do not have indexing capabilities. If you have the ability, make sure that each database table has an index. Doing so not only improves the performance of your database, but also improves the speed with which you are able to generate reports.

The answer to the question posed earlier, "Why Link?" is that links make data in one table accessible to data in another table. Without linking the customer number from the Order table to the customer number in the Customer table, you cannot find the customer address. Subsequently, when you are creating a report, you cannot print the customer address on the report if the tables are not linked via the customer number. When you design a database, you create the links between fields so that you can easily find the the that data you are looking for.

Not only does linking make finding the data you want easier, but it is also crucial to finding the correct data. Suppose that you want to find all the orders for a single customer, in this case customer number 258. The number 258 is the lowest customer number on the table, so you figure you can get all the beginning orders and those will be the orders for customer 258. Does that work? No. That method doesn't work because the orders are listed in the order of order number. Linking matches the order to the correct customer number.

You *query* (ask) the database to find all the orders for customer number 258. The computer goes to the order table and looks at order number 055. The computer asks if that is an order number for 258. The answer is no, so that order is not included in the answer to your query. The computer moves on to the next record. Is order number 056 an order for customer 258? Yes. That record is included in the answer. The computer matches the orders to customer number 258. Those orders are 056 and 058. Even though the orders are not in any sequence related to customer number, the computer finds the matching records to your request by using the links between the tables.

What Crystal Reports calls links between tables may be called other names. Some of the other names you might hear are *keys,* including primary keys and foreign keys, or *pointers.*

Working with Links

View the links already established in a report in the CRAZE database. (The CRAZE database is available in Crystal Reports 5.0 Professional.)

1. Begin by opening a report.

2. Click the <u>O</u>pen button on the toolbar.

The Open dialog box displays.

3. Double-click the reports folder.

4. Double-click the craze folder.

5. Double-click the adconds **file, or click on the** adconds **file until highlighted, and then click the Open button.**

The Design window of the report opens.

6. Click the Link Expert button on the Supplementary toolbar, or choose Database➪Visual Linking Expert.

The Visual Linking Expert dialog box opens.

In the Visual Linking Expert dialog box, you see the underlying tables from which this report collects its data. The tables display in the dialog box with the indexed fields highlighted by a colored symbol next to the field name and the links drawn between the tables. See Figure 13-1.

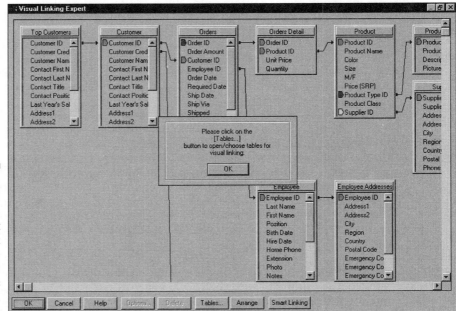

Figure 13-1:
The Visual Linking Expert dialog box with Craze Tables and Links Displayed.

The tables from the database used for this report display in the Visual Linking Expert dialog box. They include the Top Customers, Customer, Orders, Orders Detail, and Employee table.

Arrows indicate the links in the tables. For example, you can see that the Customer ID field in the Top Customers table is linked to the Customer ID field in the Customer table, which is linked to the Customer ID field in the Orders table. The Order ID field in the Orders table is linked to the Order ID field in the Orders Detail table. By using these links, you can navigate through the tables to collect and match information from any of the linked tables.

A colored arrow head with a number sign inside it indicates that the field is part of more than one index.

Use the scroll bars at the bottom and side of the Visual Linking Expert Dialog box to view all of the tables. Move the bottom scroll bar all the way to the right to see the tables shown in Figure 13-2. This view shows more of the tables used in this same Visual Linking Expert dialog box.

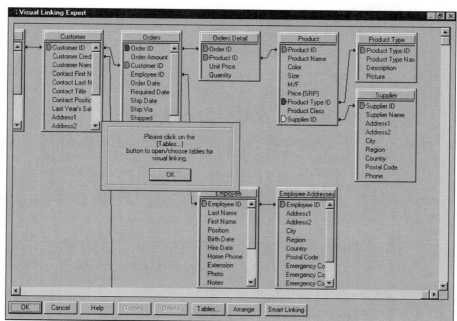

Figure 13-2:
The Visual
Linking
Expert
dialog box
scrolled to
the right.

From this group of tables you can see that the Product table has three links. One comes from the Orders Detail table, connecting Product ID to Product ID. The Product Type ID fields are connected in the Product table and the Product Type table. The third link is the Supplier ID field to the Supplier ID field in the Supplier table.

You probably have noticed a pattern here: All of the linked fields have identical names. They just appear in different tables. If you take a closer look, you will see that the linked fields have the same characteristics, too. The data length is the same, as is the data type. This is why smart linking works!

Moving a table

The little black arrows show you precisely where the links appear. You can click on any table and drag it to a different position. When you do, the links remain to connect the linked fields.

1. **Click the title bar of a table. Hold the mouse button down.**

2. **Drag the table to a new location in the Visual Linking Expert Dialog box.**

3. **Release the mouse button.**

   The table displays in the new location with the link still attached.

Looking at field properties

Looking at the Product table in Figure 13-2, notice that it has three fields linked to other tables. Each field that is linked to or from has an arrow head pointing to or from it. Each arrowhead may be a different color. In the Visual Linking Expert dialog box, you can look at the properties of the indexed fields with the arrowheads. Doing so helps you learn how the fields are connected.

1. **Right-click the Product ID field in the Product table.**

   The field menu displays. From this menu, you can browse the field to see what data is in the field, look at the table description, or cancel the menu.

2. **Click the Description option.**

   The Table Description dialog box opens as you see in Figure 13-3.

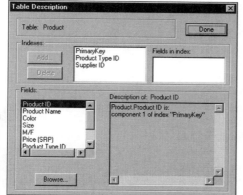

Figure 13-3:
The Table
Description
dialog box.

At the top of the Table Description Dialog box is the name of the table, in this example, Product. Below that, the indexed fields are listed. At the bottom left, all the fields in the table are listed. You can use the scroll buttons to move up and down to see all the fields. You can even add new indexes (files) if you want.

If you click on any of the indexed fields in the list of fields, the Description box on the right displays a description of that field. That description is generated by Crystal Reports. When you select an indexed field, the Description box shows index information.

Browsing through the fields

As with other boxes in Crystal Reports, if you click a field in the Fields list (from the Table Description dialog box) and then click the Browse button, the actual data in the field displays in a separate dialog box. Something important for linking also displays. This important information includes a field definition with the type of data and the size of the field.

1. **With the Table Description dialog box open, click the Product Name field to highlight it.**

2. **Click the Browse button.**

   The Product Name Dialog box opens as shown in Figure 13-4.

Figure 13-4:
The
Product
Name
browsing
dialog box.

Important information displays in this box. At the top, you can see the Type of data in this field. In this example, the data type is a string. Below that you see the length of the string. In this example, the product name is no more than 50 characters. A string is alphanumeric characters up to 50 characters. For example, a string could include "1888 Production Blvd." While this address includes numbers, the database does not treat it as a number. Instead it is treated as part of the address.

This information is very useful if you want to create links between tables. You can link between two fields where the string is 50 characters in both fields and they contain identical information and one field has an index. In some circumstances you may be able to link when one field has a string of 20 characters and another has a string of 50 characters. (This may occur when you want to link an address field from one database where it is defined as 20 characters with the address field from a different database that allows 50 characters.)

You are not able to link numeric data with string data. Numeric data is data that could be used in some mathematical calculation, for example a date field, a value, a measurement, or currency. String data, while it may include numbers, is not used as part of a mathematical calculation.

Crystal Reports can link two records based on a partial match of a string of data. In Crystal Reports terms, this feature is called a *partial link*. To turn this option on, open the Link Options dialog box. Click the check box to allow partial text matches. Partial linking only works when the string in the lookup table is longer than the string in the primary table.

Closing the Table Description dialog box

When you are finished perusing the Table Description dialog box, simply click on the Done button. After clicking the Done button, you are ready to start creating your report.

Looking at the links

The arrowheads show you the indexed fields. The black lines between tables show you the link between tables. Click a link line to select it. The line changes color to show that it is selected.

When you select a link and the link changes colors, the text in the linked tables changes colors, too. In this way, the fields from the linked tables are highlighted.

When you link tables with Crystal Reports, you need to know a few important concepts. One concept is that you have a primary table and a lookup table. The *primary table* has a link to a field in the *lookup table*. Using that link, a query of the primary table goes to the matching record in the lookup table to find the correct data. The primary table is the table you link *from*. The lookup table is the table you link *to*.

In the Visual Linking Expert dialog box you have on the screen, the Product table is a *primary* table. From this table you would link to the Product Type table via the Product Type ID field. The Product Type table is the *lookup* table.

Conversely, the Orders Detail table may be the primary table from which you link to the Product table via the Product ID field. In this example, the Orders Detail table is the *primary* table and the Product table is the *lookup* table. Orders Detail is also a lookup table to Orders.

Exploring the Visual Linking Expert buttons

The buttons along the bottom of the Visual Linking Expert dialog box allow you to initiate different activities. Table 13-3 reviews the descriptions of these buttons. You use these buttons to complete a report.

Table 13-3	**Buttons on the Visual Linking Expert Dialog Box**
Button	*What It Does*
OK	Click this button when you have all your links set up the way you want and you are ready to create a report.
Cancel	Cancels your activity in the Visual Linking Expert dialog box.
Help	Accesses the context sensitive Help. When you press this button Help displays on the Visual Linking Dialog box.

(continued)

Table 13-3 *(continued)*

Button	What It Does
Options	Specifies options for the link. Select a link line and click Options. The Link Options dialog box displays. From here you can choose what type of index you want to use, and you can choose other options about the selected link.
Delete	Select a link line and click this button to delete the link.
Tables	Click this button to open the Table To Use In Visual Linking dialog box. From this box you can choose the tables you want to link in order to create your report.
Arrange	Click this button to arrange all the tables in the Visual Linking dialog box. Use this feature to arrange tables after you have added many tables and want them automatically arranged.
Smart Linking	When you have added several tables to your Visual Linking dialog box, click this button to create logical links between those tables. Crystal Reports does so automatically. If Crystal Reports can't create links, a message displays telling you that links are not possible.

Using link options

When you link two fields from two tables, they may have more than one index on the link. Crystal Reports selects one of the indexes available to use for the link. If you want to adjust the index used for the link, open the Link Options dialog box. You may want to change the index to improve the report performance or to make indexes consistent for one report. To open the Link Options dialog box, choose one of these methods:

- ✔ Click the link line and click the Options button.
- ✔ Right-click a link line. When the menu displays, choose the Options menu option.
- ✔ Double-click the link line.

The Link Options dialog box displays as shown in Figure 13-5.

At the top of the Link Options dialog box is a description of the link. It gives you the direction of the link by telling you the table the link travels from and the table the link travels to.

The middle section tells you the index in use. In the dialog box, you see that the primary key is the index in use. If you click the drop down box, you will see any other options. If you select the option no specific index, Crystal

Reports will select an index for you at the time you display the report to the Preview Window. To the right of the index in use information is a list of the fields in the index.

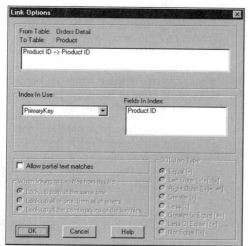

Figure 13-5: The Link Options dialog box.

Below the middle section is a text box that lets you make partial text matches. This feature can be very useful when you are going to try to link one field with 50 characters and another field with 20 characters, but with similar data in the fields. Click this box to allow a match on the partial text in the fields, instead of an exact match of the text. An example of using the partial text match might be when you have an address field from one database, defined as 20 characters, and an address field from a different database, defined as 50 characters. Allowing a partial text match will allow you to match "10789 Rancho Pen. Bv" with "10789 Rancho Penasquitos Boulevard".

Note: Partial text match only works when the string in the lookup table is longer than the string in the primary table.

At the bottom left of the Link Options dialog box are three options that allow you to determine how you want to link two records from these tables. Click the radio buttons (the circular icons next to the text — they look like old-fashioned radio buttons) for these options to choose the one you want. Table 13-4 lists the three options and a brief description of how they work. These are available only on Data files (non-SQL data sources).

Table 13-4	Options for Linking Records
Look Up Option	*Description*
Look up both at the same time	Check this option to look up one record in the primary table (Table A) and a matching record in the lookup table (Table B). Crystal Reports looks for the next matching record in one lookup table and then for the next matching record in the next lookup table (Table C) until it finds all the matching records. Crystal Reports repeats this process for every record in the primary table (Table A).
Look up all of one, then all of the others	This option directs Crystal Reports to look up each record in the primary table (Table A) and then all the matching records in the lookup table (Table B). After all the matching records are found in Table B, Crystal Reports looks for all the matching records in the second lookup table (Table C). Crystal Reports goes back to the primary table and repeats this with each record in the primary table. In other words, it links from Table A to Table B first, then Table A to Table C next.
Look up all combinations of the two files	For each record in the primary table (Table A), this option looks for a matching record in the lookup table (Table B), after which it finds all the matching records in the next lookup table (Table C). After it finds all the matching records in Table C, Crystal Reports repeats the process with the next record in the first lookup table (Table B). After all the matches are found for that record in the first lookup table (Table B), the process returns to the next record in the primary table (Table A).

At the bottom-right of the Link Options Dialog box are the SQL join options. I address these a little later in this chapter under the section "Using SQL Joins."

Creating a new report

When you open Crystal Reports, you get a screen that asks if you want to create a new report or open a report already created. In the example that follows, a new report is created.

1. **Choose to create a new report.**

   Do so in either of the following ways: Click the New Report button on the opening screen or click the New button on the toolbar.

   The Report Gallery Dialog box opens.

2. **Click the Custom button on the Report Gallery dialog box.**

3. **Choose the Data File option by clicking the Data File button.**

   The Choose Data File Dialog box opens.

   From the Choose Data File dialog box, you are going to navigate through the file to choose a database to use for the source data.

4. **Choose the database you want by clicking it and then clicking OK.**

   When you select a database, the Visual Linking Expert dialog box displays with all the tables in the selected database. You can see this dialog box in Figure 13-6.

In this example, you will see the Nursing Complications database. This database has one table with medical diagnoses. Each diagnosis has a number and a description. Another table lists nursing complications. Each nursing complication has a number and a description. Another table has the medical procedure number, the same number as in the table with medical diagnoses, associated with the name of the medical specialist you would call for this procedure.

Because more than one nursing complication can occur with each medical procedure, a lookup table is provided. This table matches each medical procedure with several of the nursing complications that could occur with that procedure. For example, if a person had surgery, one complication could be post-surgical infection, another complication could be post-surgical pain.

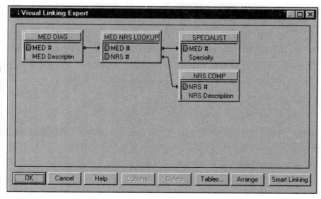

Figure 13-6:
Visual
Linking
Expert
dialog box
with four
tables.

For all the database aficionados out there this is an example of a one to many relationship, therefore a lookup table in a normalized database is required. The report you can create with this set of data is one where you list the medical procedure and then list the nursing complications associated with that procedure.

Creating links

Suppose that you added a table to this Visual Linking Expert dialog box that wasn't linked. You could create a link to the new table in two ways. One way is to manually draw a link; the second way is to press the Smart Linking button.

With the same Visual Linking Expert dialog box open, delete all the links and then recreate them.

1. **Click a link between two tables so the link changes color.**

2. **Click the delete button at the bottom of the Visual Linking Expert dialog box.**

   Continue until all links are deleted.

3. **For this example, move the mouse pointer to the MED DIAG table and click the Med # field. Hold the mouse button down.**

4. **Drag the mouse pointer to the Med # field in the Med Nrs Lookup table.**

   A linking icon appears that looks like a zigzagged line with an arrow on one end.

5. **Release the mouse button.**

   A link is created between the Med # fields in the two tables.

6. **Click the Smart Linking button at the bottom of the Visual Linking Expert dialog box.**

   All the fields that one would expect to link now have a link between them.

Deleting a linked table

For this example, you can delete the Specialist table. The Specialist table is not necessary for the report.

While in the Visual Linking Expert, follow these steps to first delete a link and then a table:

1. **Click the link between the MED NRS Lookup table and the Specialist table.**

2. **Click the Delete button at the bottom of the Visual Linking Expert dialog box.**

   Figure 13-7 shows that the link between the two boxes has been deleted.

Figure 13-7:
The Link
between
tables
removed.

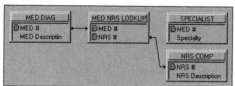

3. **Click the Tables button at the bottom of the Visual Linking Expert dialog box.**

   The Choose Tables To Use In Visual Linking dialog box displays. In this dialog box, the Linked Tables are listed on the left. The unlinked tables are listed on the right. The Specialist table is now an unlinked table located in the Visible Tables box. To remove the table, move it to the Invisible Tables box.

4. **Click Specialist in the Visible Tables box.**

   Specialist is highlighted.

5. **Click the Add> button.**

   Doing so moves Specialist from the Visible Tables box to the Invisible Tables box.

6. **Click OK.**

   The Choose Tables To Use In Visual Linking Expert dialog box closes. As you can see in Figure 13-8, the Specialist table is no longer visible.

If you want to delete tables and links at the same time, follow these easy steps.

1. **Choose Report⇨Remove from Report.**

2. **Select the table you want to remove from the report.**

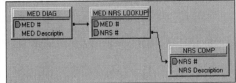

Figure 13-8:
Poof! The
Specialist
table is
gone.

3. Click the Remove button.

4. Repeat Steps 2 and 3 for each table you want to remove.

The preceding steps will automatically remove any links that you had.

Adding tables in the Visual Linking Expert dialog box

You can add tables from the Visual Linking Expert dialog box. In the opposite way you made a visible table invisible, you make an invisible table visible.

1. Click the Tables button in the Visual Linking Expert dialog box.

2. Click the name of the tables in the Invisible section until they highlight.

3. Click the Add button.

Doing so moves the selected table from the invisible side to the visible side.

After the table is visible, you can either choose to smart link the table, or you can draw a link by clicking the field in the new table and dragging to the field with which you want to link it.

Creating the report

Now that you have selected all the tables you want for your report and removed any you didn't, click OK in the Visual Linking Expert dialog box.

Return to the Design window for your new report. The Insert Fields dialog box is open, ready for you to select the fields you want and insert them into the Design window. The Insert Fields dialog box can be seen in Figure 13-9.

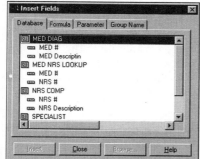

Figure 13-9:
The Insert
Fields
dialog box.

Before you click the Insert Fields button, you must remove the table from
the report or it will still be visible in the Insert Fields dialog box. You can
accomplish this task by choosing Database➪Remove from report.

Because the three tables are linked in the Visual Linking Expert dialog box,
you are able to create a report with fields from any of the three tables. With
these three tables, you can create a report that lists the Medical Procedure
number and the procedure description. After each procedure, the report will
list the nursing complications associated with that medical procedure.

At your nursing station, you can hand the head nurse a report for each
patient procedure. The report lets the nurse know that this patient has had
this procedure. You now have a list of the most likely complications you will
see following this procedure. The nurses know what to look for in any
patient under their care.

Using SQL Joins

The people who make the Crystal Reports software say that 60 percent of
their customers use SQL databases, so this information is important. You
don't have to be an expert in SQL to use SQL joins. Some of this information
is handy reference material if you are making an SQL connection.

SQL is the underlying language used in many databases. *SQL* stands for
Structured Query Language. The language is fairly easy to learn but is
beyond the scope of this book. You may purchase many books written on
the SQL language. In addition, many colleges and technical schools offer
classes in the subject. If you are familiar with working with databases in
Access, you know you can create a query and then view the SQL language
written to produce that query.

Crystal Reports allows you to link SQL tables to create reports. Crystal Reports also allows you to specify the kind of join you want to use to link SQL tables. The type of join you specify determines in what order the lookup is made between tables. SQL join types are listed in the Link Option dialog box. In order to use these join types, you must add a table via ODBC. ODBC is the acronym for Open Database Connectivity. This is the Microsoft standard for connecting client-server systems.

Adding tables via ODBC

You add tables via ODBC much the same as you would add any tables.

1. **Click the Tables button on the Visual Linking Expert dialog box.**

   The Choose Tables To Use In Visual Linking dialog box displays.

2. **Click the Add SQL/ODBC button on the right side of the Choose Tables To Use In Visual Linking dialog box.**

   The Log On Server dialog box opens as shown in Figure 13-10.

From Log On Server dialog box you can select the ODBC Server Type you want to use to select a database table, or you can select different database files. Here are some options:

✔ Click the Database Files button to open files from any other database file on your system or network. These will be .mdb files.

✔ Click the ODBC Server Type for the database to which you are connecting and then click OK.

Crystal Reports and SQL

SQL is primarily a query language, but also has capabilities for creating, managing, and organizing tables in a database. Usually used in a client/server application, SQL sends statements to an SQL database server. The statements ask (or query) the database to return certain information. The SQL database server receives the SQL request for information, analyzes the request, finds the requested information, and then returns that data to the source of the query statement.

Crystal Reports provides you a graphical user interface (GUI, pronounced gooey) with which to query an SQL database. So Crystal Reports creates the actual SQL statement with the information that you provide in the various dialog boxes. With Crystal Reports, you don't have to be a programmer to get results. Crystal Reports is one of many SQL-compliant application products that use SQL when querying a database.

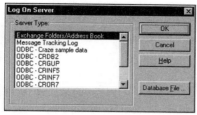

Figure 13-10:
The Log On
Server
dialog box.

When you connect to an ODBC server, you will need to know which library files to use. Table 13-5 shows the Database name in the left column with the ODBC data source in the right column. Use this table to guide you when deciding which library file to use in your ODBC connection.

Table 13-5	ODBC Drivers
Database	*ODBC Data Source*
IBM DB2/2	CRDB2
Microsoft SQL Server 6.*x*	CRSS
Oracle 7	CRORA7
Informix 7	CRINF7
SQLBase	CRGUP
SYBASE SYSTEM 10/11	CRSYB

Note: Check with your ODBC administrator if you are connecting to a different database. Other databases are supported by other drivers.

If you are connecting to a database by using ODBC, Crystal Reports uses ODBC syntax in the SQL statement. If you are connecting to an SQL database without using ODBC, Crystal Reports uses a syntax recognized by the SQL database.

Using SQL join types

Delving into the nitty-gritty of SQL is beyond this book. However, Table 13-6 can be used as a guide to help you choose the SQL join type you want to use. If you are experienced with SQL, this guide will make sense. If you are not experienced with SQL, find your nearest SQL guru and bring this guide along to help you make use of the various SQL join types.

The symbol used for the SQL join type is included in the SQL Where clause.

Table 13-6		Defining the SQL Join Types
SQL Join Type	**Symbol**	**Description**
Equal join	=	Includes all records where the linked field value is an exact match
Left outer join	*=	Includes all records where the linked field value is an exact match, plus a row for every record in the primary table whose linked field has no match in the lookup table
Right outer join	=*	Includes all records where the linked field value is an exact match, plus a row for every record in the lookup table whose linked field has no match in the primary table
Greater join	>	Includes all records where the linked field value in the primary table is greater than the linked field value in the lookup table
Less join	<	Includes all records where the linked field value from the primary table is less than the linked field value in the lookup table
Greater or Equal join	>=	Includes all records where the linked field value from the primary table is greater than or equal to the linked field value in the lookup table
Less or Equal join	<=	Includes all records where the linked field value from the primary table is less than or to the linked field value in the lookup table
Not Equal join	!=	Includes all records where the linked field from the primary table is not equal to the linked field value in the lookup table

If you are connecting to an Oracle database, the syntax is different for a left and right outer join. For a left outer join, use =(+). For a right outer join, use (+)=. If you are connecting to an Access database, the syntax is different for a left and right outer join. In Access you use the actual words, Left Outer Join, or Right Outer Join. Place this syntax in the SQL *From* clause instead of the SQL *Where* clause.

Using the equal join

Use this option when you want to find all matching instances in one table with another table. For example, in a table that lists the ID number of a product that was ordered, you want to find every matching product name that goes with that ID number. Doing so helps you find any errors in data entry. If you have two products that have the same ID number, you know you have to change the number for one of the products.

At the bicycle shop you can use the equal join to find every product ID and the product name that goes with it. You may find a helmet with two different ID numbers. This could lead to confusion in ordering or selling this product. Using the equal join helps you find these instances.

Using a left outer join

Using the same idea as in the preceding section, using a left outer join gives you a list of the ID number of a product that was ordered and every matching product name. Plus, this join would list all the ID numbers where no product name was listed. Your data-processing folks would have to return to the database to make sure that each product ID had an associated product name.

You may find several ID numbers with no product names at the bicycle shop. You would need to look through your hard copies or a source database to find the products that go with the ID number. This helps you keep your inventory straight by making sure every number has an associated product.

Using a right outer join

Using a right outer join gives you a list of the ID number of a product that was ordered and every matching product name. Plus it would list all the product names that have no ID number. How can your customer order the product if the product has no number? You can easily correct this omission by going back and adding a product ID number for each product.

Using a greater join or greater or equal join

Suppose that you sell bicycles, as exemplified in the CRAZE database. You also sell many accessories for bicycles. You want to make sure that no accessory to a bicycle costs more than the bicycle itself. The Greater than join helps you verify that information. Determine the cost of the most expensive bicycle. By using a greater than join, you can generate a list of all accessories where the cost was *greater than* the cost of that bicycle. You would enter in a single value. With this type of join, every record that is greater than that value is listed. If your pricing strategy works according to plan, you will have no accessories listed that cost more than the price of the most expensive bicycle.

Using a greater or equal join would result in a list of accessories that are equal to the cost of the most expensive bicycle or cost more than the most expensive bicycle.

Using a less join or a less or equal join

Using the opposite idea, use a less than join to list all the accessories that cost less than the price of the most expensive bicycle. If your pricing strategy works, all the accessories listed would be listed because they cost less than the bicycle. In this example, using the greater join would be better at answering this query because you would have a much smaller list as a result.

Using a less or equal join would result in a list of accessories that are equal to the cost of the most expensive bicycle or cost less than the most expensive bicycle.

Using a not equal join

The most common use for a not equal join is to compare a table to itself. In your bicycle business you may decide to hold a sale. This sale is "buy one accessory, get the second accessory for half price," Using your Product table, you would run a query to list just the accessories (excluding all bicycles). Call this table the Accessory1 table. You would make a duplicate of the Accessory1 table and call it the Accessory2 table.

Now, use a not equal join to list all the possible combinations of products. Because each accessory table has a distinct name, Crystal Reports considers them to be two separate tables. The not equal join links the accessories by name. In one column, it will list all the accessories from the Accessory1 table. In the next column, it will list all the accessories from the Accessory2 table that are not equal to the accessory listed in column 1. Using the not equal join, you will not get any helmets matched with helmets, you will get helmets matched with gloves or water bottles.

Part VI
Disseminating Reports without a Hitch

The 5th Wave   By Rich Tennant

"It's all here, Warden. Routers, hubs, switches, all pieced together from scraps found in the machine shop. I guess the prospect of using Crystal Reports was just too sweet to pass up."

In this part . . .

Would you rather be rich or famous? No, "both" is not an option in answer to this question. Seagate Crystal Reports has the capability to take your reporting *masterpieces* and share them with the world! Herein lies the ticket to fame. Imagine… your report is distributed to every salesperson in the company. Or, better yet, it's posted to that new Orwellian device known innocently as the World Wide Web. (In numerology, World Wide Web translates to the number 666.) Undoubtedly, the end is near. Better get that report done before Armageddon, or there will be heck to pay. Your report is spreading everywhere at the speed of light! Supplicants are sending you e-mail from all over the world acknowledging your greatness. This is your moment in time! *Music up, lights fade to a single spotlight on a lone worker at a computer terminal. On the desk, a copy of the IDG Books catalog and* Crystal Reports 6 For Dummies. *The look on the face of the worker resembles Caesar crossing the Rubicon. . . .*

Chapter 14

Distributing Reports

*I*n this chapter, I show you how to share your reports with a variety of software programs other than Seagate Crystal Reports. After you have created a magnificent report, you naturally want to share it with the world! Other people can see your handiwork in three general ways:

✔ You can send them a Crystal Reports file, and they can open the file in their copy of Crystal Reports.

✔ You can export the report to specific formats such as Microsoft Word and Microsoft Excel.

✔ You can create a *run-time version* of the report, which allows others to see the report in a Crystal-like environment without having a copy of Crystal Reports on their computer.

Understanding an Export File

All computer programs are composed of files, and computer programs create files. Crystal Reports creates report files. Underlying all files is a common data structure which, with the proper settings, will be understood by other programs. So, an *export file* is simply a Crystal Reports file that has been translated into a structure that other programs can read and interpret. Some programs can interpret all of the aspects of Crystal Reports files, and others cannot.

When you export a report file you can retain some or all of the fancy formatting you have created, depending on the program to which you are exporting the report file.

Exporting Reports

Exporting a report file requires similar steps each time. You always select the *file format* (the data structure) into which you want to export the report file, and then you choose the physical destination for the translated report.

Here are the steps to follow every time you export a report:

1. **Open the report you wish to export in Crystal Reports.**
2. **Click the Export button on the toolbar.**
3. **Choose the format for exporting the report.**
4. **Choose the destination for the report.**
5. **Click the OK button.**

   Crystal Reports exports your report to the specified location in the specified format.

Choosing a file format

Each time you export a report file you must specify a report format. Table 14-1 lists some of the export formats that you can use. The table gives you information on deciding which file format to choose. The main thing that you have to know for this process to work is what type of software the other person has.

Table 14-1	Export Formats	
Software Application	*Format*	*Who Can Read the File*
Crystal Reports	.RPT	Those who have Crystal Reports or Crystal Info.
Word Processing	.DOC, .RTF	Those who have a word-processing program available. Word for Windows reads the .DOC files. The Rich Text Format (.RTF) is used by almost all word-processing programs.
Spreadsheets	.XLS, .WKS	Those who have spreadsheet programs available. Excel reads the .XLS files. Lotus reads the .WKS files.

Software Application	Format	Who Can Read the File
Lotus Notes	Any format	Those who have access to Lotus Notes.
Exchange	Any format	Those who have access to Microsoft Exchange.
ODBC	data	Those who have access to an ODBC data source set up through an ODBC Administrator.
HTML	HTML	Those who have Netscape, Internet Explorer, or other Web browsers.

For example, if all the employees in your office use Crystal Reports and have Crystal Reports on their systems, export the file in the Crystal Reports format. This format is sometimes called the *native format* (referring to the product you are using to distribute the report, not aborigines).

If your office uses Microsoft Exchange and all your co-workers have Microsoft Office (but they don't all have Crystal Reports), export the report in one of the Microsoft formats. Choose either Excel (.XLS) or Word (.DOC).

Choosing the report destination

The next decision you have to make is choosing the destination of the report you are exporting. Table 14-2 lists the export destination options and where the report will go if you select that option.

Table 14-2	Export Destination Options
Export Destination	*Destination Description*
Disk file	Saves the report to a disk file. Select this option and a dialog box opens for you to select the destination file. The file can be exported to a hard disk on your system, or a disk in the A (or any other) drive.
Mail Application	Attaches the report to an electronic mail application document. Crystal Reports supports MAPI, the Microsoft Mail format used for either Exchange or Microsoft Mail. Crystal Reports also supports VIM, the format for Lotus cc:Mail.
Exchange Folder	Stores the report in a Microsoft Exchange folder. A dialog box opens from which you select the destination folder.
Lotus Notes Database	Exports the report to a Lotus Notes database. This option displays if you are on a network.

For example, if you are exporting a report file to Excel (.XLS), you select *disk file* as your destination. When the dialog box opens for you to select the destination file, choose the file name you want, such as DOUGRPT, and click OK.

If you work in a company that uses Microsoft Exchange, select Exchange Folder as the export destination. A dialog box opens where you designate which Exchange folder is the destination folder.

Exporting a report with saved data

You can either save a report definition layout, or you can save data with a report. The difference is as follows: When you save a *report definition,* you are saving the sorting, grouping, summaries, and so on with no data. If you save the *report with data,* you save the definition plus all the records that make up the report. The saved data does not include the source tables or the databases from which you selected the individual records.

So, if you are the sales manager for a company, you may want the salespeople to have just the report definition into which they would insert their own records. Or you may decide to give them the reports with the records, so they could only work with the records you select. Either way, this tool is a powerful one for any business.

If you export only the report definition:

- ✔ Your report requires less disk space.
- ✔ The program you use to open the report will need to retrieve data before it prints the report. In other words, the person receiving the definition will have to have access to the database.

If you save data with the report:

- ✔ Your report requires more disk space.
- ✔ The program you use to open the report will not need to retrieve data before it prints the report, as that data is already part of the report.

Note: Along with the preceding options, you need to know that when Crystal Reports saves the data with a report, it compresses the data to take up less disk space. When you open the report, Crystal Reports decompresses the data.

You can change the options in Crystal Reports to save the data with the report or just the report definition.

1. Choose File➪Options.

Figure 14-1 shows the File menu with Options highlighted. Note that the menu is different when no report file is open.

Figure 14-1:
The File menu with Options highlighted.

2. From the File Options dialog box, click the Reporting tab.

Figure 14-2 shows the Reporting tab.

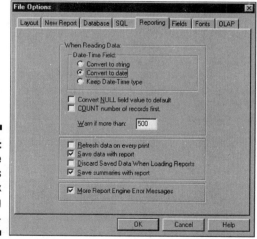

Figure 14-2:
The File Options dialog box Reporting tab.

In the middle of the Reporting tab, you see the option, Save data with closed report. The option is checked, which means that it is turned on and that the data will be saved with the report.

This option is to be turned on by default. If you want to just save the report definition, you have to turn the option off.

3. **Click the Save data with closed report check box.**

   The check is removed. Now Crystal Reports will save only the report definition when you save a report.

4. **With a report file open, open the File menu.**

   The File menu is shown in Figure 14-3.

Figure 14-3:
The File
menu.

From this option you can save a file three ways:

- **Save:** Use this command to save the active report to a disk under its current name. All changes you have made to the report will overwrite the previous version of the report.

- **Save As:** Use this command to save the report to a disk under a new name. This feature is handy when you want to save an original copy separate from the copy to which you make changes. By choosing this option, you now have two files (under different names): the untouched original and the report to which you've made changes.

- **Save Data with Report:** Use this option to save the underlying data that goes with the report. The data that is saved with the report is like a snapshot of how the data looked at the moment you ran the report. You still have to use Save or Save As to create a saved report file.

Opening a saved report

Crystal Reports includes a series of example reports. I'm going to show you how to open one of these reports in order to use it for exporting practice. You must open a report before you can export it. Open a report file to export by following these steps:

1. **Choose <u>F</u>ile⇨<u>O</u>pen (or click the Open button on the toolbar).**

   The Open dialog box displays with the Crystal Reports folder open.

2. **Double-click the Reports folder.**

3. **Double-click the Craze folder.**

4. **Click the file name, gocdir2p.**

   Figure 14-4 shows the highlighted file in the Open dialog box.

5. **Click the Open button.**

   The gocdir2p report file opens.

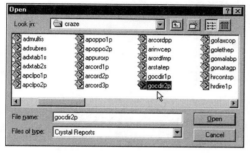

Figure 14-4: gocdir2p highlighted in the Open dialog box.

If you wish, you can use any report file you want to experiment with this example yourself. The report itself is not changed in any way, so you can safely export any report you want to.

Exporting to a Lotus Notes Database

The Lotus Notes Database is a _groupware application_ often used in an organization to provide information-sharing between departments. Here are the steps to export a Crystal Reports report file to the Notes environment.

Note: You must have version 3.0 or above of the Lotus Notes Windows client; Crystal Reports will not export to previous Lotus Notes clients or OS/2 clients.

Lotus Notes will display as a destination option only when you are on a computer that has Lotus Notes client installed.

Open the file you want to export, and then follow these steps:

 1. **Click the Export button on the Crystal Reports toolbar.**

   The Export dialog box displays, as shown in Figure 14-5.

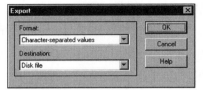

Figure 14-5:
The Export
dialog box.

2. **Under Format, click the drop-down box.**

The export formats display, as you see in Figure 14-6.

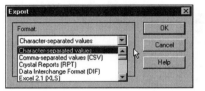

Figure 14-6:
The Export
dialog box
with format
options.

3. **For this example, choose the Excel 5.0 (.XLS) format.**
4. **Under Destination, click the drop-down box.**

The possible report destinations display.

5. **For this example, choose Lotus Notes Database.**
6. **Click OK.**

The Select Database dialog box displays.

7. **Click the Lotus Notes Database server from the Servers list.**
8. **Click the name of the database to which you want to export the report.**
9. **Click OK.**

The Comments dialog box displays.

10. **Type in any comments you want associated with the report.**

You may want to add a brief description of the report.

11. **Click OK.**

Crystal Reports exports the report.

Any user who logs on to Lotus Notes with access to the Lotus Notes database you specified will be able to view your report, provided she has Excel software. The user double-clicks the report file name to display your comments and can double-click the report icon to view the report itself.

Exporting to an Exchange Folder

Microsoft Exchange is a successor to Microsoft Mail, but with many more features. It includes electronic mail, group scheduling features, contact lists, and Internet connectivity. Exchange is often used as a communications tool within working groups of people or between departments.

Export a report to an Exchange Folder by following these steps (have a file open in Crystal Reports before you begin):

1. **Click the Export button on the Crystal Reports toolbar.**

   The Export dialog box displays.

2. **Under Format, click the drop-down box.**

   The export formats display.

3. **For this example, choose the Crystal Reports (RPT) format.**

4. **Under Destination, click the drop-down box.**

   The possible report destinations display.

5. **For this example, choose Exchange Folder.**

   Note: In order to export files to an Exchange Folder, you must have been granted that privilege by the *system administrator* in your company (sometimes known as the Maximum Leader). The system administrator is the person in charge of overseeing the local area network in your computers.

   The Export box should look like the one shown in Figure 14-7.

Figure 14-7:
Exporting
to an
Exchange
Folder.

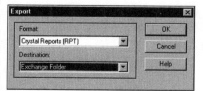

6. **Click OK.**

7. **The Choose Profile dialog box appears.**

   If the profile is correct, meaning that your name is visible, click OK. Otherwise, click the New button to create a new Inbox in order to be on the Exchange system. Follow the prompts presented by the Expert dialog boxes to do so.

8. The Select a Folder dialog box appears.

Click the folder to which you want to export the file. Normally, you send the file to a public folder, making the file accessible by other users.

9. Click OK.

The Exporting Records dialog box appears, and the export process begins. You have the option of canceling the export while it is in progress if you decide you have exported the wrong report file. Otherwise, when the dialog box closes, the file has been successfully exported.

Any user who logs on to Exchange with access to a shared folder will be able to view your report. The user double-clicks the report file name to view the report.

Exporting to Excel format

In a situation where you are networked but other users do not have Crystal Reports, you can export reports in other file formats directly to their machines. If you are in a small shop, you may have to use *sneaker net* (carrying a disk to another computer, otherwise known as troglodyte net) to get a file from your machine to another. Or, you may be going to a meeting and need to bring the report with you on a disk. Export the report to an Excel file on a floppy disk.

Begin with a report open in Crystal Reports, and then follow these steps:

1. Click the Export button.

The Export dialog box displays.

2. Under Format, click the down arrow.

The export format choices display.

3. Click Excel 5.0 (XLS).

4. Under Destination, click the down arrow.

The destination choices display.

5. Click Disk file.

Figure 14-8 shows how the Export dialog box appears with these selections.

Figure 14-8:
The Export
dialog box
with Excel
5.0 and
Disk file
selected.

6. **Click OK.**

The Choose Export File dialog box displays. The folder open in this dialog box is the one from which you opened the report. Your next step is to choose the destination for the report file.

7. **Click the button with the folder with the up arrow on it.**

Continue clicking that button until My Computer displays in the Save in: box. Figure 14-9 shows how the Choose Export File dialog box looks now.

Figure 14-9:
My
Computer in
the Choose
Export File
dialog box.

8. **Click the 3¹/₂ Floppy (A:) option.**

9. **Before you take another step, make sure that a 3¹/₂ inch floppy disk is in the A: drive.**

10. **Click the Open button.**

The Choose Export File dialog box remains on the screen with a few minor changes.

11. **Click the Save button.**

The Exporting box displays. This box is not a dialog box. It just displays during the exporting process.

You can easily tell if the export worked. Take a look at the disk in the A: drive to see if the file is there:

1. **Click the Start button.**

   Move the mouse pointer to Programs and then to Windows Explorer.

2. **Click Windows Explorer to open it.**

3. **Click the 3¹/₂ Floppy (A:) option.**

   (The 3¹/₂ Floppy (A:) option is the third item in the list.)

The file you exported, in this example gocdir2p, displays on the right side of the Explorer window. Figure 14-10 shows that this file is a Microsoft Excel Worksheet.

Figure 14-10:
gocdir2p
saved in
Microsoft
Excel
Worksheet
format to
the A: Drive.

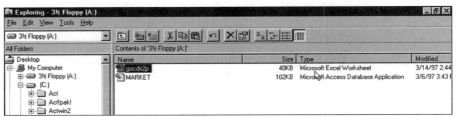

You can compare the formatting differences in the exported Excel file with the original Crystal Reports file. In Figure 14-11, you see the opened gocdir2p report in Crystal Reports. Figure 14-12 shows the opened gocdir2p Excel file. You can see that some of the formatting is lost in the export process. Excel does not support all of the features of Crystal Reports; therefore, the displayed report is different.

Exporting to Microsoft Word

Export your Crystal Reports report to a Microsoft Word file to convert the file to a .DOC document. All the Microsoft Word users will have ready access to your report. You can export a report to a file that already exists. Suppose that you want to export a report into a Word document file, and you are working in Word:

1. **Choose File⇨New (or use the New button).**

2. **Select a new blank document as the new file.**

   A blank document opens in Word.

3. **Choose File⇨Save (or hit that Save button).**

   The Save File dialog box opens.

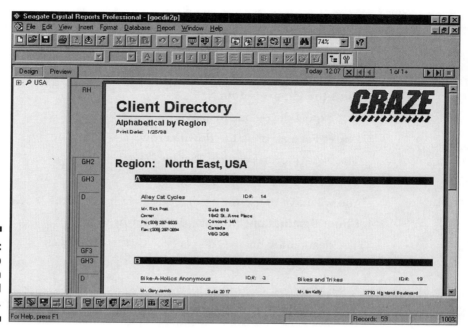

Figure 14-11:
gocdir2p
opened in
Crystal
Reports.

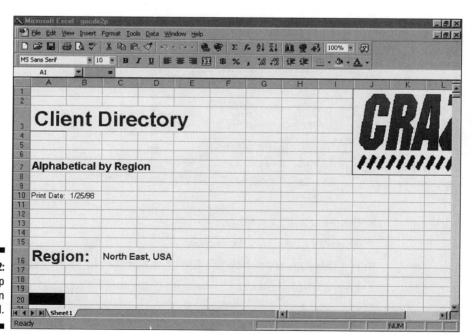

Figure 14-12:
gocdir2p
opened in
Excel.

4. **In the Save File dialog box, enter a name such as** cr example.

5. **Close this blank document by choosing File⇨Close.**

Go back to Crystal Reports, open a report, and then follow these steps:

1. **Click the Export button.**

    The Export dialog box displays.

2. **Under Format, click the down arrow.**

    The export format choices display.

3. **Click Word for Windows document.**

    You will have to use the scroll buttons to move to the bottom of the list.

4. **Under Destination, click the down arrow.**

    The destination choices display.

5. **Click Disk file.**

6. **Click OK.**

    The Choose Export File dialog box displays (as in Figure 14-13). Your next step is to choose the destination for the report file.

7. **Locate the folder you want to export to.**

Figure 14-13:
Choose
Export File
dialog box
with C:
drive
selected.

8. **Double-click that folder.**

    The files in that folder display.

9. **For this example click the file** cr example **to highlight it.**

    Figure 14-14 shows the cr example file highlighted.

Figure 14-14:
The cr
example file
highlighted.

10. **Click the Save button.**

    The File Already Exists dialog box opens.

11. **Click Yes when Crystal Reports asks if you want to overwrite the existing file.**

    The Exporting box displays. Crystal Reports is actually running the report again against the database. The Exporting box alerts you to the progress of Crystal Reports in reading the source database. This way, you are getting the latest information in your exported report.

Canceling an export

When the Exporting box displays, you can cancel the export by clicking the Cancel button. Doing so stops the export in progress.

Comparing the Word Document with Crystal Reports

Figures 14-11 and 14-12, shown earlier in this chapter, compared the exported Excel file with the Crystal Reports report file. You can also open a Word document to see how much of the formatting displays in the Word document.

1. **With Microsoft Word open, click the Open button on the toolbar.**

2. **Highlight a Word file and click the Open button in the Open dialog box.**

    Figure 14-15 shows a typical report opened in a Word document.

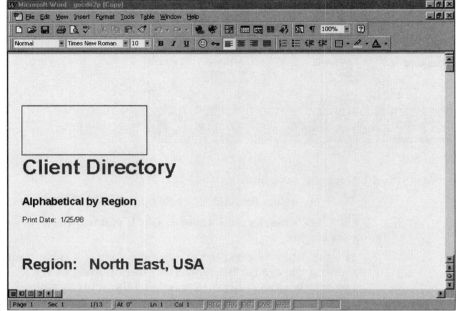

Figure 14-15:
A report as
a Word
document.

Exporting to an ODBC data source

With Crystal Reports you can export reports to any ODBC data source.
ODBC stands for Open Data Base Connectivity and is a Microsoft standard
for network communications between databases. (You may want to call
ODBC *Obfuscation Daily By Computer.*) You may ask yourself, why would you
want to export reports to an ODBC data source, anyway? Here are a few
reasons:

- ✔ You can change data from a centralized database into a format you can
  use in a local database. For example, you can take data from a
  Microsoft SQL Server and change it to data that you can use with
  Microsoft Access on your local database.

- ✔ Conversely, you can change data from a local database to data compatible with a centralized database. For example, you can take data from a
  Paradox database on your machine and change it to data you can use
  with Oracle on a centralized database.

- ✔ You can take a report and convert it to a new database table that can be
  used as a separate data set. Then you can create reports from that set
  of data.

When exporting to ODBC, the following assumption is made: You have an
ODBC data source set up through ODBC Administrator for Crystal Reports.
If not, follow the steps in the next section.

Setting up an ODBC Data Source

Each database with which you work has specific libraries for the database. For example, a database created by the Microsoft SQL Server can be read by Crystal Reports. Crystal Reports has a library file that is installed with Crystal Reports that translates requests to the SQL Server and then returns data from the SQL server.

The library file in Crystal Reports called PDSSQL.DLL talks to the MSDBLIB.DLL file in the Microsoft SQL Server. Each application has its own language. The library files allow one application to talk to another via ODBC. (By the way, DLL stands for Dynamic Linking Library. Drop that one at the next party and you have established your dynamic link to geekville!)

Files with the .DLL extension are library files used for translating between application programs. When you export a report using ODBC, you will need to know which library files to use for the destination database. Table 14-3 shows the database name in the left column and the ODBC data source as it displays in the Export dialog box. Selecting the correct data source assures that you are using the correct libraries.

Table 14-3	Library Files
Database	*ODBC Data Source*
IBM DB2/2	CRDB2
MICROSOFT SQL SERVER 6.*x*	CRSS
ORACLE 7	CROR7
Informix 7	CRINF7
SQLBase	CRGUP
SYBASE SYSTEM 10/11	CRSYB

Use this chart to guide you when deciding which library file to use in your ODBC connection.

Begin with a report open in Crystal Reports, and then follow these steps to export to an ODBC data source.

 1. Click the Export button on the toolbar.

The Export dialog box displays.

2. Under Format, click the down arrow.

The export format choices display.

3. **Click an ODBC format.**

   You will have to use the scroll buttons to move to the ODBC options. Use Table 14-3 to select the correct ODBC format. In this example, select ODBC-CRSS for SQL Server.

   Note: When working with ODBC, disregard the Destination section.

4. **Click OK.**

5. **If your ODBC data source specifies a particular database, the report will be exported to that database. If not, the Select Database dialog box displays.**

6. **Click the database that this report will be added to as a new table.**

   The database name is highlighted.

7. **Click OK.**

   If the ODBC data source you highlighted requires a logon ID and password, the Log on dialog box displays.

8. **Enter your ID and password, and click OK.**

   The ODBC Table Name dialog box displays.

9. **Type the name for the new table in the database, and click OK.**

   Crystal Reports exports the report as a new table in the destination database.

Mailing Your Report

Each electronic mail system is unique. Because of the differences in how mail systems work, the exporting instructions are presented generically. The figures shown are from a real-life example, but you have to use your own mail application program.

Anytime you are combining the activities of one program with another, things get a little bit more complicated. You need to know about some caveats and assumptions regarding exporting to e-mail. Both Microsoft Mail and Microsoft Exchange use MAPI. Crystal Reports supports exporting to MAPI. Crystal Reports also supports VIM, used by Lotus cc:Mail.

MAPI and VIM are just different standards for e-mail. MAPI is Microsoft's Mail API (Application Programming Interface), which many companies use. VIM is just another standard of getting mail. It has a different format though. It was created and maintained by Lotus. Notice the competitive aspect of this.

1. **Click the Export button.**

   The Export dialog box displays.

2. **Under Format, click the down arrow.**

   The export format choices display.

3. **Click Crystal Reports (RPT).**

   You will have to use the scroll buttons to move to this selection.

4. **Under Destination, click the down arrow.**

   The destination choices display.

5. **Click E-mail.**

   Figure 14-16 shows how the Export dialog box appears with these selections.

Figure 14-16:
The Export
dialog box
with Crystal
Reports and
Microsoft
Mail
selected.

When you export to e-mail, Crystal Reports asks you to log on to your e-mail application the normal way. If you want to export to e-mail, you have to log on to your e-mail system.

6. **Click the names of the individuals to whom you want to send the report.**

   The message screen displays. An icon showing that a report is attached to the message appears. If you choose to export an Excel file, the icon indicates an Excel file. For the purposes of this example, you will see a Crystal Reports icon.

7. **Type in the message you want to include in the report.**

8. **Click the Send button to send the message.**

   The Exporting box displays to show the progress of your export.

Faxing Your Report

You can fax a report directly to a fax machine if you have a fax application installed on your system. Microsoft Fax and Delrina WinFax are two examples of fax applications. You must have installed a fax before you can use this aspect of Crystal Reports. Use these generic instructions to fax directly from Crystal Reports:

1. **Choose Crystal Reports, and open the report you want to fax.**

2. **In Crystal Reports, choose File⇨Printer Setup.**

   The Print Setup dialog box displays.

3. **Next to the name of the printer, click the drop-down box.**

   All the available printers are listed.

4. **From the list of available printers, choose the fax driver.**

   Figure 14-17 shows the screen with your fax printer driver selected.

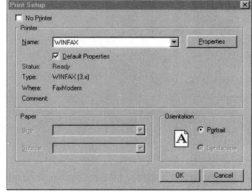

Figure 14-17:
The fax printer driver selected.

5. **Click OK.**

6. **Choose File⇨Print⇨Printer.**

   The Print dialog box opens, as seen in Figure 14-18.

Figure 14-18:
The Print dialog box.

7. Click OK.

The fax application displays. From the fax application you can select a cover page and fill in the number to which you are faxing and other required information. Figure 14-19 shows the fax application WinFax with the required information.

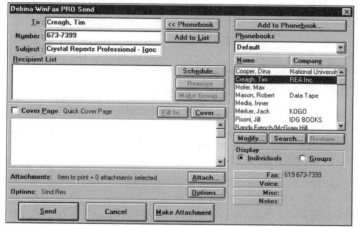

8. Click the option that lets you send the fax from your fax application.

Compiling a Crystal Report

Compiling a report creates an *executable version* of your report, which means you can create a report that can be printed on demand. You simply click an icon. You do not need to open Crystal Reports first in order to print the report.

By compiling a report, you can create a report and share it with others. If the others do not know how to use Crystal Reports, they can still print the report. They do not even have to have Crystal Reports on their system in order to take advantage of a compiled report.

When you want to create reports that can be printed by anyone, whether they have Crystal Reports or not, or distribute a report widely without regard to an individual's application products, use a compiled report. Keeping a compiled report on your own desktop means that you can open that report with the click of a button. The report displays instantly because you don't have to open Crystal Reports.

Here are some more things you can do with a compiled report:

✔ Print a compiled report to a window, a printer, or a file.

✔ Print a report immediately.

✔ Print a report at a later time, such as after hours when the printers are more available.

✔ Tailor a compiled report to individual needs.

Creating a compiled report is a six-step snap:

1. **Choose the Report menu.**

2. **Click the Compile Report option.**

   The Compile Report dialog box displays.

3. **The name of the report file you have open displays in the Compiled File Name box. You can compile this report, type in a new name, or click the Browse button to find the report you want to compile.**

4. **Click the Yes radio button to create a program item for the report in the program.**

5. **Click the Yes button to be able to distribute the report after.**

   Figure 14-20 shows the Compile Report dialog box with the selections.

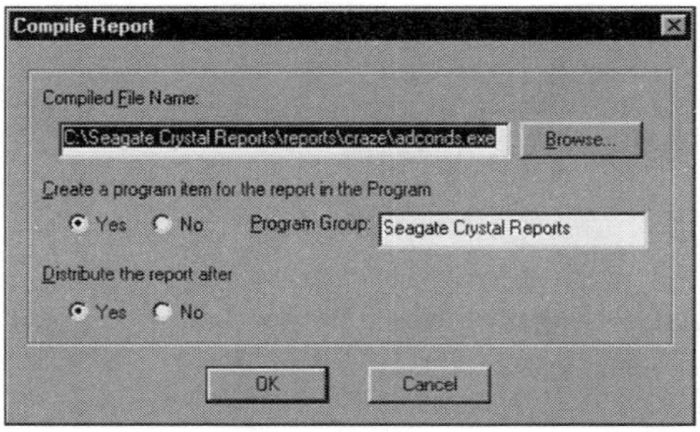

Figure 14-20:
The
Compile
Report
dialog box.

6. **Click OK.**

   Crystal Reports creates a report icon in the Crystal Reports Professional window. Next, the Report Distribution Expert displays. From the Report Distribution dialog box, you can control the distribution of the report. This dialog box also helps you identify and gather the required files to make the executable compiled report run. Figure 14-21 shows the Report Distribution dialog box as it displays.

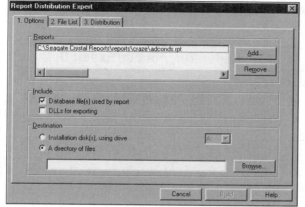

Using the Report Distribution Expert

After you compile a report using the Compile Report command on the Report menu, Crystal Reports asks if you want to distribute the report. In the steps shown in the preceding section, the option to distribute the report was selected. When you select that option, the Report Distribution Expert dialog box displays.

You will use the Report Distribution Expert when you compile reports, save reports to a disk for mass distribution, send a report to a network drive so many others can use it, or ship reports with an application you develop using the Crystal Reports Engine. In other words, you have reached a higher peak when you start doing these sorts of things, and you just became a much more valued employee.

With any open report you can see the Report Distribution Expert by taking the following steps:

1. **Choose the Report menu.**

2. **Click the Report Distribution option.**

   The Report Distribution Expert dialog box helps you gather the required files to distribute a report. From this dialog box you can also ship data with the report, compress the component files, and build a SETUP.EXE file. The SETUP.EXE file is the file that is created in this process so that the person receiving the report can install it on his or her computer. It is actually a small computer program. Any user can run the SETUP.EXE file to install the report you are distributing. When the user runs SETUP.EXE, Crystal Reports decompresses the files, installs the files where the user designates, and then creates an icon for calling up the report.

The options on the Report Distribution Expert Options tab are reviewed in Table 14-4.

Table 14-4	Report Distribution Expert Options
Report Distribution Expert Option, Options Tab	**Description**
Reports to be distributed:	Displays the list of files you want in your report distribution file
Add to list...	Adds files to the Reports to be distributed box
Remove...	Removes highlighted files from the Reports to be distributed box
Include Database files used by the report(s)	Lets you decide if you want to include data files with the report
Include DLLs for exporting	Lets you decide if you want to include the DLLs for exporting
Destination: Build install disk(s) to carry to client site, using drive:	Chooses the destination of the report distribution file after you create it (with this option, files are saved to a floppy disk)
Destination: Build directory of files to share out to install on other machines.	Chooses the destination of the report distribution file after you create it (with this option, files are saved to a directory on the hard disk; you can either type in the directory or click the browse button and select a directory)
Browse	Browse the folders and files on the hard drives
Build for Distribution	Creates the Report Distribution file

The program identifies the files you need to go with the report. Use the File List tab to add or delete files. The options to select files are described in Table 14-5.

Table 14-5	Options for Selecting Distribution Files
Report Distribution Expert, File List Tab	**Description**
File name	Lists the names of the files to be included in the distribution file. You can click the radio button in front of Description to see the type of file being included. Click the radio button in front of Path to see the DOS path for the file location. Click the radio button in front of Size, date, and version to see those details.

Report Distribution Expert, File List Tab	Description
Add	Click the Add button to open the Choose Distribution File dialog box and add the current report to an existing report.
Remove	Highlight a file and click the Remove button to determine that that file is not distributed with the report. The file is added to the Don't copy box.

The final tab in the Report Distribution Expert dialog box is the Distribution tab. When you click the tab, you have the opportunity to create the distribution file. Click the Build button to begin. The speed of your computer and the number of records in the report will determine the time it takes to create the file. If you have more than 500 records in the report, time for a long lunch with dessert. Crystal Reports displays a dialog box alerting you that the report is finished. Click OK to close the dialog box.

Printing a Compiled Report

A compiled report opens without Crystal Reports. Close Crystal Reports now, and then locate the compiled report. It is installed as part of the Windows desktop.

1. **Click the Start button.**

2. **Select the Programs menu.**

3. **Move the mouse pointer to Seagate Crystal Reports.**

   (Do not select Seagate Crystal Reports 6.0.)

4. **Move the mouse pointer to Statement of Account.**

   This selection is the report file that is now a compiled report.

5. **Click Statement of Account.**

   The Statement of Account dialog box displays. From this dialog box, you determine where you want the report to print.

6. **In the Print box, click the down arrow.**

   You have three choices: print the report to a printer, print the report to a window, or export the report. For this example, choose print the report to a window.

7. **In the Time box, click the down arrow.**

You have many choices of when to print the report. You can print it right now, specify a time, or specify an amount of time from now to print the report. For this example, choose right now.

If you elect to specify a time, click the up and down buttons next to the time values to specify the exact time you want the report to print. Figure 14-22 shows the Statement of Account dialog box with the example selections made.

Figure 14-22:
The
Statement
of Account
dialog box.

8. **Click the Print button.**

The Select Records dialog box appears. If you have a compiled report with several select record formulas, you can select one before printing.

9. **A single option is available in this example, so click OK.**

The Statement of Account Report displays in a window of its own. Figure 14-23 shows the compiled report printed to a window.

Web Reporting

The World Wide Web is the graphical portion of the Internet. The Web is the newest way of spreading information to many people at a very low cost. By posting your reports to the Web, you give access to information that heretofore would have required human attention to receive. No more faxing or mailing reports; simply tell your salespeople or customers to point their browser to your Web site.

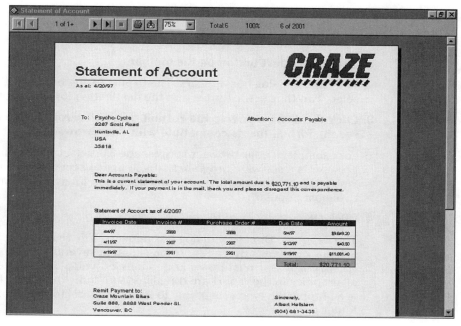

Figure 14-23:
The
compiled
report
printed to a
window.

The Internet itself is a collection of high-powered computers all connected via telephone lines. A standard system for addressing a computer and then a site on the computer have been established, making it easy for people to locate your Web site.

So, in order to post your reports to the Web, you need to have an Internet site. To get an Internet site, either your company must have an internal computer system that is an Internet host or the company must have an account with an ISP — an Internet Service Provider.

After you have established your account, the ISP will give you the information on how to access your account.

Exporting to HTML

The World Wide Web uses a standard language to create graphic pages. The name of that language is HTML (HyperText Markup Language). In the olden days, you would have had to learn to rewrite your reports in HTML in order for them to be usable on the Web. Not so anymore. Crystal Reports exports its reports directly to HTML format!

To export a report to an HTML format:

1. **Open the report you wish to export.**

2. **Click the Export button on the toolbar.**

   The Export dialog box appears. The Export dialog box allows you to select two things: the format and the destination for the report file.

3. **Click the down arrow in the Format box, and scroll the list until you see the format that is compatible with your browser.**

   For example, if your browser is Netscape 2.0, select that format. (A browser is a software program that you use to access the World Wide Web pages; Netscape Navigator and Microsoft Internet Explorer are the two most popular.)

4. **Click OK.**

   The Export to Directory dialog box appears. The reason that a *Directory* is being created is that a report may contain several elements that, for HTML purposes, must be separated into individual files. For example, all graphics in the report are translated into individual JPEG files, which is a graphic file type acceptable to HTML. (A directory is the same as a folder.)

5. **Enter the directory name and press OK.**

Checking your Web page

The main page (or *home page* in Web jargon) is always named DEFAULT.HTM, and this is the file you open using your Web browser — which, by the way, is a good way to check the layout and readability of your report in HTML. You do not have to post your report to the Web before you can view the report. View an exported HTML report this way:

1. **Start Netscape (or the browser that matches your export format).**

2. **Choose File⇨Open.**

   In the Open dialog box, locate the directory (folder) in which you have exported the report.

3. **In the directory, locate the `DEFAULT.HTM` file, and click it.**

   If everything has gone according to plan, the report will open inside your browser. After checking the layout, you can then follow the directions of your ISP to post the report to your Web site.

Chapter 15

Setting Your File Options

. . . .

In This Chapter

▶ Environment settings

▶ Field formats

▶ Font formats

▶ Default report dictionary

. . . .

*F*or those of you who have worked with computers, you may recognize the term *default*. It's not your fault if you do not; what it means is the automatic setting in computer software, such as the size of text you add to a Crystal Reports report. With a default setting, every time you add a text object to a report, you can direct Crystal Reports to make the text 18 points in size. That way, you do not have to format every piece of text every time you add one to a report. In this chapter, I show you a variety of default settings that make your report creation much easier.

Environment Settings: The File Options Dialog Box

The Crystal Reports environment consists of settings that determine how every report is formatted. For example, you can enter a setting that formats all numbers with two decimal places. Of course, you can override the setting if necessary; you can always change the format to what you need. The point is that when you create a report, you can have most of the settings you want already in place, as opposed to having to add them with every new report.

These settings only work for reports you create in the future. An existing report is not affected by these settings. But, if you add a new object to an old report, the new settings will be in effect for that object. Take a look at the File Options dialog box and the accompanying report environment settings.

With any report open, take a look at the default options in Crystal Reports by choosing File⇨Options. The File Options dialog box appears, as in Figure 15-1.

Figure 15-1:
The File
Options
dialog box.

Note: If a setting is on, it has a check mark in the box leading the option. Click the setting to remove or add the check mark.

The Layout Tab

In Figure 15-1, the File Options dialog box is open and the Layout tab is selected.

View Options

The View Options are settings you can customize. The default settings include rulers and guidelines in both Design and Preview. The section names are similar to the group tree in that each of the sections is listed to the left of the report body. Figures 15-2 and 15-3 show the difference in the way the section names are presented. Figure 15-2 shows the full name and 15-3 shows the abbreviated name.

Grid Options

Crystal Reports automatically turns on the Snap to Grid option, and in my opinion that is where you should leave it. The idea is that when you insert objects into a report, Crystal Reports moves the object so that it is in alignment with a grid of horizontal and vertical lines. This feature gives the report a well spaced layout without a struggle on your part with each object. If you wish, you can have the underlying grid visible in both Design and Preview windows.

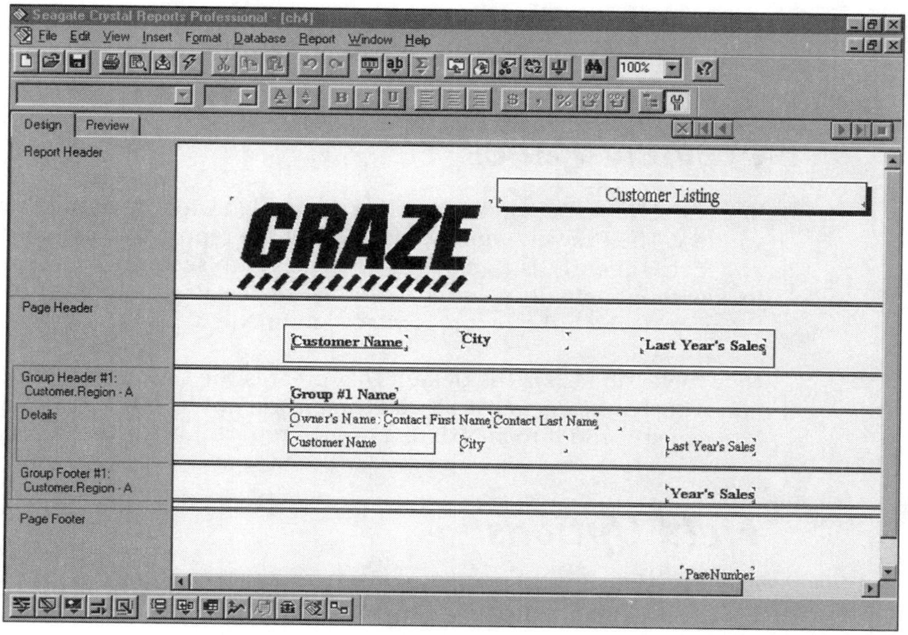

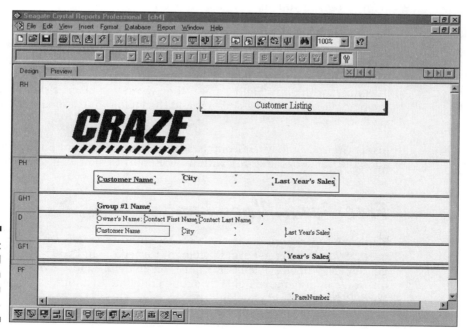

Figure 15-2:
Long
section
name in
Preview.

Figure 15-3:
Abbreviated
section
name in
Preview.

The grid size determines the spacing between the individual lines. The smaller the number, the more closely packed the lines.

Preview Pages

In Crystal Reports, you can work in the Design window or the Preview window. The Preview window is a view of the report that includes live data, and, consequently, is as close as you can get to seeing how the report will look without actually printing. Use the Preview Pages settings to determine the way in which the report is viewed in Preview.

New to version 6.0 is the default that creates the Group Tree. If you find it annoying, you can click it off and then it will not be created automatically. You can still add it to an existing or new report if you wish.

Field Options

Show Field Names is an option that I would turn on. When you insert a database field into a report with this option set to on, the field name is inserted in place of a series of XXXs. If seeing the space allotted for the field is important to you, leave this setting off.

Insert Detail Field Titles is on when you begin a new report. When you insert a database field, the field name is inserted as a heading above the Details section where you inserted the database field. The idea here is that you can easily determine which field is where on your report. If you use this setting in concert with Show Field Names, then when you insert a database field, the field name appears as header and the Field Name appears in the Details section, too.

Insert Group Name with Group is a setting you may want on, too, because it adds the name of the group within the Report Design window.

Free-Form Placement

The Snap to Grid option always decides whether Free-Form Placement is used. If you have Free-Form Placement turned on and you have many guidelines, you can place fields between guidelines. If this option is turned off, you can only move fields from one guideline to another. Play with Free-Form Placement and check it out.

The New Report Tab

This tab is used to determine two things: where new reports are going to be saved and where reports you are mailing are going to be sent by default. The New Report tab is shown in Figure 15-4. The Browse button for the report directory has been clicked, revealing the folders.

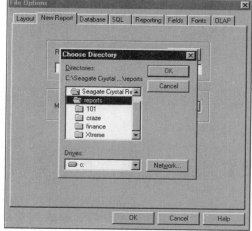

Figure 15-4:
The New
Report tab
selected
and the
Browse
button
clicked.

The Mail Destination setting on this tab determines where a report is sent by default when you want to use electronic mail to send a report.

The Database Tab

Clicking the Database tab opens the dialog box shown in Figure 15-5.

If you need to change the default location of the source of your databases, type in the path (an old DOS term to which we are wedded), such as C:\MSACCESS\DOUGS or click the Browse button — the easy way — and click on the location of the database tables that you want to use to create reports.

If you are trying to access a database that has an extension not listed in the Database Selector field, add the extension you need. Similarly, add the index extension if needed. Don't forget the semicolon (;) separator. Check *DOS For Dummies* from IDG Books Worldwide, Inc., for more on extensions.

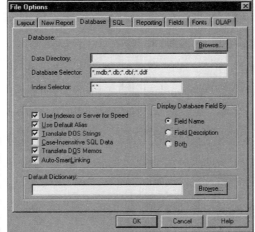

Figure 15-5:
File Options,
Database
tab
selected.

The default settings for Indexes, Default Alias, and so on are best left alone unless you know exactly what you are doing, except for the Auto-SmartLinking option which is used to link tables as described in Chapter 13.

The next setting in this dialog box that you need to think about is Display Database Fields By. The automatic setting is Field Name. You can select the Field Description, which provides more information about the type of data in the field, or you can have Crystal Reports display Both.

The SQL Tab

If you are working with SQL databases, here is where you can enter the settings that you need to make Crystal Reports work with your system. SQL databases are large databases and are explained in Chapters 13 and 14. I would advise that beginners ask your company's system administrator to assist in entering the settings here. The SQL tab is shown in Figure 15-6.

Here's a quick rundown of what each edit box represents:

- ✔ **Server type:** Sets the default datasource for you.
- ✔ **Skip server type dialog box option:** Turning this option on forces the server type (specified in the server type edit box) to be used with no chance for the user to change it. That way, you don't have to hunt it down every time you create a new report.
- ✔ **Server name:** Name of your database server.
- ✔ **Database:** Name of the database on the server.

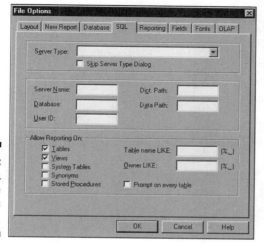

Figure 15-6:
The SQL
tab in File
Options
dialog box.

✔ **User ID:** The personal code to log onto the database. Kind of like your network logon ID.

✔ **Dictionary path:** If your database supports dictionaries, you can specify one of them as a default dictionary. That way, you don't have to keep picking it every time you create a new report.

✔ **Data path:** Where the data is in the database server.

✔ **Allow reporting on:** These options allow you to show just the objects that you need. If you don't want to see the *views* (a virtual table), then don't check this box. With this turned off, only physical tables will be available to you for reporting.

✔ **Prompt on every table:** This option basically gives you the opportunity to give a new name to each table for the purpose of the report (like a nickname). If the box is not checked, it automatically takes whatever name is in the database.

✔ **Table name like and owner like:** Sometimes, in database servers, there are *thousands* of tables and getting them all in a list would take forever. You can narrow down the tables by finding something generic. For example, DAV% will return DAVE, DAVID, DAVIDO, and so on. This is kind of like the * and ? notation used in Windows and DOS to find files.

The Reporting Tab

The Reporting tab has some more-sophisticated settings that you probably will not need until you have used Crystal Reports for a time. The Reporting tab is shown in Figure 15-7.

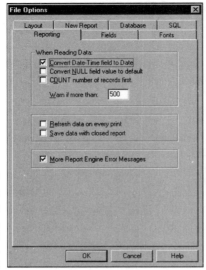

Figure 15-7:
File
Options,
Reporting
tab.

The first option, Convert Date-Time field to Date, is specific to Microsoft Access. If the setting is on, fields in Access that are combined date-time fields are converted to strictly date fields.

The second option, Convert NULL value to default, is to handle converting data in a field that are Null values (usually zero, or an empty field) to a specific value as determined by the source database.

The next option is the COUNT number of records first option. This option is important if you work with extremely large SQL databases. Why? Because when you are in the process of designing or previewing a report, you do not have to have a multitude of records in the report to determine if the design is giving you the report you want. Crystal Reports gives you the opportunity to retrieve only a portion of the records. The Count option works in concert with the next field, Warn if more than. Enter a number into this field to set the maximum number of records you want to retrieve during the design phase.

✔ Refresh data on every print

 When you have made changes to the report and are going to print or preview the report, Crystal Reports prompts you with a dialog box asking if you want to use the saved data or refresh the data. By setting the Refresh data option on, the dialog box does not appear, and Crystal Reports goes ahead and refreshes the data automatically.

✔ <u>S</u>ave data with closed report

I would recommend that you set this option on, because most of the time you will want the data included with the report. If you don't, you can simply choose <u>F</u>ile⇨Save Data <u>w</u>ith Report to toggle the command off. For more information on saving or not saving data with a report, see Chapter 14 on report distribution.

✔ <u>M</u>ore Report Engine Error Messages

This option is for the tech types who need to know why the special code they added using the Report Engine doesn't work. The option opens the flood gates on the Crystal Reports messages for run-time reports. Instead of holding back any errors, *all* the errors are shown. All error messages are already given when you are in the Crystal Reports Design Tab view, but you get to decide what the run-time user sees by using this option.

The Fields Tab

The Fields tab, shown in Figure 15-8, lists all of the types of fields that you can insert into a report. This tab allows you to set up how to format a field upon inserting.

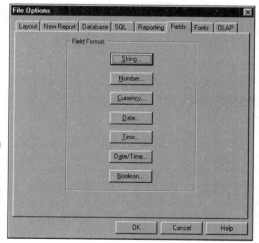

Figure 15-8:
The Fields tab with field type buttons.

Each of the field types has its own particular formatting attributes and therefore, when you click one of the field type buttons, a dialog box appears that is specific to that field. For example, clicking the <u>S</u>tring field type button opens the dialog box seen in Figure 15-9.

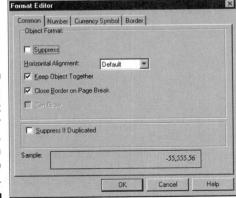

Figure 15-9:
The dialog
box for the
String field
type.

A *string field* is made up of characters — not considered numbers or dates. That does not mean that the field can't have numbers or dates, it is just that Crystal Reports treats characters not specifically formatted as dates or numbers as character strings. Crystal Reports doesn't make this decision, however. The data type comes from the database itself.

The Border tab in this dialog box allows you to add a Drop Shadow, a single- or double-lined border, and so on automatically, every time you insert a text object. If you have established a consistent style for every text object you insert, this tab is where you make those settings automatic.

In Figure 15-10, the Number Field Format has been selected, opening the Format Editor dialog box, which in turn has four more tabs: Common, Number, Currency Symbol, and Border.

Figure 15-10:
The Format
Editor
dialog box,
Common
tab
selected.

From this dialog box, you can click the Number tab to set the number of decimal places that will appear with numbers, the degree of rounding that occurs, how negative numbers are displayed, and so on. Click the Currency Symbol tab to set the manner in which numbers are displayed relative to the type of currency symbol that is included. When you make a change in the format, it is reflected immediately in the preview box at the bottom of the dialog box.

The remaining buttons in this dialog box are of the same nature — they set the automatic format for the type of field associated with the button.

The Fonts Tab

The Fonts tab gives you the tools to set the automatic (which is the same as default) sizes and type of fonts for each of the fields listed. This tab should be used in conjunction with the Fields tab to develop the look you want in your reports. Clicking the Fields button in this tab opens the Font dialog box shown in Figure 15-11.

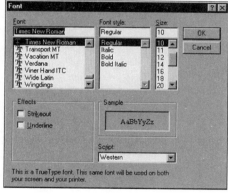

Figure 15-11:
The Font dialog box opened after clicking the Fields button.

In the Font dialog box, you can select the preferred font and size for each of the fields you insert into the report. As you try different fonts and sizes, the change is reflected in the preview box at the bottom of the dialog box.

Each of the Fields buttons on the Fonts tab, when clicked, opens the identical Font dialog box. Click each button in succession and make the settings you want for each of the fields.

OLAP

The OLAP tab is specific to OLAP reports based on OLAP databases, which, as far as I can tell, are from Arbor Essbase. So if you know what OLAP is, you know what you want from these options. I do not. Figure 15-12 shows the exotic options on the OLAP tab.

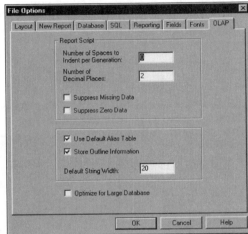

Figure 15-12:
File
Options,
OLAP
tab.

Part VII
The Part of Tens

The 5th Wave   By Rich Tennant

CLARENCE'S REWARD FOR DILIGENTLY COMPILING ALL OF HIS COMPANY'S DATABASE INFORMATION INTO ONE USEABLE REPORT.

DOWNLOADING FILE... ALTHOUGH IT WON'T MAKE ANY DIFFERENCE SINCE YOU WON'T BE WORKING HERE NEXT MONTH.

In this part . . .

In April 1990 I happened to be at a writer's conference where another unknown, relatively poor author, Dan Gookin, was in attendance. He told me of the idea he had of writing a real beginner's book on DOS, including humor, with the cover name *DOS For Dummies*. I told him it was a great idea and I bet no publisher would do it — their groupthink was that no person would self-identify as a *Dummy*. He replied that the title had indeed been sniffed at by several major publishers. Well, history agrees with Dan and me — over 3.5 million copies of *DOS For Dummies* have been sold. Dan is no longer worrying about paying the rent.

So the Part of Tens, a Gookin original, lives on. In this Part of Tens, I try to convey some of the more important concepts regarding planning and executing your reports. Hand the Ten Questions to Ask before You Create a Report to your boss the next time she demands a report but does not convey any guidance. Ask for the answers before starting. Then, with the report under construction, look at the enhancement ideas to create a dynamic report.

Chapter 16

Ten Questions to Ask before You Create a Report

. . . .

In This Chapter

▶ Finding the special purpose for your report

▶ Determining what to include in your report

▶ Getting your report out to the audience

. . . .

*Y*our boss comes in to your office in a rush stating that she needs a sales by salesperson report right away! Now what do you do? Remain calm. You need to ask the person, boss or not, requesting a report the following ten questions. Ten is not a magic number, but Dan Gookin made the Part of Tens famous in Dummies books, so here I go.

What is the purpose of the report?

Is the person requesting this report allowed to access the data? Does the report contain any confidential information?

While writing down the purpose of the report may seem like a useless exercise, it is very important. Doing so allows you to focus on what should or shouldn't be in the report and how the information should be displayed. This question also allows report recipients to know if this is the report that they want to see or if they should go look for another one.

Anytime you write a goal or purpose, you know where you are going with the report. If you don't know where you are going, how do you know if you have arrived?

More and more, companies and institutions are careful about security issues, such as who sees what data. In a hospital, a corrections facility, a school, or a business, some information may not be available to all people.

In a company, a person may have to have a security clearance to see certain data. Some financial data may only be distributed to certain people. Some information may be company private or proprietary. Keep these security issues in mind when you create a report.

From what databases, views, or tables do you need to include information in this report, and what fields do you want to include in the report?

Data for a report may come from different sources. Record the databases, tables, or views that hold that data you need. You may need to know the exact directories that hold information. You may need to know what network to access. You may need a password to obtain access to some data.

If you have more than one table involved, linking will be needed.

Do you want all the records in the report or a subset?

Women only? Over 60 years old? Transactions for March?

Many reports are run on a monthly, quarterly, or yearly basis. You need to know this information before you create your report. If you don't know, you may be in a position where you are waiting for 15 minutes for a report preview to display because you are looking at data for the last ten years. Whether you are looking for data from a certain region, a certain gender, or a certain time period, you're better off if you can reduce the number of records in your report. The Select Expert can be helpful to you.

How do you want the data grouped?

Find out if the data should be grouped by region, by date, or by alphabet. Some reports may have several groups. A report could be grouped by state, then by gender, and then by age.

How do you want the data sorted?

Usually the two choices are ascending order or descending order. In addition you will want to know if the data should be sorted in ascending or descending order by amount, alphabetically, or some other criteria. As with groups, you may sort alphabetically by state and then sort by amount within those groups.

Another feature of Crystal Reports is that you can create your own style of grouping called *custom groups*. For example, if you want to group regions by their geographic location, feel free. For more information on this feature, please see the online help.

What summary calculations do you want in the report?

Monthly totals? Grand totals? Averages?

Find out if you need to count the records in the report, get a running total, add summaries at the end of the groups, and other information. Consider whether you want summaries after every group.

What text do you want to appear in the:

- ✔ Report Header?
- ✔ Page Header?
- ✔ Page Footer?
- ✔ Report Footer?
- ✔ Other Text?

Record the text you want to display in each of these report sections. Decide on which pages you want this text to display. You may want to display some text on the first page, but not on the others. Find out if any other text is required. You may need to describe some of the summary calculations. You may need to add some quotes or expressions.

Do you want certain data to stand out?

You can make data stand out by using flags, special formatting, or conditional formatting. If the person for whom you're creating the report wants the data to stand out, find out how.

This step is for the more sophisticated presentation quality report. Will the report be printed? Will the report be distributed on a network? Do you have a color printer? You can make totals greater than 10,000 appear in red. If you are presenting in black-and-white, then you want to make totals greater than 10,000 appear in reverse image. Based on the report's purpose you can make the critical data stand out.

How should the report be distributed and to whom?

You may have a network, where all the reports are distributed to an Exchange folder or to Lotus Notes. You may want reports uploaded automatically to a company Intranet page. Perhaps you are distributing a report to a group who does not have access to Crystal Reports. Find out if you want to send them a compiled report or if you need to export the report so it can be read by another software product. Table 16-1 gives you some ideas for report format and distribution.

Table 16-1	Report Distribution or Showing Your Brilliance to the World!
Report Format	**Distribution**
Crystal Report*	Exchange Folder
Compiled Report**	Uploaded to HTML (Web site)
Excel Spreadsheet	E-mail
An Existing Application	E-mail
Word Document	Other

  * Receiver has access to Crystal Reports.

** Receiver does *not* have access to Crystal Reports.

Again, the security issue raises its head. Can anybody see the information in this report, or is it company private, proprietary, or confidential? You're better off to find this information out before you distribute the report.

When do you need to see this report, and when should it be distributed?

You should get into the habit of finding out the due date for activities assigned to you. The person requesting the report may want to see and approve the report before you send it out. Find out if the report has a critical deadline.

Is this how the report should look?

Before you start creating the new report, draw a picture of the report with all the titles, columns, groups, and so on. Get the drawing approved. Then you will have a guideline made for creating the report. Here is how you might make the report look:

	Title	
Header		
Group		
Field	Field	Field
XXXXXXXXX	XXXXXXXXX	XXXXXXX
	Summary Data	XXXXXXX
Footer		

If you follow these steps, even in an oblique way, the stress and strain of creating reports is greatly reduced.

Chapter 17

Ten Tricks to Enhance Reports

In This Chapter

▶ Remaining consistent

▶ Adding enhancements appropriately

▶ Using pictures to convey data

*T*he purpose of a report often is to summarize and identify key information necessary to manage your enterprise. (Unless you work in government, then your purpose is to obfuscate and befuddle, thereby guaranteeing the need for more reports and securing your job!) So the following ideas are not tricks really, just some guidelines that will make your reports easier to understand and interpret.

Use a predictable format

Being predictable does not mean being boring. Life is simpler for everyone if you and your readers can identify a report with a glance.

 ✔ Be clear and consistent.

 ✔ Note selection conditions in the Report Footer.

By using standard formats for specific reports, you engender consistency for all concerned. At a glance, anyone can then identify the kind of report by its format. Adding the selection conditions in the Report Footer tells the reader what data has been used to generate the report.

Another way to record information regarding the report is to enter the information into the Report Comments dialog box. To do so:

1. **Open the report.**

2. **Choose File⇨Summary Info.**

3. **Add the comments you want and close the dialog box.**

4. **Add the Comments field in the report by choosing Insert➪Special Field and selecting Report Comments.**

   Insert the Report Comments field in the Report Footer or wherever you feel appropriate.

Another labeling aspect is to use the same labeling format for the same type of report object — subtotals, summaries, and grand totals.

Allow generous white space

The acronym used to describe reports that are too busy and number laden is MEGO, meaning My Eyes Glaze Over. Keep this fact in mind when you start adding detail to the report. Your report is only as good as the information that is easily conveyed to the reader.

Another way to add readability is to format every other line of the Details section in a different color.

Position report headings and page numbers in the same place for every report

Many reports are generated on a regular basis. Therefore the design should remain the same to avoid the need to recreate and edit the look of a report with each generation.

- ✔ Your report reader can easily locate crucial information.
- ✔ Display data in a predictable order.

Consistently paying attention to format makes the information in your report accessible. To do this easily, create a report template with all the major formatting in place, save the report, and then use the Another Report button from the Report Gallery dialog box to select the saved template.

Make data easy to understand

Insider terms and jargon should always be avoided. If your report includes calculations, you should have a key to how they were constructed.

- ✔ Wrap or use abbreviations rather than truncate data.
- ✔ Use standard terminology.

All of the field headings in a report are editable. If the field name that is copied from the database is cryptic, change the field name to something that everyone can understand. Wrap field headings, that is, carry the full heading to a second line, rather than truncate, which means to shorten, because not all readers will be able to interpret the truncation properly.

Place and align columns appropriately

Readers can easily become confused if the data is not correctly labeled. Keeping the headings with the proper data and positioning data in a consistent, logical order is very important.

- ✔ List fields from left to right, consistent with the sort specification.
- ✔ Use ascending order, or note descending order in a header or footer.
- ✔ Align data.

Keeping the data aligned with the accompanying headers and using a logical order is another way to make the report more understandable.

Keep columns consistent

The following may be difficult, but arrange your report columns of data so that readers can easily determine where one set of data ends and another begins. Carrying over headings from page to page relieves the reader from moving back and forth to confirm the heading for the data.

- ✔ Space columns evenly to make boundaries obvious.
- ✔ Keep columns near enough so a reader can scan a line.
- ✔ Repeat column headings on each page.

Use column headers strategically

Any numeric columns must have a clear heading that defines what the column contains.

- ✔ Use meaningful column headers above each field space.
- ✔ Specify units (meters, units, millions of dollars) when not clear.
- ✔ Use abbreviations in field labels that the reader will understand.

Visually group data

Reading a report that resembles a dictionary is quite tiring to the eye. Effective use of white space relieves eye fatigue.

- ✔ When record information is on more than one line, separate each record with a blank line.
- ✔ Leave a blank line between groups of data.

Crystal Reports does leave space between groups, but you may want to increase the distance for added clarity. Or you may choose to draw a box around the individual groups.

Add graphs to make your reports more descriptive

Graphs are far superior to numbers when it comes to relating relationships or trends. The graphing capabilities of Crystal Reports make including the right kind of graph in the right place an easy task.

Add graphics to your report to make it visually interesting

You want to avoid graphic clutter, but keep in mind that a photograph, designs, or a logo can convey a great deal of information.

What company report is complete without your photo adorning the title page? Maybe you should save that idea for when you become company president.

Index

• *D* •

• Z •

Notes

Notes

Notes

Notes

Notes

Notes

Notes

Notes

Notes

Notes

YOUR ONLINE RESOURCE

WWW.DUMMIES.COM

Discover Dummies™ Online!

The *Dummies* Web Site is your fun and friendly online resource for the latest information about *...For Dummies®* books on all your favorite topics. From cars to computers, wine to Windows, and investing to the Internet, we've got a shelf full of *...For Dummies* books waiting for you!

Ten Fun and Useful Things You Can Do at www.dummies.com

1. Register this book and win!
2. Find and buy the *...For Dummies* books you want online.
3. Get ten great *Dummies Tips™* every week.
4. Chat with your favorite *...For Dummies* authors.
5. Subscribe free to *The Dummies Dispatch™* newsletter.
6. Enter our sweepstakes and win cool stuff.
7. Send a free cartoon postcard to a friend.
8. Download free software.
9. Sample a book before you buy.
10. Talk to us. Make comments, ask questions, and get answers!

Jump online to these ten fun and useful things at
http://www.dummies.com/10useful

WWW.DUMMIES.COM

SURF THE NET

For other technology titles from IDG Books Worldwide, go to
www.idgbooks.com

Not online yet? It's easy to get started with *The Internet For Dummies®,* 5th Edition, or *Dummies 101®: The Internet For Windows® 98,* available at local retailers everywhere.

IDG BOOKS WORLDWIDE

Find other *...For Dummies* books on these topics:
Business • Careers • Databases • Food & Beverages • Games • Gardening • Graphics • Hardware
Health & Fitness • Internet and the World Wide Web • Networking • Office Suites
Operating Systems • Personal Finance • Pets • Programming • Recreation • Sports
Spreadsheets • Teacher Resources • Test Prep • Word Processing

IDG BOOKS WORLDWIDE
BOOK REGISTRATION

Register This Book and Win!

We want to hear from you!

Visit **http://my2cents.dummies.com** to register this book and tell us how you liked it!

- ✔ Get entered in our monthly prize giveaway.
- ✔ Give us feedback about this book — tell us what you like best, what you like least, or maybe what you'd like to ask the author and us to change!
- ✔ Let us know any other *...For Dummies*® topics that interest you.

Your feedback helps us determine what books to publish, tells us what coverage to add as we revise our books, and lets us know whether we're meeting your needs as a *...For Dummies* reader. You're our most valuable resource, and what you have to say is important to us!

Not on the Web yet? It's easy to get started with *Dummies 101*®: *The Internet For Windows*® *98* or *The Internet For Dummies*®, 5th Edition, at local retailers everywhere.

Or let us know what you think by sending us a letter at the following address:

...For Dummies Book Registration
Dummies Press
7260 Shadeland Station, Suite 100
Indianapolis, IN 46256-3945
Fax 317-596-5498

...FOR DUMMIES™

BESTSELLING BOOK SERIES